# PERSPECTIVES ON WAR
# IN THE BIBLE

# PERSPECTIVES ON WAR IN THE BIBLE

JOHN A. WOOD

MERCER UNIVERSITY PRESS
MACON, GEORGIA
1998

PERSPECTIVES ON WAR IN THE BIBLE

Book Design: Marc A. Jolley
Cover Design: Mary Frances Burt
Cover Art: *David with Head of Goliath*, Caravagio

Printed in the United States of America.

Library of Congress Cataloging-in-Publication Data
Wood, John A.
    Perspectives on War in the Bible/John A. Wood
        pp. viii+ 181; 6"x9" (15x23 cm.)
    ISBN 0-86554-564-2
    1. Bible—NT—OT

∞The Paper used in this publication meets the minimum requirements
of American National Standard for Information Services—Permanance of
Paper for Printed Library materials.

# CONTENTS

# ACKNOWLEDGMENTS

This book is the result of research done while on a sabbatical from my teaching duties at Baylor University. I am most grateful to the administration of the University for granting me this summer and fall, 1991, sabbatical.

The research was done at the University of Notre Dame while I was a Visiting Scholar at the Hesburgh International Institute for Peace Studies. The Institute provided me with splendid office facilities and with the opportunity to participate in many of the events associated with the Institute. The ambitious program and the magnificent building grew out of the vision of Father Hesburgh and from generous gifts by Joan Kroc. Three people at the Institute merit special thanks. Dr. John Attanasio, Director of the Institute until June, 1992, provided me with everything I needed, including scheduling me for two lectures, which brought me feedback during my research. Dr. George Lopez, Director of the Undergraduate Program, graciously consented to meet with me on a weekly basis to discuss the philosophy and the "nuts and bolts" of the Peace Studies Program. Last, but not least, Rosemarie Green was always available to answer questions that enabled me to save an enormous amount of time and to keep me from becoming lost on either the campus or in South Bend.

Special thanks must also go to the great people of the First Baptist Church of South Bend who opened their doors and their hearts to my wife and me. Pastor Ken Wilson and his flock bent over backwards to make us feel like we were an integral part of the congregation even though we would be there only for a short time.

I must also note here that my dear wife, Sue, who passed away on June 18, 1993, left the comfort of our home to live with me in a 28-foot trailer for five months. Couples find out how deep their friendship is when they live in cramped quarters. We confirmed that we were indeed each other's best friend. It was also a delightful experience to return each day to the quietness and beauty of the Spaulding Lake Campgrounds just across the Michigan state line. This time of rest proved to be particularly helpful for Sue because she had discovered a serious heart problem only a few months earlier which caused her to take a medical leave from her elementary school teaching duties. In the providence of God she was able to get away from the stress and responsibilities of her normal existence to experience rest, healing, and the wonderful opportunity of extended reflection and reading. This time not only prolonged her life but added a depth to her remaining days. The entire experience was a sheer delight for both of us.

My thanks to my colleagues in the Department of Religion for their encouragement in this endeavor. Dr. James Kennedy and Dr. W.C. Christian were kind enough to read parts of the manuscript and offer helpful suggestions. Dr. John Jonsson also contributed useful information. Of course, they cannot be held responsible for the deficiencies that remain. I alone bear that responsibility.

# INTRODUCTION

The issue of warfare during the biblical period was not a subject of interest to a few intellectuals who happened to gather at times to discuss the subject. Warfare was at the forefront of ancient Israel's consciousness and a brutal fact of life. Israel was and is a country so small it could be dumped into Lake Michigan without splashing any water on the sidewalks of Chicago. Yet this vital piece of land located in the Syro-Palestinian corridor was so strategic that all of Israel's neighbors desired it. The Egyptians saw it as a buffer zone against the Mesopotamian empires. Those hegemonic empires viewed it as a buffer zone against powerful pharaohs of Egypt. Israel was then what it is today—a disputed piece of land with many claimants and many people willing to fight to the death to secure and keep it. As Norman Gottwald, commenting on only a part of this history, observes that "the life of Israel is shaped amidst and punctuated by civil and international strife during the six centuries from the Exodus to the Exile. This military preoccupation imparts a vigor to the biblical records but also often casts about them an aura of somber realism and a sense of the fragility of human life."[1]

Lord Byron artistically states this martial climate in "The Destruction of Sennacherib":

> The Assyrian came down like the wolf on the fold,
> And his cohorts were gleaming in purple and gold;
> And the sheen on their spears was like stars on the sea,
> When the blue wave rolls nightly on deep Galilee.

Consider, for example, what W. F. Albright observed over a half century ago, that the important city of Bethel was destroyed four times from BCE 1200-1000, so "one can hardly be surprised if under such conditions Israel became martially minded."[2] This event is equivalent

---

[1]Norman K. Gottwald, "'Holy War' in Deuteronomy: Analysis and Critique," *Review and Expositor* 61 (1962): 296.

[2]W. F. Albright, *From the Stone Age to Christianity* (Baltimore: Johns Hopkins,

to the city of Philadelphia being destroyed four times since the Declaration of Independence. Americans, who have enjoyed secure borders for over 200 years, may have difficulty identifying with ancient and modern nations who were and are surrounded by hostile neighbors. This argument is not to defend Israel's past or present martial attitudes, but it does, at least, make them understandable. All who lived in this land during the biblical period could count on one fact—during their lifetime many armies would camp on their doorsteps and threaten their very existence.

Surprisingly, however, this kind of situation, Israel being under nearly a constant state of siege, did *not* lead to a unified understanding of war. Instead, there existed, as I will demonstrate, several competing traditions or ideologies about warfare.[3]

War not only was variously understood in biblical times but, of course, was and is a focus of intense debate since that time. This fact is true in many religious traditions and is particularly true within the Christian faith. For two thousand years Christians have debated the relationship of the Christian faith and warfare In his classic work, *Christian Attitudes Toward War and Peace*, Roland Bainton traces the historical development of the crusade, the just war, and the pacifist viewpoints.[4] Many sound theological, philosophical, psychological, historical, and sociological reasons can be brought forward and defended as to why these views have persisted so strongly over such a long period of time. This book is written, however, to illustrate one reason why these views have persisted—each of them is firmly rooted in the biblical texts. No matter how deep the differences between Christian denominations, one thing is held in common among these views—the Bible is seen as the foundation of Christian beliefs. Reason, experience, tradition, and culture all play important roles in understanding and expressing one's faith, but they all must interact with the Bible in order to present a coherent and genuine Christian theology.[5]

---

1940), 219.

[3]We can note here that these ideologies exist today in modern Israel.

[4]Roland H. Bainton, *Christian Attitudes Toward War and Peace* (Nashville: Abingdon, 1960).

[5]Roman Catholics, for example, who for centuries have grounded just war theory almost exclusively in natural law, have more recently sought to take the Bible more seriously as the Church seeks to establish a relevant contemporary statement about the ethics of war.

On the subject of the Bible and war there are two rather common paradigms that are unsatisfactory and need to be dismissed at the outset. First, one view identifies the Old Testament with holy war, the New Testament with pacifism, with the just war doctrine developing after the biblical period through Augustine, Aquinas, and others. This view is a caricature and is inaccurate. Second, a more appealing paradigm suggests that there is a line of development throughout the Old Testament, beginning with a primitive, warlike ideology that gradually develops into a more pacifistic view by the time of the eighth-century prophets. This view is also an oversimplified approach. In place of these two approaches, this book demonstrates that throughout the entire biblical period there were several variations of a holy war ideology that existed alongside pacifistic and just war teachings.

Because of the sheer amount of attention given to war, anyone interested in studying the Bible must deal with this issue. Millar Burrows was correct when he observed years ago that the Bible is concerned with three subjects: religion, agriculture, and war. In noting the now-lost "Book of the Wars of Yahweh" mentioned in Numbers 21:14, Burrows goes so far as to say that "much of the Old Testament might be aptly characterized by that title."[6] This perspective is not only true of biblical history but true of history in general. There is a sense in which all history is a history of warfare. Because so many wars from the earliest times to the present were faithfully recorded or commemorated historians have a wealth of material that shows how the outcome of wars has determined the course of history like no other series of events.

To study the subject of war in the Bible is to raise some important hermeneutical questions.[7] Are the descriptions found in the Bible merely literary inventions intended to portray some deeper religious perspectives? Do the battles report actual events or were they embellished by later redactors? Are the battles, and especially the interpretations of them in the Bible, culturally conditioned? Is it possible to distinguish between confessional content and merely descriptive content? Does the Bible actually concern itself with war theologically and ethically; that is, does it seek an integration of the fact of war with

---

[6]Millar Burrows, *An Outline of Biblical Theology* (Philadelphia: Westminster Press, 1946), 317.

[7]These questions are raised in many places but are most cogently stated by Dianne Bergant, "Yahweh: A Warrior-God?" *The Bible Today* (May 1983): 156, and by Waldemar Janzen, "War in the Old Testament," *The Mennonite Quarterly Review* 46 (1972): 155f.

an understanding of its relationship to what God is like and what God wills? Can we say that all or most ancient Israelites held to one view about war? Can we say that the Bible, taken as a canonical text may be read as supporting one view about war?

These questions to a large degree are not questions of fact but rather questions of belief and of a general worldview or general approach to the Bible as a whole. A writer can only answer these questions in the form of assumptions and hope that the analysis will demonstrate the validity of the assumptions. It is at this point, then, that I state my assumptions.

(1) *This study assumes that the record of the events in the Bible is based to a large degree on actual events.* I find it much harder to believe that the ancient Israelite faith, which was and is a historical religion, would simply manufacture historical narratives. In my judgment a single focus on the texts themselves is not enough. The texts grew out of historical events. I am not arguing that the narratives describe exactly what happened. Rather, biblical history is interpreted history and history which was often written down many years after the events which inspired the narrative. Interpreting a story does not necessarily rob it of its historicity. One does not have to foist on ancients a modern understanding of history in order to derive historical meaning from their texts. In sum then, the texts in the Bible that describe and interpret war reflect events as well as the beliefs of at least some of those who recorded the events. Blending historical fact, theological reflection, and their own literary creativity allows us to emphasize not Israel's war as much but rather God's presence in every event of life, even war. The main focus becomes not the historicity of an event, but rather the faith that lies behind the theological and literary telling of the event. [8]

(2) *The writings of the Bible were, to some degree, historically and culturally conditioned.* They were not written in a vacuum. Writers, even under inspiration, did not magically escape the thought patterns and worldviews of the cultures in which they lived. They were people of their times and they drew upon ideas available to them. "The shutters of understanding are always conditioned by the environment."[9] The

---

[8]Bergant, 160 (emphasis added).

[9]Henry J. Flanders, Jr., Robert W. Crapps, David A. Smith, *People of the Covenant*, 2nd ed. (New York: John Wiley & Sons, 1973), 192. This assumption is valid, of course, with our own process of interpretation because we are also influenced profoundly by our environment. As Philip LeMasters notes: "Moral knowledge gained from Scripture is always *mediated* knowledge which is appropriated through a variety of historically conditioned procedures,

Bible is a divine-human book containing not only a revelation of God but also containing human viewpoints incompatible with the overwhelming picture of Yahweh that shines through its pages.

(3) *Statements in the Bible do not necessarily reflect prevailing theological or ethical opinions of that time.* Walter Eichrodt is wrong to imply that if an attitude is expressed by a character in a biblical narrative that it reflected a prevalent attitude in early Israel.[10] We can, however, modify this idea to say that such an attitude was present and that it was preserved by those who believed that it merited consideration in the community of faith. In fact, it cannot always be determined whether or not a writer or redactor approves, disapproves, or is indifferent to the words and actions in a biblical story.[11]

Furthermore, it is a distinct possibility that some writers held minority or atypical views in comparison with the "conventional wisdom" of their day. This view is certainly evident in many, if not all, of the pre-exilic prophets who seemed to have clashed head–on with the views of the political and religious leaders of their time.[12]

(4) *Instead of the common view stated earlier that the Bible contains a linear development in its understanding of war, I offer instead the idea that great diversities of opinion existed simultaneously throughout most of the biblical period.* The biblical texts faithfully record both serious disagreement and heated debate within the community of faith (both in the O.T. and N.T.). *There was, in fact, no one normative view about warfare.* Rather, there were several normative views competing in the marketplace of ideas. Underneath this remarkable diversity among the writers of the texts and among reflective people within the community, however, stood one unifying theme — *trust in Yahweh.* Whether one believed in non-violent conflict resolution, or in allowing God only to

---

assumptions, and institutions. The Bible is by no means reducible to those mediating factors, but they will shape and inform any use of the Bible." "A Critique of Yoder's 'Biblical Realism'" (unpublished paper delivered at the AAR: Southwest Regional meeting, March 14, 1992)

[10]Walter Eichrodt, *Theology of the Old Testament*, II, trans. by J.A. Baker (Philadelphia: Westminster, 1967), 317f.

[11]John Barton, "Understanding Old Testament Ethics," *Journal for the Study of the Old Testament* 9 (1978): 55.

[12]As Barton, 48, states, "Since our written evidence comes, inevitably, mostly from the more articulate and memorable representatives of particular periods, we shall run a considerable risk of exaggerating the degree of sophistication attained by the period in question if we treat our sources as normative rather than as at least possibly atypical."

engage in war, or in joining with Yahweh in engaging in holy war, or in fighting in a justified war, all of these sought to operate out of an attitude of trust in the only true God. The text, then, contains a diversity of what may be called "theologies of warfare" but the theological core was faith in Yahweh.[13]

(5) *The fact that this book is a study of both the Old and New Testaments indicates a belief in the unity of the Bible.* I see elements from the traditions about war in the Old Testament carried over into the New Testament in spite of a significantly different historical-political situation. A major difference, of course, is the fact that whereas the New Testament documents were written within roughly a one hundred year period, the Old Testament documents were written, redacted, and compiled over a period lasting more than a thousand years. Ideas about war in the Old Testament had a longer time to confront the realities of history and to interact with conflicting viewpoints than was the case in the New Testament. As Victor Furnish reminds us, unlike the Old Testament, the events in the New Testament took place when Israel was relatively secure and free from the threat of invasion, and the New Testament community of faith had no national history of its own and no experience of political or military power.[14] In spite of these differences, however, we reject the old Marcionite view that places a huge cleft between the Testaments. We affirm, instead, Paul Hanson's view that "believe(s)…(in) a biblical theology in which both Old and New Testaments are viewed as bearing witness to one universal redemptive drama…Of course, those bearing witness to God's initiative in both Testaments are humans, and hence the records we receive are richly diverse. Their unity resides solely in the oneness of the divine initiator whose will can be known only by studying diligently all of the biblical traditions."[15]

---

[13]This statement is an effort to combine von Rad's "chain of theologies," which he sees in the O.T., with Eichrodt's effort to find a theological core to the O.T. These approaches can be, but are not of necessity, incompatible, at least when it comes to the subject of war. I do not insist on the term "theologies of warfare" but the term is used to indicate the shared and sometimes conflicting attitudes toward war which resulted from one's understanding of God's will for His people. This perspective, in general, seems to be compatible with the view of T.R. Hobbs, *A Time for War: A Study of Warfare in the Old Testament* (Wilmington, DE: Michael Glazier, 1989), 211.

[14]Victor Paul Furnish, "War and Peace in the New Testament," *Interpretation* 38, 4 (1984): 364.

[15]Paul D. Hanson, "War and Peace in the Hebrew Bible," Interpretation 38, 4

After beginning with a general discussion on the concept of holy war in ancient Israel, I will examine several aspects of the holy war tradition: war in which Israel participated, war in which either Yahweh alone fights or will fight for his people, holy war which is characterized by vengeance, and holy war which was seen as ultimately redemptive in nature. Then the pacifist tradition as developed in both Testaments will be explored followed by a chapter on just war motifs. The final chapter seeks to draw some conclusions.

The study is an effort from a generalist to arrive at a broad synthesis regarding war in the Biblical texts. Those who seek to take the Scriptures seriously as normative for faith and practice have often found themselves ambivalent about war. This ambivalence stems, at least in part, from the sacred texts themselves. Thus, one purpose of this study is to illustrate how the major historical positions on war— i.e., pacifism, just war, and holy war—are firmly embedded in the Biblical texts. Whatever philosophical, socio-political, and psychological bases undergird these positions, it is clear is that each of them can be traced to Biblical events and teachings.

In sum, the purpose of this study is to bring together the work of Biblical scholars in a new way. It is largely a descriptive and derivative work, drawing upon the vast stream of Biblical scholarship that touches on this subject. What is creative here is the taxonomy employed to arrange and interpret the texts. I leave it to the reader to determine if the taxonomy is a valid one.

This study reflects the broad and deep interest that I have had on the subject of war which began for me in the Viet Nam era. That senseless war and the problem of nuclear proliferation propelled me into a search for answers which continues to this day. This study is a necessary part of the process because, for me, the Bible is the basis for Christian ethics and theology. It is, of course, not the only source, but it is the first among a special set of sources (thus not "*sola Scriptura*," but "*prima inter pares*").

I entered this project with a deep ambivalence about war. I was and am strongly attracted to the power and beauty of the pacifist tradition but cannot embrace it fully because of the compelling logic and realism of the just war tradition. Now, after examining the biblical materials I now know the source of some of this ambivalence. It is evident to me that the people in the biblical era, whose situation differed greatly from

---

(1984): 344.

mine, also experienced profound ambiguity about this issue and this ambiguity is faithfully recorded for us.

F. Braudel expresses a sentiment I agree with, and possibly for many biblical authors when he observes that "Historians refer constantly to war without really knowing or seeking to know its true nature—or natures. We are as ignorant about war as the physicist is of the true nature of matter. *We talk about it because we have to: it has never ceased to trouble the lives of men.*"[16]

I undertook this study because I had to and because war has never ceased to trouble me. I now see that it never ceased to trouble the people of the Old and New Testaments.

---

[16]Fernand Braudel, *The Mediterranean and the Mediterranean World in the Age of Philip II*, vol. II (New York: Harper & Row, 1972), 836 (emphasis added).

# Chapter One

# THE CONCEPT OF HOLY WAR
# IN ANCIENT ISRAEL

## The Centrality of Warfare in Ancient Israel

War was not a peripheral concern in ancient Israel. For one thing, "war was a normal state in the ancient world of the Near East,"[1] and, like modern war, "was candidly a plundering expedition."[2] While war was not the only method used to settle the Promised Land, "it is evident that without the use of force the state of Israel would not have come into existence."[3] Furthermore, their location in the strategic Syro-Palestinian corridor guaranteed that they would be engaged in constant warfare to secure the land and to protect themselves from the hegemony of the Egyptians and Mesopotamian kingdoms.[4] Over a hundred years ago Julius Wellhausen observed how warfare was central to Israel's identity saying that "the camp was, so to speak, at once the *cradle* in which the nations was nursed and the *smithy* in which it was welded into unity; it was also the primitive *sanctuary*. There Israel was, and there was Jehovah."[5]

---

[1]John L. McKenzie, *Dictionary of the Bible* (Milwaukee: Bruce Publishing Co., 1965) 919.

[2]John L. McKenzie, *A Theology of the Old Testament* (Garden City, NY: Doubleday, 1974) 152.

[3]Peter C. Craigie, "War, Idea of," *International Standard Bible Encyclopedia* IV, ed. by G. W. Bromiley (Grand Rapids: Eerdmans, 1988) 1019.

[4]This phenomenon is not new of course. Included in expansionist policies is also the desire of countries to establish a "buffer zone" around them. The former Soviet Union is a good modern example. The many invasions of Russia throughout the centuries led to an understandable desire to protect themselves and let other peoples absorb the brunt of any attack. The defensive and offensive postures are often conflated so that neither outsiders nor insiders remember what gave rise to the policies.

[5]Julius Wellhausen, *Prolegomena to the History of Ancient Israel* (New York: Meridian Books, 1957) 434. Emphasis added.

Or, as Walter Eichrodt states, relating warfare to Israel's understanding of the nature of Yahweh, "Undoubtedly it was Yahweh's warlike activity, affording as it did sensible experience of his power, which evoked the most powerful response in ancient Israel."[6]

Israel's beginnings as a people occurred in the contest with Pharaoh in Egypt and at the Sea of Reeds, where Yahweh is declared to be "a man of war" (Ex. 15:3). Later passages illustrate the persistence of this title:

> The LORD goes forth like a soldier, like a warrior he stirs up his fury; he cries out, he shouts aloud, he shows himself mighty against his foes. (Is. 42:13)

> The LORD, your God, is in your midst, a warrior who gives victory; he will rejoice over you with gladness, he will renew you in his love; he will exult over you with loud singing. (Zeph. 3:17)

> Who is the King of glory? The LORD, strong and mighty, the LORD, mighty in battle. (Ps. 24:8)

The theme of Yahweh as warrior is evident in the early events of Israel's history, particularly during the exodus and post-exodus traditions. It is also used in creation texts in hymnic material, especially regarding the fighting against mythological creatures. More, it is even present in the traditions of the exile and restoration, and eventually in apocalyptic texts.[7]

Thus, from the beginning to the end of the Old Testament this theme is in the forefront. One cannot dismiss it "as 'primitive' without in effect dismissing the Old Testament."[8] The concepts of salvation, judgment, and kingship are inextricably tied to Yahweh's involvement in Israel's wars.[9]

---

[6]Walter Eichrodt, *Theology of the Old Testament* I, trans. by J. A. Baker (Philadelphia: Westminster, 1961) 228.

[7]Richard Nysse, "Yahweh Is a Warrior, " *Word and World* 7 (1987): 193.

[8]Patrick D. Miller, Jr., *The Divine Warrior in Ancient Israel* (Cambridge: Harvard University Press, 1973) 171.

[9]Miller, *The Divine Warrior in Ancient Israel*, 173-175. Also see, H. D. Preuss, *Old Testament Theology*, vol. 1 (Louisville: Westminster/John Knox, 1995) 129-38.

# Terminology

Several designations of Yahweh possess military imagery. Moses refers to Yahweh as "Yahweh is my banner (of war)"(Ex. 17:15). More common is the title Yahweh Sabaoth, "Lord of Hosts."[10] Whether it is rendered "Yahweh, the Great Soldier" or "Yahweh of the Armies," its military impact is graphic.[11] Scholars generally agree that this term designates Yahweh as commander of both the heavenly armies and Israel's earthly armies.[12]

This belief that God was actively involved in warfare gave rise to the use by scholars of the term "holy war." Since the Hebrew Bible does not employ the term some scholars prefer "Yahweh War," which is derived from such texts as Ex. 17:16; Num. 21:14; 1 Sam. 17:47; 18:17; 25:28.[13] Of course, "Yahweh war," would be limited to Israelite or Old

---

[10]The phrase occurs some 267 times but not at all from Genesis through Judges. It appears first in 1 Sam. 1:3, 11 and is associated in 1 Sam. 17:45 with "the God of the army of Israel." John Polhill, "Lord of Hosts," *Mercer Dictionary of the Bible* (Macon, GA: Mercer University Press, 1990): 522.

[11]Richard J. Sklba, "A Covenant of Peace," *The Bible Today* (May 1983) 151.

[12]Norman Gottwald, "Holy War," *Interpreters Dictionary of the Bible*, Supp. Vol. (Nashville: Abingdon, 1976) 943; J. Carter Swaim, War, *Peace, and the Bible* (Maryknoll, NY: Orbis Books, 1983) 5; and Frank M. Cross, Jr., "Yahweh and the God of the Patriarchs," *Harvard Theological Review* 55 (1962): 256. However, Roland de Vaux, in contrast to most scholars, says that it is not certain that this term had any connections with military institutions. *Ancient Israel: Its Life and Institutions*, translated by John McHugh. (New York: McGraw-Hill, 1961) 259. Walter Eichrodt, 138f., accepts the view that the term is used to designate Yahweh as a Warrior, but he also thinks that the term is much broader and refers to "all bodies, multitudes, masses in general, the content of all that exists in heaven and in earth." See also the helpful discussion by Patrick D. Miller, 152-155. A more recent and thorough study by Tryggue N. D. Mettinger sees the term as referring to "the enthroned God who reigns and determines the destiny of the world." *In Search of God: The Meaning and Message of the Everlasting Names*, trans. by Frederick Cryer (Philadelphia: Fortress, 1988) 150. Chapter 7 is devoted solely to the analysis of this title. Mettinger subsumes the term under God's Kingship and posits that it affirms that God is both ubiquitous and omnitemporal.

[13]Gwilym H. Jones, "Holy War or Yahweh War?" *Vetus Testamentum* 25, 3 (1975): 643f. Walter Zimmerli, *The Old Testament and the World*, translated by John J. Scullion (Atlanta: John Knox Press, 1976) 57. Nu. 21:14 refers to "the Book of the Wars of Yahweh," apparently a collection of ancient war songs which has been lost. Peter Craigie prefers the term "Yahweh War," because it "conveys the

Testament usage, whereas the term "holy war" may be used to describe
a similar phenomenon in the ancient Near East. In a more technical
sense it may be best to refer to the term "Yahweh war" as applying to
Israel's early experience or tradition of warfare and the term "holy war"
to the theologically elaborate schema of holy war characteristic of the
Deuteronomistic history. For our purposes, however, we will use the
terms interchangeably to refer to the broader phenomenon of Israel's
understanding that warfare was related to their worship of, and obedience to, Yahweh. Furthermore, we concur with Ollenburger that the
term "Yahweh as Warrior" is found in a broad range of contexts which
reflect different traditions.[14] Many scholars have noted the striking
parallels to the Old Testament understanding of war found in texts from
Ugarit, Mari, Egypt, Assyria, Moab, and elsewhere.[15] Gwilym Jones
summarizes the view of many when he observes that an examination of
historical records and other documents from areas surrounding Israel
make it clear that by "accepting the general presupposition that the affairs of a nation were controlled by its deities, territorial conquests and
military successes were attributed to effective surveillance by the national gods."[16]

Thus, Israel's life and faith were molded in a world where war was
regarded as a religious enterprise.

---

religious character of Israel's warfare without implying that the conduct of the
war had moral or religious worth." Craigie, "War, Idea of," 1019. The ancient
Israelite engaged in Yahweh War, however, undoubtedly believing that the conduct of the war did have moral and/or religious worth.

[14]Ben Ollenburger, *Zion the City of the Great King: A Theological Symbol of the
Jerusalem Cult* (Sheffield: JSOT Press, 1987) 101. Ollenburger expands on these
distinctions: "While it would not be correct to maintain that these three—Israel's
experience in the 'wars of Yahweh,' the tradition of holy war and the motif of the
Divine Warrior—were unrelated at various points in the history of Old Testament traditions, it would be equally inaccurate to claim that these three can be
simply collapsed into each other, so that when we speak of the Divine Warrior
we are thereby talking about a holy war tradition or an actual experience of
warfare" (101f.).

[15]A brief listing and discussion of some of these texts are found in Jones,
"The Concept of Holy War," *The World of Ancient Israel*, ed. by Ronald Clements
(New York: Cambridge University Press, 1989) 300-302. Mark Smith also
chronicles the remarkable similarity between the imagery of Baal and Yahweh
as warriors in *The Early History of God: Yahweh and the Other Deities in Ancient
Israel* (New York: Harper and Row, 1990) 1-79. See esp. pp. 48-55.

[16]Gwilym H. Jones, "The Concept of Holy War," 300.

## Israelite Distinctiveness

Having acknowledged the similarities between Israel and her neighbors with reference to warfare, we must ask: Did the Israelites hold any distinctive beliefs and/or practices from those found in the surrounding nations? Jones notes that some scholars see no differences at all,[17] but the evidence points to several significant differences between Israel's religious understanding of war and those of their surrounding cultures.

(1) In contrast to cultures which glorify military exploits, Swaim points out that the Hebrew calendar contains no memory of men of war, and that whereas foreign kings set up monuments to celebrate their victories, "the monuments of the Old Testament do not mark the places where battles were fought; they do not show generals astride prancing steeds; they do not represent beaten enemies bowing in submission."[18]

Or, as Zimmerli states it, "The Old Testament, whose stories are full of men of war, never developed any kind of hero worship."[19] Furthermore, as Edward Ryan observes, the Jews did not form a militaristic nation according to the Spartan model nor did they give undue prominence to military training. They did not maintain large standing armies for the purpose of conquest, although their political leaders clearly believed that military force was necessary to resist invasion.[20]

(2) Related to the first difference is the fact that Israel's war methods, however brutal they seem to the modern reader, were relatively mild in comparison to many other ancient cultures.

> Slaughter out of sheer lust for blood, which often features so repulsively in the Assyrian inscriptions, is unknown. Similarly there is nowhere any mention of the raping of women by Israelite warriors, and fruit trees were protected by the laws of war (Deut. 20:19f.).[21]

In fact, the Israelite kings had a reputation of being merciful kings (1 Kgs 20:31).

---

[17]Ibid., 302.

[18]Swaim, 15.

[19]Walter Zimmerli, *Old Testament Theology in Outline,* trans. by David E. Green (Atlanta: John Knox Press, 1978) 61.

[20]Edward A. Ryan, S. J., "The Rejection of Military Service by the Early Christians," *Theological Studies* 13 (1952) 3.

[21]Eichrodt, 140.

(3) A notable theme found in the Old Testament which is absent in other ancient Near Eastern literature is the use of the holy war imagery by some of Israel's prophets *against* their nation. In 2 Kings 8:7-13, Elisha prophesies that the Syrian warrior Hazael will defeat Israel as "God's gruesome instrument"[22] because of Israel's sinfulness. Similarly, Isaiah sees brutal Assyria as Yahweh's chosen instrument to judge wicked Israel in comments.

> Ah, Assyria, the rod of my anger—the club in their hands is my fury! Against a godless nation I send him, and against the people of my wrath I command him, to take spoil and seize plunder, and to tread them down like the mire of the streets. But this is not what he intends, nor does he have this in mind; but it is in his heart to destroy, and to cut off nations not a few. (Is 10:5-7)

Amos employs this theme:

> Also I brought you up out of the land of Egypt, and led you forty years in the wilderness, to possess the land of the Amorite. And I raised up some of your children to be prophets and some of your youths to be nazirites. Is it not indeed so, O people of Israel? says the LORD. But you made the Nazirites drink wine, and commanded the prophets, saying, "You shall not prophesy." So, I will press you down in your place, just as a cart presses down when it is full of sheaves. (Amos 2:10-13)

Amos' contemporary Hosea echoes this theme:

> Therefore I am like maggots to Ephraim, and like rottenness to the house of Judah. When Ephraim saw his sickness, and Judah his wound, then Ephraim went to Assyria, and sent to the great king. But he is not able to cure you or heal your wound. For I will be like a lion to Ephraim, and like a young lion to the house of Judah. I myself will tear and go away; I will carry off, and no one shall rescue. (Hos. 5:12-14)

Jeremiah in particular uses this imagery with stunning force.

---

[22]Zimmerli, *The Old Testament and the World*, 60.

Then Jeremiah said to them: Thus you shall say to Zedekiah: Thus says the LORD, the God of Israel: I am going to turn back the weapons of war that are in your hands and with which you are fighting against the king of Babylon and against the Chaldeans who are besieging you outside the walls; and I will bring them together into the center of this city. *I myself will fight against you with outstretched hand and mighty arm, in anger, in fury, and in great wrath.* And I will strike down the inhabitants of this city, both human beings and animals; they shall die of a great pestilence ... For I have set my face against this city for evil and not for good, says the LORD: it shall be given into the hands of the king of Babylon, and he shall burn it with fire. (Jer. 21:3-10; see also 6:1-6)

Jeremiah's employment of this imagery illustrates that "the prophets were well aware that the choice of a holy war was 'dialectical:' for the same offenses for which Israel at one time was sent to punish other peoples by means of a holy war, Israel herself could now be punished by the same holy war with other peoples being used by Yahweh for this purpose."[23]

Jeremiah, like Elisha and Isaiah earlier, boldly announces that Yahweh has chosen an evil nation, Babylon, to punish Israel.

I am going to send for all the tribes of the north, says the LORD, even for King Nebuchadrezzar of Babylon, my servant, and I will bring them against this land and its inhabitants, and against all these nations around; I will utterly destroy them, and make them an object of horror and of hissing, and an everlasting disgrace. (Jer. 25:9; see also 27:6; 43:10)

In other words, "Yahweh is never merely a 'victory God of Israel.'"[24] Yahweh is free to give victory or to deny it. Jeremiah and other prophets took the holy war concept and, as it were, "stood it on its head."

(4) The foregoing distinction points to a broader and more significant difference between Israel and its neighbors. Israel perceived Yahweh as the God of all nations. The prophets refused to allow Israel to look upon

---

[23]J. Alberto Soggin, *Old Testament and Oriental Studies* (Rome: Biblical Institute Press, 1975) 67f. See also Edgar W. Conrad, *Fear Not Warrior: A Study of 'al Tira' Pericopae in the Hebrew Scriptures* (Chico: CA: Scholars Press, 1985) 48-51.

[24] Zimmerli, *Old Testament Theology*, 63. See also Nysse, 198.

Yahweh as a tribal god who was consumed with Israel's interests. Yahweh's judgment was upon evil wherever it was found. His calling of Israel through Abraham was for the purpose of blessing all humankind (Gen. 12:1-3). Amos even stated boldly that Yahweh initiated the migration of the Philistines to the land (Amos 9:7). The prophets envisioned that one day all nations would recognize the God of Israel as the only true God (Is. 2:2-4; 11:1-9; 19:24). To these prophets, as we shall examine later, Yahweh's wars were ultimately redemptive.

(5) Roland de Vaux points to another difference between Israel and later uses of the holy war concept. The Israelite holy war was *not* a war of religion, that is, it was not undertaken, like some forms of the Muslim jihad, to spread their faith.[25] Thus he maintains a distinction between wars which were essentially religious, and wars of religion.

(6) As we shall examine in chapter 3, a strong belief persisted in some circles throughout Israel's history that wars were to be fought *only* by Yahweh. Human warriors were not only unnecessary but an evidence of lack of faith in Yahweh's power to bring victory over the enemy. In this view, Israel limited itself to "passive participation."

(7) In addition to the above differences, another element of humility was injected into Israel's understanding of war, viz., wars which secured for Israel the promised land and the blessings which followed

---

[25]de Vaux, 262. Other differences between "holy war" and "jihad" are cited by Norman Gottwald, "War, Holy," *Interpreter's Dictionary of the Bible*, Supp. Vol. (Nashville: Abingdon, 1976) 942: "... jihad, was among other things, an attempt to control blood revenge among nomadic converts who did not easily assimilate to the larger Moslem brotherhood. Characteristically, jihad was directed either at the conversion of pagans or the subjection of Christians and Jews to poll and land taxes under Moslem rule. Prior to the monarchy, holy war in Israel did not function in an analogous way, and it is doubtful that it did so even during the monarchy." Efraim Inbar agrees: "The campaign against idolatry is important, but the missionary impulse has no institutional expression such as the Jihad in Moslem tradition. The normative emphasis in the war against Amalek is not transferred to other military activities." "War in Jewish Tradition," *The Jerusalem Journal of International Relations* 9, 2 (June 1987) 90. We must note, however, that some scholars do not view mainstream Islam as teaching jihad as holy war but, rather, as a commitment to justice and human rights. See Muhammad Qutb, *Islam: The Misunderstood Religion* (Kuwait: Ministry of Awqaf and Islamic Affairs, 1964) 29; Sayyid Qutb, "Social Justice in Islam," in *Islam in Transition: Muslim Perspectives*, ed. John J. Donohue and John L. Esposito (New York: Oxford University Press, 1982) 127; Abul A'la Maududi, *Jihad in Islam* (Beirut, Lebanon: The Holy Koran Publishing House, 1980) 1.

were a result of God's grace. Nowhere did Israel ever claim that she deserved the land.[26] Deuteronomy underscores this in 8:11-18.

> Take care that you do not forget the LORD your God, by failing to keep his commandments, his ordinances, and his statutes, which I am commanding you today. When you have eaten your fill and have built fine houses and live in them, and when your herds and flocks have multiplied, and your silver and gold is multiplied, and all that you have is multiplied, then do not exalt yourself, forgetting the LORD your God, who brought you out of the land of Egypt, out of the house of slavery, who led you through the great and terrible wilderness, an arid wasteland with poisonous snakes and scorpions. He made water flow for you from flint rock, and fed you in the wilderness with manna that your ancestors did not know, to humble you and to test you, and in the end to do you good. Do not say to yourself, "My power and the might of my own hand have gotten me this wealth." But remember the LORD your God, for it is he who gives you power to get wealth, so that he may confirm his covenant that he swore to your ancestors, as he is doing today. (Deut. 8:11-18)

These differences do not address the question as to whether or not Israel viewed every war as a holy war. Were there wars which were simply "profane," and, if so, what distinguished them from holy wars? The evidence is mixed. Certainly the biblical texts do not ascribe every war to the initiative of Yahweh.[27] Examples are found which do seem to contrast sharply from the strongly religious flavor of the holy wars. The war against Sihon the Amorite in Num. 21:21-32 makes no mention of Yahweh in the narrative or in the victory song that follows. Gideon's campaign against Zebah and Zalmunna in Judg. 8:4-21 contains one reference to Yahweh but lacks the usual elements connected with a holy war. Some scholars believe that the Deuteronomic historian(s) gathered profane war stories like Ehud's assassination of Eglon in Judg. 3:15-30 and Jephthah's war experiences in Judg. 11 and transformed them into holy war narratives.[28] One may argue, on the other hand, that the re-

---

[26]J. E. West, *Introduction to the Old Testament* (New York: Macmillan, 1971) 170.

[27]A. Gelston, "The Wars of Israel," *Scottish Journal of Theology* 17 (1964) 331.

[28]See Jones, "The Concept of Holy War," 308 for references. Of course, this

dactors found it unnecessary to include the religious dimension in every instance because they were working out of the general framework, obvious to their readers, that Yahweh was intimately involved in all that Israel did and in all that happened to the nation. Perhaps von Waldow is correct when he asserts that Israel's wars do not describe a special kind of war, but "express the belief that war as such is something sacred because the decision to go to war was made by Yahweh."[29] It may be necessary to go one step further in concluding that "war is not holy because God commanded it; it is holy only in the sense that the victory is totally ascribed to God.[30]

Clearly, one's solution to this question is contingent on a host of judgments made about the nature of the biblical narratives in their final form. For our purposes a solution is not necessary. Wars, whether fought explicitly under Yahweh's leadership or not, were viewed by the authors/redactors as falling under the providence of God and instructive to Israel regarding its relationship to Yahweh. In sum, we can point to at least four types of wars involving Israel in the Old Testament: (1) defensive wars against Israel's aggressors, (2) wars in which Israel is the aggressor but under Yahweh's approval, (3) wars in which Israel is the aggressor, but "presumptuously," i.e., against Yahweh's will, and where she suffers defeat, and (4) wars in which Israel herself is the object of Yahweh's judgment.[31] The title "holy war" or "Yahweh war" would apply most clearly to all but the third type, but, even here it is related because the people apparently *believed* they were engaging in holy war.

## Elements of an Israelite Holy War

Can we discern any pattern in Israel's understanding of and conduct of war? Are there any elements which appear consistently which would allow us to arrive at some systematic conclusions? The work of Gerhard von Rad is especially important in examing this dimension. Von Rad's basic thesis is that holy war was not only a tradition in Israel, but it was

---

type of judgment is based on the assumption that one can discern the various layers of redaction.

[29]H. Eberhard von Waldow, "The Concept of War in the Old Testament," *Horizons in Biblical Theology* 6, 2 (Dec. 1984): 37.

[30]James A. Fischer, "War and Peace: A Methodological Consideration," *Blessed are the Peacemakers*, ed. by Anthony J. Tambasco (New York: Paulist Press, 1989) 28.

[31]Gelston, 329.

a *religious (or cultic) institution* and consequently contained a highly stylized pattern.[32] Although he admitted that not every element is specifically stated in every war, by examining all the narratives we can discern the following schema:

1. The call to Yahweh's war comes through the blast of the trumpet (Judg. 6:34f; 3:27; 1 Sam. 13:3).

2. The Israelites maintained ritual purity throughout the camp through severe sacral regulations (Josh. 3:5; 1 Sam. 21:5; 2 Sam. 11:11f.; Deut. 23:9-14; 2 Sam. 1:21).

3. Sacrifices are made to Yahweh and/or He is consulted (1 Sam. 7:9; 13:9-10, 12; Judg. 20:13, 18).

4. The leader proclaims to the army: "Yahweh has given the enemy into your hand" (Josh. 6:2 plus 19 additional references, so von Rad sees this element as one of the most important factors).

5. The army marches out with certainty that Yahweh is with them and that the enemies of Israel are the enemies of Yahweh (Judg. 4:14; 5:31; Deut. 20:4; 2 Sam. 5:24). The ark accompanies them in Josh. 3:11.

6. Leaders admonish the people not to be afraid (Ex. 14:13f.; Deut 20:3; Josh. 8:1; 10:8, 25; 11:6; Judg. 7:3; 1 Sam. 23:16-17; 30:6; 2 Sam. 10:12).

7. The enemy loses courage (Ex. 15:14-16; 23:27f.; Deut. 2:25; 11:25; Josh. 2:9, 24; 5:1; 10:2; 11:20; 24:12; 1 Sam. 4:7f.).

8. The battle cry is sounded (Judg. 7:20; Josh. 6:5; 1 Sam. 17:20, 52).

9. The enemy is terrified and incapable of real opposition and sometimes turn their swords on each other (Ex. 23:27; Deut. 7:23; Josh. 10:10; 24:7; Judg. 4:15; 7:22; 1 Sam. 5:11; 7:10; 14:15, 20).[33]

10. The highpoint and the conclusion of the war culminate in the *herem*, the consecration of the booty to Yahweh (Josh. 6:18f.).

11. Leaders dismiss the militia with the cry, "To your tents, O Israel" (2 Sam. 20:1; 1 Kings 12:16) or it is simply stated that they went (or fled) to their tents (1 Sam. 4:10; 2 Sam. 18:17; 19:8; 20:22; 2 Kings 8:21; 14:12).

A few elements here merit further discussion.

---

[32]Gerhard von Rad, *Holy War in Ancient Israel*, trans. and ed. by Marva Dawn (Grand Rapids: Eerdmans, 1991) 41-51. All references to von Rad are from this book unless otherwise noted.

[33]Bernhard Anderson thinks that this element is especially important: "The strategy of holy war was not so much to fight pitched battles as to frighten the enemy with the 'terror of God' so that they would flee in panic and confusion." *Understanding the Old Testament*, 4th edition (Englewood Cliffs, NJ: Prentice-Hall, 1986) 217.

*The Ark of the Covenant*

Because the people carried the Ark of the Covenant into battle in Josh. 6:6 and implies that they should have done so in Num. 14:44, and because it is indirectly connected with the war effort in Josh. 7:6 and 8:33, some have surmised that Israel understood it to function as a war palladium.[34] Rudolf Smend appears to both affirm and reject this notion. He notes that in Israel's battle with the Philistines in 1 Samuel 4, the Ark was brought along in desperation in the *second* battle, but not in the first one (vv. 3ff.), and that the Philistines observed that the Ark had not accompanied the Israelite warriors in previous battles (v. 7). Consequently, it would appear at this time it was not being used as a true war standard.[35] Thus, the notion of the Ark as a war palladium is wrong if it supposes that the Ark was present at every war or that its sole purpose was warlike, because as the ark embodied God's presence in war, it also did in peace. However, the concept has some validity "if the war was the sphere in which the efficacy of the god was most perceptible and most characteristic, then one has the right to speak of the ark according to its most important function, a palladium in war."[36]

But if its most important function was in war, why was it used only on some occasions but not on others? It would seem that if the Ark was widely understood in this manner that it would demand much more prominence in the narratives. It seems best, then, to conclude with Jones that the people, in general, did not view the Ark as a war palladium.[37]

*Ḥerem*

The concept of *ḥerem* is a crucial but difficult one. The word (חרם), in both its verb and noun forms, appears 84 times, usually but falsely translated as "ban." Furthermore, it is concentrated in the Deuteronomistic history.[38]

---

[34]The word comes from the Greek statue of Pallas, the preservation of which insured the safety of Troy. Thus it refers to anything that affords effective protection and security.

[35]Rudolf Smend, *Yahweh War and Tribal Confederation* (Nashville: Abingdon, 1970) 77.

[36]Smend, 78. Eichrodt accepts the view that the Ark functioned as a palladium in war (273).

[37]Jones, "The Concept of Holy War," 309f.

[38]Norbert Lohfink, "ḥerem," *Theological Dictionary of the Old Testament*, ed. by G. Johannes Botterweck & Helmer Ringgren, trans. by David R. Green (Grand

A few key passages illustrate the various uses. Leviticus 27:28 and Deut. 7:26 use it in the sense of something which has been removed from the sphere of the profane and set apart for Yahweh or things, like idols, which God has condemned and, consequently, cannot be set apart for Yahweh.[39]

> Nothing that a person owns that has been devoted to destruction for the LORD, be it human or animal, or inherited landholding, may be sold or redeemed; every devoted thing is most holy to the LORD. (Lev. 27:28)

> Do not bring an abhorrent thing into your house, or you will be set apart for destruction like it. You must utterly detest and abhor it, for it is set apart for destruction. (Deut. 7:26)

The most prominent usage of the word, however, revolves around the practice of extermination of entire populations in warfare.

> All the spoil of these towns, and the livestock, the Israelites took for their booty; but all the people they struck down with the edge of the sword, until they had destroyed them, and they did not leave any who breathed. (Josh 11:14)

Thus, there is "the destruction of everything among the enemy which the victor might have retained and enjoyed,"[40] "a renunciation of private enrichment."[41] Some speculate that this practice had its basis in the idea that persons or things contaminated by idolatry carried with them a dangerous force which was to be avoided.[42]

---

Rapids: Eerdmans, 1986) 181.

[39]Lohfink, *TDOT*, 184.

[40]Roland H. Bainton, *Christian Attitudes Toward War and Peace* (Nashville: Abingdon Press, 1990) 48.

[41]Zimmerli, 58.

[42]Louis F. Hartman, "Ban," *Encyclopedic Dictionary of the Bible*. A translation and adaptation of A. Wander Born's *Bijbels Woordenboek*. (New York: McGraw-Hill, 1963) 196. Johannes Pedersen, *Israel, Its Life and Culture III, IV* (London: Oxford, 1940) 27-31. Pedersen believes that one source of this understanding lay in the belief that an alien spiritual power permeated the persons and possessions of the enemy and could only be made harmless by concentration to Yahweh.

Walter Eichrodt believes that this custom cannot "be explained either as a sacrificial or as an oblatory act. It is part of the discipline laid on the warrior, by which he renounces something in thanksgiving to the deity present in the camp. This means that the enemy is regarded as holy or dedicated, and so no longer available for human possession."[43]

Eichrodt defends this understanding by pointing out that human beings were killed, not burnt, and the booty not consecrated, but utterly destroyed. The fact that the ban was a vow does not suggest that it was seen as a sacrifice, but only that it was a duty of solemn importance.[44]

Although the notion of unqualified devotion to Yahweh seems to be the basis of *herem*, other reasons are cited: judgment upon the Canaanites (Gen. 15:16; Lev. 18:25, 28) and the cruel Amalekites (1 Sam. 15:2, 33), and the fear, noted above, of idolatrous contamination (Deut. 7:1-6).[45] The fact that the text emphasizes judgment on the Canaanites and the Amalekites reflects the conviction among at least some Israelites that these wars had an *ethical* basis. It was not that Yahweh was blindly partial to Israel, but, in this instance, Israel was the means whereby Yahweh punished wickedness. The warning of Deuteronomy 9:4 indicates that Israel tended to forget this truth.

> When the LORD your God thrusts them out before you, do not say to yourself, "It is because of my righteousness that the LORD has brought me in to occupy this land"; it is rather because of the wickedness of these nations that the LORD is dispossessing them before you. (Deut. 9:4)[46]

Millar Burrows points out that Israel's felt need to justify their wars is true even of the most unscrupulously aggressive nations, but "the ques-

---

[43]Walter Eichrodt, *Theology of the Old Testament* I, trans. by J.A Baker (Philadelphia: Westminster, 1961) 139.

[44]Eichrodt, 139. His notion of the booty doesn't square with the discussion which follows here.

[45]Eichrodt, 140.

[46]Gottwald views this as a curious bit of reasoning because it seems to enable Israel to say that they were *relatively* more righteous than the Canaanites. Thus, he sees this statement's basis more from a cultic perspective than a moral perspective. "If Israel had been more stable, she could have lived uncontaminated among the Canaanites.... Israel being so cultically fickle, her territory must be morally and religiously sanitized by herem." "'Holy War' in Deuteronomy," 304.

tion always is how profound the feeling is and how far it influences conduct."[47] One of the purposes of this entire study is to illustrate that within the entire scope of Israel's history we find a broad range of "feelings" about the morality of war and the complex ways those feelings affected conduct.

For the Deuteronomic historians the carrying out of the *herem* originally always involved the killing of all Canaanites, but there are several variations regarding non-Canaanites and regarding booty. Sometimes the Israelites were to burn everything in the city.

> The images of their gods you shall burn with fire. Do not covet the silver or the gold that is on them and take it for yourself, because you could be ensnared by it; for it is abhorrent to the LORD your God. (Deut. 7:25)

At other times all was to be burned except the silver and gold.

> They burned down the city, and everything in it; only the silver and gold, and the vessels of bronze and iron, they put into the treasury of the house of the LORD. (Josh. 6:24)

Some passages in the Deuteronomic history exclude livestock from destruction,

> At that time we captured all his towns, and in each town we utterly destroyed men, women, and children. We left not a single survivor. Only the livestock we kept as spoil for ourselves, as well as the plunder of the towns that we had captured. (Deut. 2:34, 35)

---

[47]Millar Burrows, *An Outline of Biblical Theology* (Philadelphia: Westminster, 1946) 318. The Persian Gulf War of 1991 provides some illustrations on the need that nations feel to justify war. Sadaam Hussein justified his invasion of Kuwait on the basis of land taken from Iraq and given to Kuwait by the British and the fact that Kuwait was pumping oil on the border which rightfully belonged to Iraq. President Bush countered by trying to downplay the economic dimensions (e.g., that oil was needed to maintain American and Western lifestyles) and sought to focus on the moral dimensions (e.g., Hussein was a brutal Hitler who ordered an unprovoked invasion of helpless and innocent Kuwait). Examples could be found from both sides of every modern, and possibly every ancient war. The urge to find, or at least to rationalize a moral justification for conflict is irresistible.

Others command the destruction of all creatures.

> Joshua took Makkedah on that day, and struck it and its king
> with the edge of the sword; he utterly destroyed every person
> in it; he left no one remaining. And he did to the king of Mak-
> kedah as he had done to the king of Jericho ... and took it, and
> struck it with the edge of the sword, and its king and its towns,
> and every person in it; he left no one remaining, just as he had
> done to Eglon, and utterly destroyed it with every person in it
> ... and he took it with its king and all its town they struck them
> with the edge of the sword, and utterly destroyed every person
> in it; he left no one remaining; just as he had done to Hebron,
> and, as he had done to Libnah and its king, so he did to Debir
> and its king. So Joshua defeated the whole land, the hill country
> and the Negeb and the lowland and the slopes, and all their
> kings; he left no one remaining, but utterly destroyed all that
> breathed, as the LORD God of Israel commanded. (Josh. 10:28,
> 37, 39, 40)

A difficulty in the conquest narratives emerges when the text states
that the *herem* was carried out in the taking of a city, but later the city
has to be *re*captured (e.g., Hebron in Josh. 10:36-39; 15:13-17). If all were
destroyed, why would it need to be retaken? One possibility is that
many inhabitants escaped and later resettled their city since the Israelites were not numerous enough to occupy every city they captured.

First Samuel 15 recounts the vivid story of Saul failing to carry out
the *herem* against the Amalekites. Saul's motives in sparing the best of
the animals for Yahweh appear to be good but as Frank Cross notes, he
attempts "to manipulate the fixed form of holy war in his own interest."[48] This story is especially difficult because Saul is condemned for
doing almost exactly what David did a short time later against these
same Amalekites. In 1 Sam. 27:8-9 and 30:1-31, David defeats the
Amalekites but takes livestock and other valuables. Gottwald notes that
the term *herem* is not found in these accounts of David and the
Amalekites, and further observes that "it is striking that neither in 1
Sam. 27 nor in 1 Sam. 30, contrary to 1 Sam. 15, is anything said about
the command to exterminate Amalek."[49]

---

[48] *Canaanite Myth and Hebrew Epic* (Cambridge: Harvard University Press,
1973) 221.
[49] Gottwald, "'Holy War' in Deuteronomy," 299.

From a historical perspective, then, the *herem* custom seems to have undergone considerable modification with the passage of time. Cattle and booty, as noted above, and even women and children were, at times, exempted from the ban (Deut. 20:13ff.). David not only allowed his soldiers to retain booty, but instituted a liberalized policy whereby booty "should be shared equitably between the active participants and the strategic reserves" (1 Sam. 30:16-24).[50] In the latter period of the monarchy the custom of the *herem* seems to have disappeared. Clearly, it had already been disregarded in the time of Ahab[51] because, by then, the Israelite kings had gained a reputation for being merciful (1 Kings 20:31). Gottwald concludes that "perhaps in a majority of battles no *herem* vow was thought necessary. If such is the case, Deuteronomy takes the most severe form of the vow and treats it as normative for all of Israel's war in Canaan.[52]

Apparently, part of what scholars call the "Deuteronomic Reformation" under Josiah consisted of a revival of the *herem*. The historian gives meticulous attention in 2 Kings 22 and 23 to Josiah's destruction of the idols and the priests who attended them. Furthermore, these reforms and the Saul story may be illustrations of why the Deuteronomic historian(s) placed such an important emphasis on the *herem*. Viewing the history of Israel and Judah from the vantage point of the exile which resulted from the destruction of the nation, the historian points to disobedience as the basic cause for destruction (Deut. 28).[53] Deuteronomy 7:1-6 prohibits covenants and intermarriage with outsiders and com-

---

[50]Keith W. Whitelam, *The Just King: Monarchical Judicial Authority in Ancient Israel* (Sheffield: JSOT Press, 1979) 119. See also K. N. Schoville, "War; Warfare," *International Standard Bible Encyclopedia* IV, ed. by G. W. Bromiley (Grand Rapids: Eerdmans, 1988) 1016.

[51]Eichrodt, 140.

[52]Gottwald, "'Holy War' in Deuteronomy," 300. Ahab's merciful treatment of the Syrian King Benhadad is condemned by an unknown prophet (v.42). The rules about a surrendering non-Canaanite in Deut. 20, however, would seem to suggest that Benhadad should be spared.

[53]Denis Baly states that the "concept of a sustained holy war belongs to a later period, in an attempt to understand the meaning of past events rather than an interpretation called forth by the events themselves at the time when they happened. It belongs, therefore, to history as it was remembered and studied and not to the history as it was experienced.... They [the Deuteronomic editors]... were convinced that the people from the beginning ought to have eradicated more firmly the foreign ideas." *God and History in the Old Testament: The Encounter with the Absolute Other in Ancient Israel* (New York: Harper and Row, 1976) 49f.

mands that they be put under the *herem*. From the perspective of the
Deuteronomist, was not the defeat of Israel and Judah at least partially
(if not completely) a result of the failure to destroy the Canaanites and
other enemies? Apparently the historian viewed the pagan's seductive
influence on Israel's faith as a major cause of their nations' apostasy.
"Thus the failure to carry out the *herem* is used by the exilic Deuteronomist to account for the catastrophe and make it intellectually as-
similable."[54]

Von Rad believes that the old holy wars were defensive in nature
but that the author of Deuteronomy decisively changes them to wars of
religion "against the Canaanite cult which is irreconcilable with faith in
Yahweh."[55] Von Rad also sees the Deuteronomist as seeking to combat
the secular understanding of war, which had emerged in the monarchy,
by calling for the re-institution of the amphictyonic militia which represented a religious understanding of war that had been either excluded
or strongly pushed to the periphery of Israelite thought and practice.
Von Rad goes so far to say that the set of ideas about holy war com-
prised "the actual core of all their [i.e., those supporting the Deutero-
nomic/Josianic reformation] thinking about Israel around which everything else could be organically grouped."[56] Whether one takes it this
far or not, it seems clear that the Deuteronomic Reformation is closely
linked to the concept of holy war.

We should note once again that there are parallels of *herem* outside
Israel, most notably in the Moabite Stone Monument (or Mesha Stela)
where the Moabite King Mesha attacked Israel at Nebo, captured the
city, and totally destroyed the population "for I had consecrated it to
Ashtar-Chemosh for destruction."[57] This remarkable text would seem to

---

[54]Lohfink, TDOT, 198. This comment would address de Vaux's statement
where he finds it remarkable that herem should be emphasized in Deuteronomy
since the book was written when the custom was little more than a memory. *Ancient Israel*, 260. If the book were written, as many scholars believe, during
Josiah's reign, then it is not surprising that *herem* is prominent because the historian is calling for a revival of the custom.

[55]Von Rad, 118.

[56]Von Rad, 126.

[57]Note that the only differences here between Israelites holy war and
Moabite holy war are: (1) the substitution of Chemosh for Yahweh and Moab for
Israel, and (2) Mesha drags the vessels of Yahweh before his god—"presumably
to subordinate and annex them rather than destroy them. Yahweh, by contrast,
would have no truck with other cult-objects. They must be burnt." F. Derek Kidner, "Old Testament Perspectives on War," *Evangelical Quarterly* 57, 2 (April
1985): 103.

indicate that "there was in Israel and Moab, and perhaps also among other neighboring peoples, a common practice of *herem* and a common tradition for telling of it."[58]

*Herem* is, in sum: (1) The term refers primarily to the practice of extermination of entire populations during warfare, but that it was variously understood and unevenly observed through Israelite history; (2) The Book of Deuteronomy, written sometime around the reign of Josiah, calls for the reinstitution of this custom and blames Israel's/Judah's fall, at least in part, to the failure to carry it out; (3) The *herem* was not unique to Israel but a practice she shared with her neighbors.[59]

In spite of what we may conclude, however, about the concept of *herem*, Lohfink raises a number of interesting questions which, at this point, are still unanswered.

Did original usage of the word group derive from actual *herem* ritual involving the magical encirclement of a city (Josh. 6:3ff.) or the stretching forth of a spear (Josh. 8:18)? What originally instigated a *herem*—a vow (Num. 21:2) or the command of a military leader (Josh. 6:17)? Was the critical element the renunciation of booty or the radical extermination? Was the destruction and razing of a city considered a part of the *herem* or was it a further measure (Josh. 6:24; 8:28; 11:11)? What distinguished the punishment of *herem* from the other forms of capital punishment?[60]

## The Day of Yahweh

We should also note that the term "Day of Yahweh" is closely related to the concept of holy war. Von Rad highlights this in an article written several years after his book on holy war.[61] After examining

---

[58]Lohfink, *TDOT*, 190. According to Isa. 37:11, Sennacherib of Assyria is said to engage in the practice of herem. Max Weber points out that this practice was universal and especially seen in "Egypt, where the king, by virtue of ritualistic duty, slaughters the captives. The enemy was held as godless." *Ancient Judaism*, trans. by Han Gerth and Don Martindale (Glencoe, IL: Free Press, 1952) 93. W. F. Albright agrees: "The practice of devoting a recalcitrant foe to destruction as a kind of gigantic holocaust to the national deity was apparently universal among the early Semites." *From The Stone Age to Christianity* (Baltimore: Johns Hopkins Press, 1940) 213.

[59]No effort is made here to determine the origins of *herem*, but no one attributes its beginnings to Israel.

[60]Ibid., 188.

[61]Gerhard von Rad, "The Origin of the Concept of the Day of Yahweh," *Jour-*

passages in Isa. 13, 34; Ezek. 7; Joel 2, and elsewhere, he draws two conclusions: (1) "the Day of Yahweh encompasses a pure event of war, the rise of Yahweh against his enemies, his battle and his victory;"[62] (2) the entire material for this imagery which surrounds the concept of the Day of Yahweh is of old-Israelite origin. It derives from the tradition of the holy wars of Yahweh."[63] Von Rad views the new element introduced by Amos, which other prophets used at a later time, viz., that the Day of Yahweh is a time of darkness and *judgment against Israel*, as an interlude in the history of the concept, because the later prophets returned to the idea that the Day represented a day of *salvation* for Israel.[64] Thus, the "Day" had both a positive and negative dimension in Israel's prophetic traditions. To some it was a day of judgment on rebellious Israel while to others it was a day of salvation and deliverance from enemies.

## War and the Establishment of the Monarchy

An enduring contribution of von Rad, besides being the catalyst of holy war research, is his insistence that holy war was an instrument of prophetic criticism against the royal court, a view accepted by most scholars.[65] VonRad thus raises the crucial issue of the relationship between the concept of holy war and the development of the monarchy. A surprising amount of the debate surrounding holy war revolves around the issue of whether or not the monarchy was a legitimate or illegitimate development in Israel's history. The relationship between the establishment of the monarchy and Israel's warfare is stated strikingly in 1 Samuel 8:20 where the Israelites ask for a king "who will fight our battle for us."

The narratives describing the rise of the monarchy in 1 Samuel 8-12 have provided scholars with ample ammunition to arrive at opposing conclusions regarding the establishment of the monarchy. Scholars have

---

*nal of Semitic Studies* IV, 2 (April 1959): 97-108.

[62]Ibid., 103. Frank Cross accepts this view but also relates the term to mythological and apocalyptic motifs (111).

[63]Ibid., 104.

[64]Ibid., 104f. Although Amos was the first to use the term "Day of Yahweh," von Rad asserts that he was only employing a "firmly coined formula of tradition." (108). Von Rad thinks that this formula is only accidentally missing from the ancient accounts of holy war and that possibly the "Book of the Wars of Yahweh" (Num. 21:14) contained this phrase.

[65]Ollenburger, 31.

long noted different traditions within the text.[66] The fundamental question seems to be whether these two traditions represent pro and anti-monarchy views or whether they represent a debate within Israel as to the *kind* of kingship Israel should have.

Martin Noth's view that the final Deuteronomic redactor/theologian was fundamentally opposed to the institution of kingship became a standard position in Old Testament scholarship.[67] Those who hold this view believe that the historian rejected kingship because its establishment represented a rejection of Yahweh as king.

> And the LORD said to Samuel, "Listen to the voice of the people in all that they say to you; for they have not rejected you, but they have rejected me from being king over them." (I Sam. 8:7)

Noth cites passages such as Hosea 8:4 (they have set up kings but not by me) to indicate that there persisted for centuries in Israel a strong tradition which flatly refused to recognize the monarchy as legitimate. According to Max Weber, to many prophets, the "whole bureaucratic apparatus was an Egyptian abomination."[68] Moshe Weinfeld provides a good summary of this approach.[69] He sees the establishment of a royal dynasty and the creation of a fixed religious center as two developments which shattered the earlier sacral conceptual frameworks characteristic of the Israelite amphictyony. In the monarchy the "army of Yahweh" (Judg. 5:11, 12; 2 Sam. 1:12) becomes "the men of David." During the amphictyony Yahweh bestows His spirit on any mortal at any times he pleases, but in the monarchy this anointing is limited to the king. Thus, this tradition within Israel favored the retention of the tribal league where Yahweh alone was king and where Yahweh raised

---

[66]The "Saul source:" 1 Sam. 9:1-10:16; ch. 11 and the "Samuel source:" 1 Sam. 7:3-8:22; 10:17-27; ch. 12 are discussed in Bernhard Anderson, 206-210. Anderson, following Eichrodt, Spicer, and others, traces Israel's ambivalent attitude toward the monarchy back to its inception.

[67]Martin Noth, *The History of Israel*, trans. by Stanley Godman (New York: Harper and Row, 1958) 232: "(The deuteronomist) aimed to represent the monarchy as a fundamental cause of Israel's defection." See also pp. 175, 215.

[68]Weber, 111.

[69]See his chapter "Zion and Jerusalem as Religious and Political Capital: Ideology and Utopia," in *The Poet and the Historian: Essays in Literary and Historical Biblical Criticism*, ed. by Richard E. Friedman (Chico, CA: Scholars Press, 1983) 76-115.

up charismatic leaders who led the people in battle.[70] As Kidner states the issues, "at more than one level the new military style was a threat to Israel's character, substituting professionalism and the latest weaponry for spontaneous leadership and naked faith. It began to turn a federation of tribes into an increasingly impersonal and burdensome state, saddled with the expense of garrisons and a full-time chariot force, and tempted into military adventures with dubious allies."[71]

Millard Lind views the rejection of kingship in 1 Samuel as a rejection of "kingship like all the nations," a kingship whereby the divinity was mediated on the human scene chiefly by one who represented the "Enlil function," the violent power function. In contrast, Yahweh reserved the Enlil function to himself and mediated his covenant through a prophet, not through a king or warrior.[72]

Furthermore, the vast *structural* changes brought on by the monarchy[73] required a new *ideology* and the David/Zion tradition provided

---

[70]Anderson, 208. Inbar observes that these radical innovations of dynastic kingship and a permanent sanctuary, which many regarded as sins, were later given a new twist by those prophets who viewed the eschatological reign of peace in terms of kingship and worship at one sanctuary. "In this manner, we are witness to the paradoxical fact that dynastic kingship and a permanent sanctuary, which were regarded as transgressions at the dawn of Israelite history, became a great incentive and a lever for the heralding of salvation to Israel and to the peoples of the world." (114f.). John L. McKenzie, S. J., holds to this basic view in *The Two-Edged Sword* (Milwaukee: The Bruce Publishing Co., 1956) 132-149. Weber, 112, offers a caustic observation: "The utopian phantasies of their champions were saturated the more with bloody images of Yahweh's heroic feats the more un-military they had become in fact. Just as today, in all countries, we find the highest measure of war thirst among those strata of literati who are farthest from the trenches and by nature least military." Much of the rhetoric from the recent Gulf War confirms this analysis.

[71]Kidner, 105.

[72]Millard Lind, "Perspectives on War and Peace in the Hebrew Scriptures," *Monotheism, Power, Justice: Collected Old Testament Essays* (Elkhard, IN: Institute of Mennonite Studies, 1990) 174.

[73]Gottwald, *Hebrew Bible*, 323-325, lists four major enduring structural effects of the monarchy: political centralization, social stratification, shifts in land tenure, and domestic repercussions of foreign trade, diplomacy and war. Albright observes a substantial change from tabernacle to the beautiful temple of Solomon, where the process of Canaanization appears to reach a climax (225). The temple was not intended to be a public place of worship for all Israel but "to be a royal chapel into which the palladium of Israel was brought as a sign that the worship of Yahweh was thereafter to be under the special protection of the king."

it. Hobbs notes that this tradition, in contrast to the patriarchal, Exodus-Sinai, and conquest traditions, is the only one centered around one person who was still living while these traditions were still being formulated and propagated.[74] Drawing on Hobsbawm and Ranger's *The Invention of Tradition*, which shows how new institutions establish legitimacy and authority, Hobbs describes how the Davidic covenant/tradition reworked the older patriarchal and Sinai traditions to demonstrate how the Davidic covenant was in continuity with, and a logical progression from, the older covenants.[75] To establish legitimacy and continuity the Davidic tradition sought to find justification for the monarchy's imperialistic and economically motivated wars. Consequently, offensive wars became defensive wars, e.g., war with the Amalekites was because they resisted Israel's exit from Egypt; war against Moab was because they prevented Israel's approach to Canaan; and war against Edom was because of the jealous brother of Jacob.[76] In fact, however, David's wars were not defensive nor for some past misdeed, but they were David's means to build an empire.[77] In addition, David subjected the Moabites to cruel treatment once he had defeated them (2 Sam. 8:2) and engaged in excessive and brutal treatment of the Edomites (1 Kings 11:14-16).[78] Hobbs, following von Rad and Noth, believes that many of the prophets, representing a view held by many within Israel, rejected this process and institution and called for a return

---

[74]Hobbs, 60.

[75]Ibid., 63-66.

[76]Ibid., 67. Furthermore, as Wright has noted, the Davidic covenant was a different type than that of the Mosaic covenant. The Mosaic covenant had to be regularly renewed, but the Davidic covenant was an "everlasting covenant." "In a masterful defense of the ways of God with Israel in the Promised Land, the Deuteronomic historian uses the theme of the divine lawsuit against Israel for breach of the Mosaic covenant. It is not surprising, however, that the Chronicler, writing for the small postexilic community, should center his case in the Davidic covenant. There is a future for the community because God promised it to David." G. Ernest Wright, *The Old Testament and Theology* (New York: Harper & Row, 1969) 138.

[77]David is depicted throughout the texts as a warrior par excellence and, in contrast, his son Solomon is depicted as a just king par excellence. Whitelam, 166.

[78]Hobbs, 149. Kidner observes that David's wars varied between "sheer brigandry and responsible campaigning" (p. 106) and that he conquered territories emphatically denied to Israel in God's charge to Moses (p. 100). See 2 Sam. 8:12; Deut. 2:4f., 9, 19.

to the amphictyony ideal where Yahweh only was king and where holy war was carried out by Yahweh.[79]

Some scholars, on the other hand, view the debate within Israel regarding the monarchy, not as one where some embraced the monarchy while others rejected it, but a debate which centered on *the kind of kingship* Israel saw as ideal. These scholars argue that the Deuteronomic historians could hardly have been anti-monarchical because of the positive way that David is depicted as well as the positive assessment of the later reigns of Hezekiah and Josiah. In this view an "Israelite king insured the well-being of his people through fulfilling his responsibility as covenant administrator, and then trusting Yahweh to protect and bless them."[80] The warnings in 1 Samuel do not represent a rejection of the monarchy per se, but a warning against the possible abuses of kingship. This view holds that the Hebrews were aware they were introducing their own institution in imitation of others and under the strain of emergency, but that they did not allow it to achieve the sanctity and absolutism characteristic of neighboring kingships.[81]

---

[79]Ibid., 69.

[80]Gerald E. Gerbrant, *Kingship According to the Deuteronomistic History* (Atlanta: Scholars Press, 1986) 190. As covenant administrator the king had the power to bring about enormous changes in the life of the nation. Whitelam points to the fundamental legal and religious character of these changes: "It appears that the monarchy gained influence over local jurisdiction from an early date, limiting and ultimately subordinating priestly judicial functions at the various local sanctuaries. The important Solominic ideological development emphasized the internationalization of God-given judicial wisdom with the king over against previous reliance upon oracular guidance by the priest" (220).

[81]G. E. Wright, *The Old Testament Against Its Environment* (London: SCM Press, 1962) 66f. A. D. H. Mayes, "The Rise of the Israelite Monarchy," *Zeitshrift fur Die Alttestamentlliche Wissenshcaft* 90, 1 (1978) 1-19, agrees that it is too simplistic to describe the deuteronomistic attitude as anti-monarchical. The deuteronomistic criticism of the monarchy is set alongside the equally deuteronomistic view that the desire for a king originated in the perfectly laudable wish to replace the corrupt judges in Israel and that the king had been chosen by Yahweh (11). Ronald E. Clements, "The Deuteronomistic Interpretation of the Founding of the Monarchy in 1 Sam. VIII," *Vetus Testamentum* 24, 4 (1974): 398-410, acknowledging that the Deuteronomists wished to assert that the kingship was not an institution necessary for Israel's salvation, views the sin of requesting a king from Samuel in the fact that the request brought them the person of Saul, a king who would not save them but would rather be a hindrance to the succeeding king whom Yahweh would choose (406). But why did the Deuteronomists affirm that Saul was elected to the office? Because the inclusion of the lengthy nar-

Paul Hanson also examines the legitimacy of the monarchy to the issue of warfare in ancient Israel.[82] In discussing the nature of the wars conducted by the northern and southern kings, Hanson concludes that although a sense of justice may have played a part in the minds of some of the kings, the wars of the kings for the most part were anything but "just wars." He cites three reasons: (1) The rupture of David's kingdom occurred as a result of the ruthless use of raw power by the king. (2) In case after case kings fought wars not in Yahweh's cause of defending the weak and impoverished against the oppressor but in careless adventures aimed at adding territory and wealth to their kingdoms. (3) By defining greatness in terms of earthly power and splendor, the kings attracted the attention of greedy neighbors, thereby encouraging and abetting aggression by hostile and envious neighbors.[83] Thus, warfare under the kings was a classic example of the abuse of monarchical power.

On the basis of this discussion we draw two conclusions: (1) We can discern no clear fixed formula for Holy War in Israel. What seems to emerge is a pattern which exhibits a number of constant elements, but with room for flexibility and variety in the presentation.[84] (2) The people of Israel were highly ambivalent about the institution of the monarchy, and the way the kings conducted warfare contributed to this ambivalence. To employ ethical terms, in establishing the monarchy Israel

---

rative of the Rise of David (1 Sam. 14:14–2 Sam. 5) depicts David as Yahweh's chosen one to be Saul's *successor* (407; emphasis added). Tomoo Ishida recognizes an anti-monarchical strand in the texts but claims that it had been silenced by the time of David and Solomon. He seems to favor the view, contrary to most scholars, that Gideon actually accepted the offer of kingship (Judg. 8) but the language was later changed in order to deny Abimelech's, Gideon's son, claim to be king. In addition, Jotham's fable (Judg. 9:8-15) was directed not against monarchy as such but at Abimelech's effort to become Israel's monarch. *The Royal Dynasties in Ancient Israel: A Study of the Formation and Development of Royal-Dynastic Ideology* (New York: Walter de Gruyter, 1977) 184f.

[82]Paul Hanson, "War and Peace in the Hebrew Bible," *Interpretation* 38, 4 (1984) 341-362. See also Max Weber who earlier observed: "The seers and prophets independent of the king, the popular heirs of the military Nebiim, now without commissions, hence, hallowed the time when Yahweh himself as war leader led the peasant army, when the ass-riding prince did not rely on horses and wagons and alliances, but solely on the god of the covenant and his help" (111).

[83]Ibid., 351. See Hobbs, 148-150, for examples of how David's brutal policies brought problems for Israel years later.

[84]Jones, "The Concept... ," 309, 312.

may have done the *right thing* for the *wrong reasons*. It is most probable that Israel could not have survived without the establishment of a centralized government. However, the initial impetus for this was a result of a lack of faith in Yahweh. The people wanted a king who would fight their battles for them (1 Sam. 8:20), signifying a rejection of their Warrior-King Yahweh. Some may hold that Hosea and possibly other prophets insisted that Israel did the *wrong thing* for the *wrong reasons*, but the weight of evidence seems to be against them. It seems more accurate to say with Lind that "the Deuteronomist recognized kingship as an institution essentially foreign to Israel, and demanded its radical *transformation* from an institution based upon military power, international diplomacy, and state commerce, to an institution whose political base was the fear of Yahweh and the doing of his law (Deut. 17:14-20)."[85]

Furthermore, while Isaiah of Jerusalem was a severe critic of the *policies* of the Judean kings, nevertheless his enthusiasm for the *concept* of royal theology is clear and unambiguous. As Judah's leadership deteriorated, hoever, Isaiah had to look beyond the present leadership to a future David who would lead the nation back to Yahweh (Isa. 9 & 11).[86]

---

[85]Millard Lind, "Economics Among the People of God in the Old Testament," in *Monotheism...* , 221. Emphasis added.

[86]This type of ambivalence is aptly described in an essay by Baruch Halpern, "The Uneasy Compromise: Israel between League and Monarchy," in *Traditions in Transformation: Turning Points in Biblical Faith*, ed. by Baruch Halpern and Jon Levinson (Winona Lake, IN: Eisenbrauns, 1981) 59-96. He concludes: ". . . just as Israel's egalitarian, covenantal religion assimilated and transformed royal, messianic elements, Israel's tribes came to terms with the fact of a central administration. In the process, both the religion of the covenant, and the tribes, were profoundly transformed. But it is precisely that transformation that produced the ancient Near East's profoundest contributions to the human race. It is that synthesis from which much of the modern world has been shaped."

# Chapter Two

# HOLY WAR:
## ISRAEL ACTIVE

In warfare opposing armies engage each other in battle. In the next chapter we will examine how many of Israel's battles did *not* fit into this mold. Instead, Yahweh alone fought the battle while the people observed. Nonetheless, there are times when the text either assumes or explicitly states that the Israelites engaged in battle.

A major thrust of Patrick Miller's *The Divine Warrior in Early Israel* is that "at the center of Israel's warfare was the unyielding conviction that victory was the result of a fusion of divine and human activity .... Yahweh was general of both the earthly and the heavenly host."[1]

Miller refers to this as a "synergism," a term he took from von Rad, who, in turn, had borrowed it from Martin Buber.[2] As the next chapter will indicate, Miller has overstated his case. In many instances there was no fusion. A more accurate way to state Israel's "unyielding conviction" is to say that Israel was convinced that however they won, whether by miraculous intervention or by engaging the enemy in battle, victory was from Yahweh. The following contains a partial list of cases where victory was given *through* Israel's army or through a single warrior.

In rehearsing Israel's victories en route to Canaan, the speech of Moses affirms that "Yahweh our God delivered him (Sihon of Heshbon) over to us: we defeated him ... we captured all his cities and laid whole towns under ban ... So Yahweh our God put Og king of Bashan at our mercy too, with all the people. We struck him down and not a thing remained to him" (Deut. 2:33f; 3:3f).

The involvement of Israel is clear. Unlike Israel's experience at the Sea of Reeds, when they were told to "stand still ...." (Ex. 14:13), they

---

[1]Patrick D Miller, Jr., *The Divine Warrior in Early Israel* (Cambridge: Harvard University Press, 1973) 156.

[2]Ben C. Ollenburger, "Gerhard von Rad's Theory of Holy War" in Introduction to von Rad, *Holy War in Ancient Israel* (Grand Rapids: Eerdmans, 1991) 18.

engaged the transjordan kingdoms in battle and prevailed. The great
military strategist, Joshua, whom Edgar Conrad in his excellent study
calls "the paradigmatic warrior in the Deuteronomic texts,"[3] leads Israel
into battle against superior forces. While the text constantly reminds the
reader that Yahweh gave the victory, it was not without Israel's
participation. The battle of Jericho included the killing of men, women,
and animals (Josh. 6:21). The warriors of Ai were enticed out of their
city and the Israelites "set about them till not one was alive and none
left to flee ... When Israel had finished killing all the inhabitants of Ai
in the open ground and where they followed them into the wilderness,
and when all to a man had fallen by the edge of the sword, all Israel
returned to Ai and slaughtered all its people" (Josh. 7:22,24).

The story of the attack of five Canaanite kings against the Gibeonites
who had made a treaty with Israel illustrates the concept of synergism.
The victory was a combination of Israel's fighting and Yahweh's
miraculous intervention. "Yahweh hurled huge hailstones from heaven
on them ... More of them died under the hailstones than at the edge of
Israel's sword (Josh. 10:11). The same fate happened to a coalition of
northern kings in Joshua 11. Yahweh delivered them over to Israel but
it was a result of Joshua's strategy to attack at a place where the kings'
chariots could not maneuver.[4] "Yahweh delivered them into the power
of Israel, who defeated them and pursued them ...; Israel harried them
till not one was left to escape" (Josh. 11:8).

The covenant at Shechem (Josh. 24) sets forth the cooperative aspect
of holy war. This cooperation is in contrast, as Lind notes, to the Sinai
covenant which does not contain this element.[5] Although the emphasis
in the covenant is on Yahweh's acts of deliverance on Israel's behalf,
deliverance did not come about in the same way as it did at the Sea of
Reeds. There Israel did not fight. In the instances Joshua cites, Israel's
military participation is assumed.

The period of the Judges is important in examining the phenomenon
of the war in Israel. Von Rad's thesis is that holy war proper, that is, as
a sacral institution, was limited to this period, and that everything

[3]Edgar W. Conrad, *Fear Not Warrior: A Study of 'al tira' Pericopes in the Hebrew Scriptures* (Chico, CA: Scholars Press, 1985) 53.

[4]Joshua "caught them unawares by the waters of Merom" (v. 7) which rose in a valley 4000 feet above sea level. By doing this Joshua neutralized the kings' chief military advantage, i.e., their superior military hardware.

[5]Millard Lind, "Paradigm of Holy War in the Old Testament," *Monotheism, Power, Justice: Collected Old Testament Essays* (Elkhart, IN: Institute of Mennonite Studies, 1990) 187.

changed later as a result of "Solomonic humanism."[6] The purpose of this chapter, however, does not hinge on the proving or disproving of his thesis.

The book of Judges starts out with the Israelites requesting aid from Yahweh against the Canaanites. Yahweh leads to victory as the army routs the enemy. For good measure and to give him a dose of his own medicine, Adoni-zedek's thumbs and big toes are cut off (Judg. 1:1-8). Israel is not a passive participant in the initial episode of Judges.

The first judge mentioned, Othniel, achieves a victory over the Edomites as a result of Yahweh's spirit coming upon him (Jud. 3:9-11). Likewise, Barak, armed with a promise of victory from Deborah[7] and with 10,000 men, destroys Sisera's entire army (Judg. 4:9, 14-16). The Song of Deborah, recognized by virtually all scholars as a very ancient hymn, celebrates the victory over Sisera's army. Furthermore, the cooperative effort of Yahweh with Israel consumes most of the space in the poem. While Lind is correct to observe that the poem downgrades Israel's fighting and emphasizes rather that the decisive action of the battle was Yahweh's, he goes too far in limiting Israel's army to "mop-up exercises."[8] The army of Israel seemed to do more than merely draw

---

[6]Gerhard von Rad, *Holy War in Ancient Israel*, translated and edited by Marva Dawn (Grand Rapids: William B. Eerdmans Publishing Co., 1991) 74-84. See also his Studies in Deuteronomy, translated by David Stalker (London: SCM Press, 1948) 46.

[7]James Ackerman, "Prophecy and Warfare in Early Israel: A Study of the Deborah-Barak Story," *BASOR* 220 (1975): 5-13, argues convincingly that Deborah functions in a prophetic role, in contrast to the more usual view that prophecy emerged as a result of the development of the monarchy, in order to safeguard the religious-political ideals and traditions of the past over against the new directions inherent in monarchy. Thus, the prophetic relationship to holy war reaches far back into Israel's history. The same might also be said of Moses, who functions as a prophet during the Exodus event. Therefore, when the prophet Isaiah attempts to revive the holy war tradition, he is reaching back to a very ancient tradition. For a good general discussion of the song of Deborah see Norman Gottwald, *A Light to the Nations* (New York: Harper & Bros., 1959) 171-177.

[8]Lind, "Paradigm of Holy War in the Old Testament," 185f. Lind recognizes the difference between these two songs and deals with it by declaring that the Reed Sea experience becomes the paradigm of Yahweh's future acts with his people. However, isn't it more likely, given the diversity evident in ancient Israel, that there were several paradigms which explained Israel's experience and which formed their identity? On what basis, then, is one paradigm made to be the one normative paradigm?

the enemy into the trap and take political advantage of the event. Yahweh was indeed the main actor in this drama, but Israel's active participation was necessary. The involvement here is very different from that at the Sea of Reeds, where Israel participates in no way in the conflict but only observes the deliverance wrought by Yahweh.

The Gideon narratives provide an interesting combination of the active and passive war traditions. While the major emphasis is upon Yahweh's miraculous interventions (see discussion in chap. 3), still the army engages the enemy in combat and "utterly destroys them" (Judg. 7:25; 8:10-12). So von Rad errs when he insists that "the assumption of any kind of human synergism is carefully dismissed" in the story.[9] Gideon's army may have had the luxury of seeing the enemy defeated during the surprise attack (7:16-22), nevertheless a vigorous "mop up operation" is necessary in order to seal the victory (vv. 23-25).

The brief career of Abimelech contains similar motifs as noted above. God instigates the conflict between Abimelech and the Shechemites, whom Abimelech ruthlessly destroys (Judg. 9:22,40,44,49). The account, however, does seem to be more ambivalent about him than we find in other war narratives.[10] The narrative seems to justify Abimelech's actions and yet sees his death as a judgment from God because of the murder of his seventy brothers (vv. 56,57).

Although Samson never leads an army into battle, nor are the elements usually associated with holy war included in the narratives, nevertheless the Samson sagas relate to our discussion. Samson functions as a "one man army" against the Philistines, and he engages them in battle only after "the spirit of Yahweh has seized on him" (Judg. 14:19; 15:14). The miraculous or extraordinary elements of the sagas are not actions taken by Yahweh apart from human participation but are performed through Samson. The point of the stories is that his ability to slay a thousand Philistines with a jawbone of a donkey and his strength to carry the city gates of Gaza for several miles result from his special dedication to, and his empowerment by, Yahweh.

The story of Saul's holy war campaign against the Amalekites (1 Sam. 15) is discussed elsewhere,[11] but merits mention here because the account includes no activity of Yahweh other than the command to utterly destroy the Amalekites (vv. 2,3). Permeating the story is the

---

[9]Von Rad, *Holy War*, 87.

[10]Is it possible that the writer suggests ambivalence about this story by not using the name of Yahweh, but by referring to God as El?

[11]See the discussion in chap. 1.

assumption that Yahweh is involved in these martial undertakings, but the emphasis is upon human activity.

An experience by Saul's son Jonathan reflects the belief that victory in warfare came ultimately from Yahweh but not apart from the participation of the soldiers. As in the Gideon story, victory is not dependent on having a larger army because "nothing can prevent Yahweh from giving us victory, whether there are many or few of them" (1 Sam. 14:6). Jonathan, however, does not assume that Yahweh is automatically present in every Israelite military conflict, because he looks for a sign to indicate whether or not he ought to attack a Philistine outpost (vv. 8-10).[12] This incident adds weight to the belief that Israel did not assume that every war was a holy war or that because "God was on Israel's side" they could assume carte blanche that every battle would result in victory.

As noted in chapter one, scholars generally agree that the establishment of the monarchy signaled a change in Israel's understanding of and conducting of warfare. Whereas warfare in Joshua was to secure the land promised by Yahweh and warfare in Judges was to defend the land from enemy attack, King David institutes a policy of aggressive, expansionistic warfare. Unlike Samson, who defeated the Philistines because Yahweh's spirit seized upon him, David defeated Goliath because he was an expert marksman with a sling. Although Saul did invoke God's blessing on the endeavor (1 Sam. 17:37), there is a subtle shift here away from God's activity to the performance of the gifted and remarkable young warrior.

Even here, however, we must note that while the exploits of King David receive great emphasis, the texts are careful to show that Yahweh was the ultimate source of David's prowess. In a campaign against the Amalekites, David consults with Yahweh through the ephod, and unlike Saul, carries out the holy war ban against them (1 Sam. 30:6-20). Later, in a campaign against the Philistines, David again consults Yahweh (through the ephod?) and receives specific instructions on how to attack (2 Sam. 5:17-25). The "sound of the steps in the tops of the balsam trees" (v. 24) echoes the motif of Yahweh's heavenly army marching before the earthly army. Victory is now assured. Thus, the "synergism" theme is prominent in the military activity of one of Israel's greatest heroes. Yahweh's presence is not explicitly stated in

---

[12]As people of faith sought the will of Yahweh sometimes these signs were foretold by God or by a man of God (Ex. 3:12; I Sam. 2:34; 10:7-9; 2 Kings 19:29). At other times, as here and in Gen. 24:12f; Judg. 6:17-18,36-40; 2 Kings 20:8-10, it was suggested by the person in order to invite an answer from God.

every conflict, but it is assumed that David's great success is due to a combination of Yahweh's blessing and David's brilliant military strategy.

The campaign of Israel and Judah against the Moabites in 2 Kings 3 provides a classic example of synergistic holy war waged during the time of the monarchy. Yahweh's message regarding war comes through the prophet Elisha. While Israel and Moab prepare for battle, a miraculous element enters and plays a dominant part in the series of events (i.e., v. 17f, a wadi is filled with water without the benefit of rain). This confuses the Moabites, who, mistaking the water for blood, think that a bloody conflict has occurred between Israel and Judah. Thus, the Moabites rush to gather the booty but are surprised by an attack. The Israelites drive them back and "cut them to pieces" (v. 24). Consequently, a miracle provided through God's prophet contributes to victory, but the outcome also required fighting on the part of the Israelites.

The campaign against Moab, in which Elisha is a key figure, reflects to some degree an earlier event in the life of his mentor Elijah. In the famous contest on Mt. Carmel, Elijah demonstrates the power of the true God Yahweh and the impotence of Baal. Following the miracle of the fire, Elijah orders the seizure and slaughter of the 450 Baal prophets (vv. 22, 40). This contest takes the form of a holy war against Baal and the Baal followers function here as enemy soldiers and suffer the same fate as armed warriors. Victory comes from a synergism of Yahweh's miracle and human participation.

Two passages from the prophetic literature, Isa. 13:1-22 and Joel 3:9-17, provide examples of a synergistic understanding of holy war. Each views war as a sacred undertaking.

> Proclaim this among the nations: Prepare for war, stir up the warriors. Let all the soldiers draw near, let them come up. Beat your plowshares into swords, and your pruning hooks into spears; let the weakling say, "I am a warrior." Come quickly, all you nations all around, gather yourselves there. Bring down your warriors, O LORD. Let the nations rouse themselves, and come up to the valley of Jehoshaphat; for there I will sit to judge all the neighboring nations. Put in the sickle, for the harvest is ripe. Go in, tread, for the wine press is full. The vats overflow, for their wickedness is great. Multitudes, multitudes, in the valley of decision! For the day of the LORD is near in the valley of decision. (Joel 3:9-14)

Involved in this battle at the Day of Yahweh (Is. 13:9; Joel 3:14) are the heavenly hosts, who along with the earthly troops (Joel 4:9,10; Is. 13:3,15-18) destroy the enemies of Yahweh. Israel's war making activities, however, must be accompanied with trust in Yahweh, or the careful preparations will come to naught.

> He has taken away the covering of Judah. On that day you looked to the weapons of the House of the Forest, and you saw that there were many breaches in the city of David, and you collected the waters of the lower pool. You counted the houses of Jerusalem, and you broke down the houses to fortify the wall. (Isa. 22:8-10)

In Conrad's examination of the "Fear not warrior" terminology in the Old Testament, he demonstrates how Jeremiah uses this terminology but with a different twist.[13] The call of Jeremiah is replete with holy war language:

> [T]oday I am setting you over nations and over kingdoms, to tear up and to knock down, to destroy and to overthrow ... Do not be dismayed at their presence ... I, for my part, today will make you into a fortified city, a pillar of iron, and a wall of bronze to confront all this land ... They will fight against you but shall not overcome you, for I am with you to deliver you ...." (Jer. 1:9,10,17-19).

Here Jeremiah is Yahweh's warrior, but he does not fight *for* Israel but *against* her. Yahweh will "lay the ban on [Judah]" (Jer. 25:9). And Jeremiah has only one weapon—neither spear nor sword—but armed only with the word of Yahweh. So active spiritual warfare against his own people characterizes Jeremiah's entire ministry. His war wounds would be both spiritual (cannot have a wife or children, rejection by family, friends and country, despair and heartbreak) and physical (beaten, jailed, thrown into a pit, etc.). Jeremiah, as Yahweh's warrior, was an active participant in the conflict but his job was to *wage peace*. His message was not one of comfort and encouragement to the armies of Israel, but a message of peaceful co-existence with the new regime set up by Babylon.[14] As Conrad observes, "Gedaliah was the governor

---

[13]Conrad, 38-51.

[14]Jeremiah's situation recalls Woody Allen's quip that "More than any other time in history, mankind faces a crossroads. One path leads to despair and utter

representing Babylon, the earthly victor of the defeated nation. Jeremiah was the governor representing Yahweh, the heavenly victor of the defeated nation."[15] While the false prophets called for revolt against Babylon and assured the people that Yahweh would bring deliverance (Jer. 28:1-4), Jeremiah continually called for Judah to surrender and to submit to Babylon (Jer. 38:17f). For his stand the people label Jeremiah as a traitor, in essence a warrior who had switched his allegiance to Babylon and therefore deserved the death penalty (Jer. 26:11). However, Jeremiah was not a turncoat; he was Yahweh's warrior who remained faithful to his "commander-in-chief." Here Jeremiah turns the synergism concept upside down. If Judah will not submit to Babylon, Yahweh will join with the Babylonian army to defeat Judah.

Jeremiah's striking utilization of holy war motifs draws upon the prophetic tradition seen in Amos 1-2[16] and noted also in Is. 10:27c-34.[17] His daring and dangerous prophesying is seen most explicitly in 21:1-5.

> This is the word that came to Jeremiah from the LORD, when King Zedekiah sent to him Pashhur son of Malchiah and the priest Zephaniah son of Maaseiah, saying, "Please inquire of the LORD on our behalf, for King Nebuchadnezzar of Babylon is making war against us; perhaps the LORD will perform a wonderful deed for us, as he has often done, and will make him withdraw from us." Then Jeremiah said to them: Thus you shall say to Zedekiah: Thus says the LORD, the God of Israel: I am going to turn back the weapons of war that are in your hands and with which you are fighting against the king of Babylon and against the Chaldeans who are besieging you outside the walls; and I will bring them together into the center of this city. I myself will fight against you with outstretched hand and mighty arm, in anger, in fury, and in great wrath.

This is holy war *with Babylon, not Israel,* as the active means whereby Yahweh accomplishes his purposes. Jeremiah's use of the expression "with outstretched hand and strong arm" harks back to the Exodus-

---

hopelessness. The other to total extinction. Let us pray we have the wisdom to choose correctly." Cited in *Context*, March 15, 1986.

[15]Conrad, 48.

[16]See the chapter on Just War. In Amos 1-2 the prophet combines the holy war tradition with just war motifs.

[17]See the chapter on "Holy War: passive."

Conquest tradition (Ex. 6:6; Deut. 4:34; 5:15; 26:8; 1 Kings 8:42; Ps. 136:12) and is compatible with both active and passive holy-war traditions. The focus is so strongly on what Yahweh is doing that human military action is submerged or ignored. In commenting on Jer. 25:15-38, an oracle against both the nations and Judah, Duane Christensen notes that "the imagery is that of holy war and the agent of Yahweh's destruction, presumably the Babylonians, is unimportant to the prophet. It is Yahweh's battle."[18]

Jeremiah's use of the holy war tradition against the surrounding nations contains the same emphasis on Yahweh's actions, but the implication of human means is often clearer. For example, Yahweh's "sword" against Philistia in 47:1-7 may refer to either Egyptians or to Babylonian attacks on Philistia. Yahweh's judgment against Egypt in 46:2-12 is clearly a reference to Pharaoh Necho's defeat by the Babylonians at Carchemish. What is certain is that Jeremiah attributes the destruction of Egypt to Yahweh who engages in holy war against Egypt.[19]

In sum, Jeremiah, as Yahweh's mouthpiece, pronounces Yahweh's holy war judgments against the surrounding nations who will suffer military defeat because of Yahweh's actions. But Jeremiah's insistence on turning this theme against Judah accounts for his most enduring contribution because it illustrates that Yahweh's holy wars are against evil wherever it may be found. The synergism of God and the army is not one merely with Yahweh and Judah. Yahweh commandeers other armies to accomplish his purposes. To Jeremiah, Yahweh is not Israel's tribal god who automatically fights her enemies. Yahweh is the God of all nations who stands in judgment against sin, whether home-grown or foreign-made.

An incident during the rebuilding of the Jerusalem walls under Nehemiah's leadership illustrates how faith in Yahweh's help combined with military preparation brought victory. Nehemiah uses the common

---

[18]Duane L. Christensen, *Transformation of the War Oracle in Old Testament Prophecy* (Missoula, MT: Scholars Press, 1975) 199. Christensen also discusses briefly Yahweh's "cup of wrath" referred to in this passage. He agrees with Weiser, Cross, and others that it is not an invention of Jeremiah but may go back to the ancient ordeal custom as seen in Num. 5:11-31 or to some other ancient rite in which the cup contained blood instead of wine. "In the context of holy war the cup of wine/blood may have been a victory cup used in cultic celebration." (199). See also pp. 202-208 where he discusses the twelve occurrences of this phrase in the O.T.

[19]Christensen, 218.

holy war terminology ("Do not be afraid of them") as the people took up their defensive positions (4:14). In this case actual combat did not take place, but the willingness of the people to fight was part of what persuaded the enemies to withdraw (v. 15).

The Psalms contain many references to Yahweh's help in military encounters. In some psalms (20, 33), the emphasis is on Yahweh's work, seemingly apart from human participation. In others the stress is on Israel's actions. Psalm 149:4-9 is an example.

> For the LORD takes pleasure in his people; he adorns the humble with victory. Let the faithful exult in glory; let them sing for joy on their couches. Let the high praises of God be in their throats and two-edged swords in their hands, to execute vengeance on the nations and punishment on the peoples, to bind their kings with fetters and their nobles with chains of iron, to execute on them the judgment decreed. This is the glory for all his faithful ones. Praise the LORD!

In still other psalms, human participation is assumed but the focus is on what God did. Psalm 44 is a good example

> We have heard with our ears, O God, our ancestors have told us, what deeds you performed in their days, in the days of old: you with your own hand drove out the nations, but them you planted; you afflicted the peoples, but them you set free; for not by their own sword did they win the land, nor did their own arm give them victory; but your right hand, and your arm, and the light of your countenance, for you delighted in them. You are my King and my God; you command victories for Jacob. Through you we push down our foes; through your name we tread down our assailants. For not in my bow do I trust, nor can my sword save me. But you have saved us from our foes, and have put to confusion those who hate us. In God we have boasted continually, and we will give thanks to your name forever. (Ps. 44:1-8)

The Psalmist here refers to the bow and sword (v. 3) but victory came through Yahweh's help. The Psalmist believed that without Yahweh's presence the weapons of Israel would have been ineffectual.

Psalm 83 exhibits many of the characteristics already noted. The Psalm seems to focus so much on Yahweh's actions that the human armies are only alluded to in v. 10 where Yahweh is asked to "treat (the enemies) like Midian, like Jabin at the river Kishon." These battles involved vigorous participation by the troops under the leadership of Barak, Deborah, and Gideon. The belief was strong that without Yahweh's help the outnumbered Israelites would have suffered defeat. Psalm 60 is similar. The prayer for deliverance mentions the "bowmen" (v. 6) and "armies" (v. 12) but recognizes that they are not sufficient for victory: "O grant us help against the foe, for human help is worthless. With God we shall do valiantly; it is he who will tread down our foes"(Ps. 60:11,12).

The book of Nahum reflects the tradition of holy war with Israel active. Written sometime before the fall of Nineveh, its purpose, according to Duane Christensen, was to persuade the Judean king to take part in a revolt against Assyria because Yahweh, the Divine Warrior, had ordained the fall of Assyria.[20] Nahum presents a vivid portrayal of the battle charge and resultant carnage in 1:2, 3:

> A jealous and avenging God is the LORD, the LORD is avenging and wrathful; the LORD takes vengeance on his adversaries and rages against his enemies. The LORD is slow to anger but great in power, and the LORD will by no means clear the guilty. His way is in whirlwind and storm, and the clouds are the dust of his feet. (Nahum 1:2,3)

The Maccabean revolt provides a shining example of the synergistic view of holy war. First Maccabees 3:17-19 echoes 1 Sam. 14:6 in the belief that Yahweh's activity is the key to victory against overwhelming odds.

> But when they saw the army coming to meet them, they said to Judas, "How can we, few as we are, fight against so great and so strong a multitude? And we are faint, for we have eaten nothing today." Judas replied, "It is easy for many to be hemmed in by few, for in the sight of Heaven there is no difference between saving by many or by few. It is not on the size of the army that victory in battle depends, but strength comes from Heaven." (1 Macc. 3:17-19)

Once again, Yahweh's work does not exclude Israel's participation. Indeed, refusal to fight will result in the extermination of the Jews.

---

[20]Christensen, 175.

When Mattathias and his friends learned of it, they mourned for them deeply. And all said to their neighbors: "If we all do as our kindred have done and refuse to fight with the Gentiles for our lives and for our ordinances, they will quickly destroy us from the earth " (I Macc. 2:39-40)

The Maccabean warriors Judas (1 Macc. 3:3-9) and Simon (14:4-15), are both praised for their military prowess. Second Macc. 8:18 and 10:29-31 further reflects this understanding of holy war when the Israelites are told that God fights along side of them and that Yahweh's angelic armies put the enemies to rout.

> "For they trust in arms and acts of daring," he said, "but we trust in the Almighty God, who is able with a single nod to strike down those who are coming against us, and even, if necessary, the whole world." (2 Macc. 8:18)

> When the battle became fierce, there appeared to the enemy from heaven five resplendent men on horses with golden bridles, and they were leading the Jews. Two of them took Maccabeus between them, and shielding him with their own armor and weapons, they kept him from being wounded. They showered arrows and thunderbolts on the enemy, so that, confused and blinded, they were thrown into disorder and cut to pieces. Twenty thousand five hundred were slaughtered, besides six hundred cavalry. (2 Macc. 10:29-31)

In both cases Yahweh brings victories, but they result from Yahweh's work associated with Israel's participation in battle. In sum, the Maccabees exhibit a "peace through strength" ideology.[21]

In essence then, the decisive element in holy war was the conviction that Yahweh achieves victory,[22] and it is probably significant that human victory is expressed by a passive form—"receive help."[23] As Zimmerli notes, Yahweh's part in these human victories takes many different forms: (1) Sometimes a divine spirit is sent to empower a warrior for battle; (2) Yahweh may place instructions in the mouths of

---

[21]Leslie Hoppe, "Religion and Politics: Paradigms from Early Judaism," *Biblical and Theological Reflections on the Challenge of Peace*, eds. John Pawlikowski and Donald Senior (Wilmington: Michael Glazier, 1983) 49.

[22]Ollenburger, 31.

[23]Walter Zimmerli, *Old Testament Theology in Outline* (Atlanta: John Knox, 1978) 61.

priests or prophets and reveal his will through the casting of lots and dreams; (3) Yahweh sends terror upon the enemy so that they are put to rout. In whatever way Yahweh intervened, "we find a tendency to represent the human agents of victory in the most humble possible terms."[24] Furthermore, at times war was avoided by a miracle or by human actions or by a combination of the two. At other times, Israel did not engage in any fighting, but observed in faith as Yahweh alone routed the enemy. Also we have seen that victory often occurred when Israel participated in intense fighting, although in some instances Israel's role in battle was limited to pursuing the routed enemy. We may properly include all of these categories under the concept of holy war or Yahweh war.

---

[24]Ibid., 61, 62. Moses Hadas and Morton Smith discuss an interesting comparison between the great personages of early Israel and the heroes of Greek history and myth. Whether it was Moses, the judges, kings, or prophets, human agency was absent or downplayed because it was the transcendent God who was steadily in control. Humans had the choice of obedience or disobedience. Among the Greeks, however, it was not obedience but independence, which of necessity must often rebel against authority, which was the criterion for distinction. *Heroes and God: Spiritual Biographies in Antiquity* (New York: Harper and Row, 1965) 12, 13. Thus, for Israel, even when humans were involved in warfare or in any other significant activity, the unrelenting focus in the Hebrew Scriptures was on Yahweh who acts.

# Chapter Three

# HOLY WAR:
# ISRAEL PASSIVE

In contrast to the preceding chapter which focused on warfare where Israel was an active participant, we find in other biblical texts a powerful and ancient belief that Yahweh fought *for* Israel, not through Israel. Israel functioned as a believing observer of Yahweh's deeds. Millard Lind goes so far to assert that a scholarly consensus exists that the war narratives throughout the Bible are characterized by a belief in Yahweh's deliverance and a denial of the efficacy of human fighting.[1]

The single most important event which demonstrated this belief was the deliverance from the Egyptians at the Sea of Reeds.[2] The faith of Israel was centered in and grounded upon the Exodus event. It defined who Israel was in a fundamental way. All segments of the Hebrew Bible refer to it as the foundation of Israel's life and faith.[3] We see its importance in the celebration of the event in Psalm136 and Isaiah 63.

> [W]ho struck Egypt through their firstborn, for his steadfast love endures forever; and brought Israel out from among them, for his steadfast love endures forever; with a strong hand and an outstretched arm, for his steadfast love endures forever; who divided the Red Sea in two, for his steadfast love endures forever; and made Israel pass through the midst of it, for his steadfast love endures forever; but overthrew Pharaoh and his

---

[1]Millard Lind, "Perspectives on War and Peace in the Hebrew Scriptures," *Monotheism, Power, Justice: Collected Old Testament Essays* (Elkhart, IN: Institute of Mennonite Studies, 1990) 171.

[2]One of the best discussions of this event is found in Millard Lind, *Yahweh is a Warrior* (Scottsdale, PA: Herald Press, 1980) 46-64. Except where otherwise noted, all references to Lind will be from this work.

[3]For a partial list see Ex. 32:12(J); Ex. 33:1(E); Lev. 11:45(P); Deut. 6:21ff.(D) in the Torah; Joshua 24:4-6; Judg. 2:12; 1 Sam. 6:6; 1 Kings 8:9; Mic. 6:4; Hos. 11:1; Amos 3:1; Jer. 2:6; Zech. 10:10 in the Neviim; and Ps. 18:12ff.; 81:10; 105:23ff.; Dan. 9:15; Neh. 9:9ff. in the Kethuvim.

army in the Red Sea, for his steadfast love endures forever. (Ps. 136:10-15)

Then they remembered the days of old, of Moses his servant. Where is the one who brought them up out of the sea with the shepherds of his flock? Where is the one who put within them his holy spirit, who caused his glorious arm to march at the right hand of Moses, who divided the waters before them to make for himself an everlasting name, who led them through the depths? Like a horse in the desert, they did not stumble. (Is. 63:11-13).

Scholars have long noted the striking similarity of the scenario underlying this song with that of the common Near Eastern conflict myth. In a popular article, Paul Hanson lists six common elements:

(1) The Divine Warrior (in this case Yahweh) engaged in conflict with the adversary.

(2) The Divine Warrior, using the storm as a weapon, defeats the adversary.

(3) The incomparable strength of the Divine Warrior is celebrated.

(4) The Divine Warrior secures those he has delivered in the place of the temple abode.

(5) The perpetuity of His reign is celebrated.

(6) Yahweh, using the same implements of war employed by Baal in his defeat of Yamm(Sea) in Canaanite mythology, vanquishes the enemy by casting him into Yam(sea).[4]

Hanson believes that the writer of this ancient song, utilizing the form and content available to him, takes powerful aim at the Egyptian understanding of reality that sees the Pharaoh as secure, changeless, and true, reflecting the divine order that was incarnate in the Pharaoh. Part of that system was the position of serfs and slaves which formed an essential part of this perfect, timeless system. However the song sees the affliction and suffering of those in bondage as *not* a natural part of a well-ordered society.

Clearly this notion is based on a norm radically different from the cardinal Egyptian principles of the absolute authority of the Pharaoh vested in his divine nature, and of the eternal validity of the institutions and social structures of the land .... Pharaoh's defeat by Yahweh is thus

---

[4]Paul Hanson, "War, Peace, and Justice in Early Israel," *Bible Review* (Fall 1987): 38.

not the mere demonstration of superior raw force. It is a demonstration of the validity of the principle of universal justice over the principle of special privilege.[5]

Consequently, the contest between Israel and Pharaoh is a contest between two entirely incompatible views about how the world is and should be ordered. The song celebrates the deliverance by a gracious God of those who have been oppressed by a thoroughly dehumanizing social order. It is Yahweh's way of bringing *shalom* in the midst of chaos.

Frank Cross, Patrick Miller, and others have written extensively on how Israel's understanding of warfare relates to ancient near-eastern mythological elements. It is possible then, following Hanson' allusion above, to read the crossing of the sea story as essentially a retelling of the Chaos/Creation battle between Yahweh and Leviathan (also known as Rahab or Sea). In this way, creation language supports the attitude to simply watch Yahweh fight for Israel. Just as no human aided Yahweh in quelling the sea monster in the *Chaoskampf* motif, so no human need help him in overcoming Israel's historical enemies.[6]

Both the narrative account (Exod. 14) and the Song of Victory (Exod. 15:1-21) emphasize the activity of Yahweh during the events that transpired. For centuries Jews and Christians in general, and scholars in particular, have debated "what actually happened" at the Sea of Reeds, but this debate is not germane to our discussion here. What is clear from the accounts is that Yahweh is the main actor and that Israel was delivered by means of Yahweh's miraculous intervention. Even the towering figure of the Old Testament, Moses, is overshadowed by the key Actor in the drama.[7] Moses, who apparently experienced a

---

[5]Ibid., 39, 40.

[6]This concept was emphasized to me in a conversation with James Kennedy, who also sees the Noahic flood account as a cosmic battle-with-the-dragon story. In Genesis 6-9 Yahweh allows the primordial chaos to reign supremely but promises that creation will never again suffer such a catastrophe. As a sign Yahweh hangs His great warrior-bow (rainbow) in the sky, the same bow that he used to defeat the forces of chaos in saving Noah and his family. Does the rainbow mean that Yahweh no longer needs the bow because he hangs it like a trophy in the sky?

[7]Lind notes that J mentions Yahweh's name 12 times and Moses' name only 3 times; E mentions God 4 times and Moses once; P places Moses more into the foreground as his name is mentioned 5 times, Yahweh's 7 times. Consequently, one can asert that six centuries of tradition agree on this focus. Lind, 58f.

conversion from the way of violence (the murder in Ex. 2:11f) to a better way, functions as Yahweh's messenger of freedom.

Many scholars have noted[8] that it was common for nations in the ancient Near East to believe that their god(s) accompanied them into battle. However what is unique in this event was the way that Israel's God was involved in the contest with the powerful Pharaoh. The Israelites were not expected to engage Pharaoh's army. A key statement in the narrative is:

> But Moses said to the people, "Do not be afraid, stand firm, and see the deliverance that the LORD will accomplish for you today; for the Egyptians whom you see today you shall never see again. The LORD will fight for you, and you have only to keep still." (Exod. 14:13,14)

Israel is active in faith but passive in battle. The narrative contains the terminology of warfare (e.g., "tremble," "dismayed," "encamped," "Yahweh will fight for you"), but the focus is on Yahweh's actions, not Israel's.[9] Yahweh delivered the people through a miraculous act of nature, not through any military maneuvers by Israelite soldiers. The concept of synergism, seen in Chap. 2 as a dimension of one tradition about holy war, is absent in the Exodus. Violence, however, is not absent.

The collapse of oppressive power in the Exodus story is painful and violent. Because the oppressor is deaf to any appeal that requires relinquishment of oppressive power, his power is opposed by the great power of God in the name of freedom and justice.[10]

---

[8]See Lind, 51. See also Ben Ollenburger, citing Friedrich Schwally's contribution to holy war studies: "Israel and every other nation in antiquity claimed that their gods participated in war and were responsible for giving their warriors victory. But only Israel came to understand this claim to mean that it was unnecessary for warriors to fight." Ben Ollenburger, "Gerhard von Rad's theory of Holy War," in *Introduction* to Gerhard von Rad, *Holy War in Ancient Israel* (Grand Rapids: Eerdmans, 1991) 5.

[9]Lewis S. Hay, "What Really Happened at the Sea of Reeds?" *Journal of Biblical Literature* 83 (1964): 397-403, is an example of those who believe that an actual battle took place between Pharaoh's army and the army of Israel. His main argument seems to rest on the translation of 15:1 as "... horse and rider he has *shot* into the sea," but where did the Israelite slaves learn how to be such expert marksmen?

[10]Bruce C. Birch, *Let Justice Roll Down: The Old Testament, Ethics, and Christian Life* (Louisville, KY: Westminister/John Knox Press, 1991) 124.

Centuries later Deutero-Isaiah described the Exodus event with the same emphasis found in Exodus 14:

> Thus says the LORD, who makes a way in the sea, a path in the mighty waters, who brings out chariot and horse, army and warrior; they lie down, they cannot rise, they are extinguished, quenched like a wick: Do not remember the former things, or consider the things of old. I am about to do a new thing; now it springs forth, do you not perceive it? I will make a way in the wilderness and rivers in the desert. (Is. 43:16-19)

However much subsequent redactors may have edited the narrative or poetic accounts, scholars agree generally that the Song of the Sea is a very ancient document, composed roughly at the time of the events themselves. Lind is right to argue that the miraculous elements in the story were *not* later additions, but belong to the original.[11] This is a serious challenge to the view of von Rad and others that the miraculous elements found in many war stories were later revisions which tried to heighten Yahweh's involvement and downplay human participation.[12]

Since Yahweh alone is the deliverer at the Sea of Reeds, Israel's participation is "limited" to worship and singing (15:3).[13] Moreover, as

---

[11]Lind, 46f. Lind believes that an early date for the Song of the Sea is important, but not necessarily essential for his thesis. Lind, "Perspectives on War and Peace," 172. Elsewhere in these essays ("Paradigm of Holy War in the Old Testament") Lind argues that it is quite remarkable that the J source was so emphatic that Israel not engage in battle but wait for Yahweh's miracle because J believed so strongly in the Davidic kingdom. So it is highly unlikely that J would have invented such a "passive" tradition; rather he was writing under the influence of an old tradition which continued to influence even his strong nationalistic enthusiasm (188).

[12]Gerhard von Rad, *Holy War in Ancient Israel*, trans. Marva Dawn.(Grand Rapids: Eerdmans, 1991) 87, 89, 102. Even Patrick Miller, whose basic thesis in *The Divine Warrior in Early Israel* (Cambridge: Harvard Univ. Press, 1973) is that the holy wars were viewed by Israel as synergistic, that is, a combination of Yahweh's help and Israel's participation, admits that the miraculous elements are a part of the original Exodus accounts. However, he stops short in admitting that the Israelites were passive in the battle with Pharaoh (pp. 168ff.).

[13]Ps. 2:4 reflects the theme of Yahweh who engages the enemy while Israel worships. See also a comparison of the texts where Yahweh fights and Israel worships in Richard Nysse, "Yahweh is a Warrior," *Word and World* 7 (1987): 197-200. Furthermore, George Coats, "An Exposition for the Conquest Theme," *Catholic Biblical Quarterly* 47 (1985): 47-54, believes that the Deuteronomistic

Dianne Bergant observes, "the ritual reenactment and celebration of this victory are a commemoration of deliverance, not of conquest. Justice, not dominance, was to be served even at the expense of violence and death."[14]

The power of this story was not lost on the early Christians as they struggled to deal with the problem of Christians participating in warfare. Origen responded to Celsus' charge that Christians were aloof and irresponsible in refusing to join the Roman army by saying that Christians through prayer and faith can "overthrow far more enemies who pursue them than those whom the prayer of Moses — when he cried to God — and of those with him overthrew."[15] Origen seemed to believe that any nation, even the Romans, could call upon God to defend them as He did for the Israelites at the Sea of Reeds.

This passive stance in the face of warfare is not generally carried over to the time of the conquest under Joshua where Israel takes a much more active stance, as seen in Chap. 2 But there are those who think that Israel *could* have and *should* have taken this approach upon entry into Canaan. J. H. Yoder cites Exodus 23 as teaching that if Israel would believe and obey that the Canaanites would be driven out "little by little" (v. 29) by the "angel" (v. 23), or the "terror" (v. 27), or the "hornet" (v. 28) of God. Or, if Israel had been faithful, the other people in Canaan would have withdrawn without violence.[16] Nevertheless, the book of Joshua does highlight instances when Israel takes a more

---

historian is guided by the motif that the failure of Israel to believe, and not to fear, resulted in the *reversal* of the Exodus. "It is the thesis of this paper that the narrator marks the conquest theme with a Leitmotif. The Canaanites fear Israel, melt before the armies of the Lord, and their land falls into Israel's hands. If the deuteronomistic historian has used this motif, how does it determine the character of his work? The two points of the exposition, gift of the land and fear among the Canaanites, are balanced in 2 Kings 25:26 by the negative of the same two points. 'All the people, from the smallest to the greatest, and the captains of the armies arose and went to Egypt because they were afraid of the Chaldeans.' The people desert the land. Indeed, they desert the land in order to flee to Egypt, the reverse of the exodus, and they do so because they fear the Chaldeans. The punishment against the people is thus complete" (53).

[14]Dianne Bergant, "Peace in a Universe of Order," in *Biblical and Theological Reflections on "The Challenge of Peace,"* ed. by John Pawlikowski and Donald Senior (Wilmington, DE: Michael Glazier, 1983) 22.

[15]Celsus 8:68. Cited in C. J. Cadoux, *The Early Christian Attitude to War* (New York: Seabury, 1982) 132.

[16]John Howard Yoder, *The Politics of Jesus* (Grand Rapids: Eerdmans, 1972) 81.

passive role in battle because Yahweh is the primary Warrior. Yahweh makes the walls of Jericho fall flat (ch. 6); he makes the sun stand still so that victory can be completed (ch. 10); and he hurls huge hailstones on the attackers of the Gibeonites (ch. 10). While Israelite military participation is not denied in these accounts, the clear focus is on the one who fights *for* Israel.

The prophet Elijah embodies the holy war ideology and provides examples of both a passive Israel and an active Israel. For example, in 2 Kings 1:1-16, Elijah confronts Moabite soldiers and defeats them by calling down fire from heaven. In contrast, on Mt. Carmel, after fire from heaven has devoured the animal sacrifices, Elijah orders the Israelites to slaughter the Baal prophets (1 Kings 18:20-40).

Elisha carries on the tradition of his mentor Elijah. Both, as vigorous champions of Israel's faith, are recipients of the cryptic saying, "My father, my father! The chariots of Israel and its horsemen!" (2 Kings 2:12; 13:14). The statement, as Patrick Miller notes, refers to the prophet's role in Israel's holy wars during the 9th century.[17] Whatever the exact meaning of this saying is, it seems clear that "from a military point of view, both Elijah and Elisha were more important and more powerful than mere chariots and horsemen."[18] Thus, it appears that in the face of the secularization of war under the monarchy, Elijah and Elisha were reviving the institution of the "Judges," those charismatic leaders of Yahweh's holy wars.[19]

The belief that holy war was solely Yahweh's province and the corresponding belief that human responsibility amounted to belief in Yahweh's miraculous intervention found an able spokesman in the eighth century prophet Isaiah of Jerusalem. In Isaiah he counsels against taking military preparations.

> He has taken away the covering of Judah. On that day you looked to the weapons of the House of the Forest, and you saw that there were many breaches in the city of David, and you collected the waters of the lower pool. You counted the houses of Jerusalem, and you broke down the houses to fortify the wall. You made a reservoir between the two walls for the water of the old pool. But you did not look to him who did it, or have regard for him who planned it long ago. (Isa. 22:8-11)

---

[17]Miller, 134f.

[18]Duane L. Christensen, *Transformation of the War Oracle in Old Testament Prophecy* (Missoula, MT: Scholars Press, 1975) 21.

[19]Christensen, 31.

Later, when an invasion by a Syro-Ephraimite coalition threatens King Ahaz, Isaiah counsels him to rely solely upon Yahweh for deliverance, which he viewed as realistic foreign policy rather than the misguided "realistic" power politics of Ahaz:[20]

[A]nd say to him, Take heed, be quiet, do not fear, and do not let your heart be faint because of these two smoldering stumps of firebrands, because of the fierce anger of Rezin and Aram and the son of Remaliah. Because Aram—with Ephraim and the son of Remaliah—has plotted evil against you, saying, Let us go up against Judah and cut off Jerusalem and conquer it for ourselves and make the son of Tabeel king in it; therefore thus says the Lord GOD: It shall not stand, and it shall not come to pass. For the head of Aram is Damascus and the head of Damascus is Rezin. (Within sixty-five years Ephraim will be shattered, no longer a people.) The head of Ephraim is Samaria, and the head of Samaria is the son of Remaliah. If you do not stand firm in faith, you shall not stand at all. (Isa. 7:4-9)

Von Rad couples this passage with 30:15f:

For thus said the Lord GOD, the Holy One of Israel: In returning and rest you shall be saved; in quietness and in trust shall be your strength. But you refused and said, "No! We will flee upon horses"—therefore you shall flee! and, "We will ride upon swift steeds"—therefore your pursuers shall be swift! (Is. 30:15, 16)

to illustrate how holy war language is often used and to illustrate that, to Isaiah, "faith refers to the absolute miracle of Yahweh ... as excluding any military co-participation."[21] However, Janzen is careful to point out that these exhortations by Isaiah are "less expressive ... of a 'peace mentality' than of noninterference in 'divine strategy.'"[22] Whatever Isaiah's reasons may have been, the result was the same: Israel was to trust in Yahweh alone for deliverance.

Another expression of this belief is found in Isaiah 31:1-5:

---

[20]Lind, "Perspectives," 175.
[21]Von Rad, 102f.
[22]Waldemar Janzen, "War in the Old Testament," *The Mennonite Quarterly Review*, 46 (1972): 160, n. 16.

Alas for those who go down to Egypt for help and who rely on
horses, who trust in chariots because they are many and in
horsemen because they are very strong, but do not look to the
Holy One of Israel or consult the LORD! Yet he too is wise and
brings disaster; he does not call back his words, but will rise
against the house of the evildoers, and against the helpers of
those who work iniquity. The Egyptians are human and not
God; their horses are flesh, and not spirit. When the LORD
stretches out his hand, the helper will stumble, and the one
helped will fall, and they will all perish together. For thus the
LORD said to me, As a lion or a young lion growls over its
prey, and — when a band of shepherds is called out against it —
is not terrified by their shouting or daunted at their noise, so
the LORD of hosts will come down to fight upon Mount Zion
and upon its hill. Like birds hovering overhead, so the LORD of
hosts will protect Jerusalem; he will protect and deliver it, he
will spare and rescue it.[23]

Isaiah not only refuses to call for military action from Judah but
insists that they not forge any alliances with other nations for protection,
thereby condemning "panicky moves and reckless adventures."[24]
Their help is not needed, he insists. Judah's only responsibility is "to
expect Yahweh and to look toward his deed of deliverance."[25] As
Frank Cross states it, "The prophetic oracle against alliances stemmed
from the old ideology of war with its stress on faith in Yahweh of hosts
as the sole basis of victory."[26]

---

[23] Actually Isa. 30 & 31 should "be read in their entirety to experience the full
impact of Isaiah's bitter denunciation of all leaders who put their trust in
chariots and horses." Richard H. Sklba, "A Covenant of Peace," *The Bible Today*
(May 1983): 153.

[24] Walter Houston, "War and the Old Testament," *The Modern Churchman*
27, 3 (1985): 19.

[25] Von Rad, 105. We should note here that we take issue with von Rad's
view that Isaiah was radicalizing the tendency to suppress the human
participation in holy war which had risen rather late in the development of
Israel's faith, i.e., in the post-Solomonic novella. If our reading of Exodus is
correct, Isaiah is reaching back to the very beginnings of Israelite faith.

[26] Frank M. Cross, *Canaanite Myth and Hebrew Epic* (Cambridge: Harvard
University Press, 1973) 229.

Isaiah 19:1-3 (see also 30:27-33) echoes Isaiah's understanding of holy war.

> See, the LORD is riding on a swift cloud and comes to Egypt; the idols of Egypt will tremble at his presence, and the heart of the Egyptians will melt within them. I will stir up Egyptians against Egyptians, and they will fight, one against the other, neighbor against neighbor, city against city, kingdom against kingdom; the spirit of the Egyptians within them will be emptied out, and I will confound their plans; they will consult the idols and the spirits of the dead and the ghosts and the familiar spirits.

Isaiah held consistently to this understanding during Judah's greatest crisis in his lifetime. The powerful Assyrian army under Sennacherib lay siege to Jerusalem (2 Kings 19//Isa. 37). Although Hezekiah is "shut up like a bird in a cage,"[27] Isaiah admonishes him to have faith and promises him that Yahweh "will protect the city and save it." (2 Kings 19:34//Isa. 37:35). No battles are necessary because the angel of the Lord brings a plague to Sennacherib's camp and forces a withdrawal (2 Kings 19:35f).[28] In the parallel account of this event in 2 Chronicles 32, Hezekiah himself voices the kind of trust which Isaiah has proclaimed:

> "Be strong and of good courage. Do not be afraid or dismayed before the king of Assyria and all the horde that is with him; for there is one greater with us than with him. With him is an arm of flesh; but with us is the LORD our God, to help us and to fight our battles." The people were encouraged by the words of King Hezekiah of Judah. (2 Chr. 32:7,8)

Edgar Conrad contrasts Isaiah's emphasis with that of other traditions in Israel. "The Deuteronomist uses the (holy war) genre to place emphasis on the active participation in battle by the community and its leaders while the royal tradition reflected in Isaiah uses the

---

[27]So stated on the Prism of Sennacherib. James B. Pritchard (Ed.) *The Ancient Near East*, Vol. 1 (Princeton: University Press, 1973) 200.

[28] 2 Kings 19:7 provides an alternative explanation for Sennacherib's withdrawal, i.e., "I (Yahweh) am going to put a spirit in him, and when he hears a rumour he will return to his own country ...." This explanation would reflect a more pacifist strand where no lives on either side are lost.

genre to emphasize the action of the deity on behalf of the community
and its leader, who is to take a passive stance of trust in the action of
God."[29] Although it is not clear whether another eighth century
prophet, Hosea, advocated a totally passive view toward warfare,
certainly he went to the heart of the matter by condemning Israel's *trust*
in military hardware and in political alliances:

> Israel has forgotten his Maker, and built palaces; and Judah has
> multiplied fortified cities; but I will send a fire upon his cities,
> and it shall devour his strongholds. (Hos. 8:14)

> You have plowed wickedness, you have reaped injustice, you
> have eaten the fruit of lies. Because you have trusted in your
> power and in the multitude of your warriors, ... (Hos. 10:13)

Like Isaiah, he also rejected the practice of forming alliances with
ungodly nations who could not, in spite of their vast military resources,
save Israel:

> Assyria shall not save us; we will not ride upon horses; we will
> say no more, 'Our God,' to the work of our hands. (Hos. 14:3)

The eighth century prophets "tend to downplay acts of human heroic
endeavor in favor of emphasis on God's action" and they usually stand
against Judah's, and Isarel's, preparations for war.[30]

An incident involving Jehoshaphat provides an excellent example of
holy war where Judah's army is passive. In 2 Chr. 20:1-30, Jehoshaphat
learns of an invasion from the eastern kingdoms, proclaims a fast and
summons the people to Jerusalem. The Levites lead the people in
prayer and worship and voice the familiar holy war terminology, e.g.,
"Do not be afraid" (v.15), "stand firm and see what salvation Yahweh
has in store for you" (v.17).[31] The latter statement is a verbatim quote
of Exodus 14:14, and thus places this event in a direct connection with

---

[29] Edgar W. Conrad, *Fear Not Warrior: A study of 'al Tira' Pericopae in the
Hebrew Scripture* (Chico, CA: Scholars Press, 1985) 62.

[30] Ben Ollenburger, *Zion, the City of the Great King: A Theological Symbol of
the Jerusalem Cult* (Sheffield: JSOT Press, 1987) 104.

[31] In commenting on this verse John Howard Yoder notes that one of the
leitmotifs of this part of Chronicles concerns war as "the outworking of the
unwillingness of Israel, especially of the kings, to trust Jahweh." *The Politics of
Jesus* (Grand Rapids: Eerdmans, 1972) 83.

the Exodus holy war tradition. As was the case at the Sea of Reeds, the people do not engage the enemy.

> As they began to sing and praise, the LORD set an ambush against the Ammonites, Moab, and Mount Seir, who had come against Judah, so that they were routed. (2 Chr. 20:22)

The cultic dimension is the most striking feature of this entire event and the cultic personnel have converted the original war cry into a hymn of praise.[32] The booty from the battle which Judah did not have to fight was enormous (v. 25), and the results of this event are arresting:

> The fear of God came on all the kingdoms of the countries when they heard that the LORD had fought against the enemies of Israel. And the realm of Jehoshaphat was quiet, for his God gave him rest all around. (2 Chr. 20:29,30)

Deutero-Isaiah carries on the tradition so ably stated by Isaiah of Jerusalem. Even though Judah now lies in ruins and its army destroyed or in exile, the promise is made in Isa. 41:8-16 that Yahweh will so defeat the enemy that Israel can not even locate them (v. 12). Yet this passage seems to incorporate into it the type of promises made to Israel when they would be actively engaged in battle, e.g., "you shall thresh and crush the mountains ... you will winnow them ... " (vv. 15, 16). This illustrates how the active and passive traditions could be combined. This is not hard to explain because both traditions emphasize that it is Yahweh who brings victory, whether it is by few or by none. Yahweh alone is the sovereign and ultimate Victor. *How* He accomplishes victory is not as important as *that* he accomplishes it.

The Psalms contain elements of the theme of victory through Yahweh's miraculous action apart from human contribution.

> Some take pride in chariots, and some in horses, but our pride is in the name of the LORD our God. They will collapse and fall, but we shall rise and stand upright. Give victory to the king, O LORD; answer us when we call. (Ps. 20:7-9)

> A king is not saved by his great army; a warrior is not delivered by his great strength. The war horse is a vain hope

---

[32]Von Rad, 130, 131.

for victory, and by its great might it cannot save. Truly the eye of the LORD is on those who fear him, on those who hope in his steadfast love, to deliver their soul from death, and to keep them alive in famine. Our soul waits for the LORD: he is our help and shield. Our heart is glad in him, because we trust in his holy name. (Ps. 33:16-21)

He makes wars cease to the end of the earth; he breaks the bow, and shatters the spear; he burns the shields with fire. Be still, and know that I am God! I am exalted among the nations, I am exalted in the earth. The Lord of hosts is with us; the God of Jacob is our refuge. (Ps. 46:9-11)

Though I walk in the midst of trouble, you preserve me against the wrath of my enemies; you stretch out your hand, and your right hand delivers me. (Ps. 138:7)

His delight is not in the strength of the horse, nor his pleasure in the speed of a runner; but the LORD takes pleasure in those who fear him, in those who hope in his steadfast love. (Ps. 147:10,11)

Although the oldest Psalms were more recent than the latest holy wars, nonetheless this tradition survived, reaching "back into the times when the Israelite militia saw themselves opposed to the [technologically] superior Canaanite war chariots."[33] Von Rad adds, "We are dealing with the afterlife of the old motifs, with transposition into new situations or simply only with stereotyped reminiscences in the language of prayer out of a body of traditions which had become canonical."[34]

---

[33]Von Rad, 132.

[34]Von Rad, 131. Ben Ollenburger agrees that the strong emphasis on the lack of human participation in warfare reflect a later period in Israel's history. "It is true, of course, that even within the most historically reliable accounts there is an emphasis on Yahweh as the source of victory, but the lack of human responsibility for this victory is not made the object of theological reflection as it is in Pss. 20, 33 and 44. Furthermore, texts such as Exod. 14:13-14; Josh. 6; Judg. 7:2ff.; 1 Sam. 17:45-47, etc., which do exhibit such theological reflection, reflect not the period of the wars themselves but a later period in which Israel's war had become the object of considerable theological elaboration." *Zion*, 102.

The Israelites did not limit Yahweh's fighting on their behalf to the area of the Promised Land, nor did they apply it exclusively to the corporate sphere. Ezra's refusal to accept the Persian soldier's protection for the long trek of his small party to Jerusalem illustrates the belief that Yahweh was present wherever His people were and that protection was possible apart from military means.

> For I was ashamed to ask the king for a band of soldiers and cavalry to protect us against the enemy on our way, since we had told the king that the hand of our God is gracious to all who seek him, but his power and his wrath are against all who forsake him. (Ezra 8:22)

At this juncture we can compare the two traditions examined thus far. Although these two traditions shared a common starting point (i.e., Yahweh initiates the war and He alone is responsible for victory), they took two different routes. While both traditions downplayed human activity, one tradition eliminated it altogether. How do we explain the relationship between these two? Was the "passive tradition" the original one and the other a later corruption of it? (Lind) or was the "active tradition" the original one with the other a later idealization of it? (von Rad) Is it possible that both of them existed more or less simultaneously? Both can point to early experiences in the life of Israel (Exodus=Israel passive; the war with Amalek in Exod. 17=Israel active; etc.). There is often a fine line between being completely passive and providing only a minimal contribution. For example, even when Yahweh brought victory, the Israelites often (but not always) engaged in "mop-up" operations. How does one assess an activity that may seem both necessary and unnecessary? It seems reasonable, in the light of the fine line between these two traditions and because they shared a common foundation, that early Israelites had substantially different perspectives on how Yahweh delivered Israel and to what extent people were involved in the often confusing happenings on the battlefield.

## Apocalyptic Literature

Israel's prophetic tradition underwent a subtle shift in the book of Zephaniah. Whereas the holy war slogan, the "Day of Yahweh," had been firmly rooted in contemporary history in Amos, for Zephaniah the

Day becomes trans-historical.[35] This is the second major transformation of the war oracle in ancient Israel (the first being the transformation of the war oracle from the domain of military tactics to a literary mode of judgment speech as seen in Amos 1-2.)[36] Thus, the focus of the holy war tradition in early apocalyptic literature becomes a focus on the preservation of the nation whose very existence is threatened.

Apocalyptic literature is "prophecy in a new idiom."[37] In spite of its new style of bizarre visions and weird symbolism, it is closely related to, if not a logical development of, Israel's linear view of history. A persecuted and powerless people would understandably see the conclusion and climax of history as a time when Yahweh will judge and punish the oppressors.

For our purposes, we may view the emerging apocalyptic literature of the exilic and post-exilic period as an effort to call Israel to reaffirm its earlier faith in the miraculous action of Yahweh on the behalf of a powerless Israel.[38] At this point in Israel's history, the land lay largely in waste and Israel had no standing army. Consequently, Yahweh is seen more and more as a lone Warrior (Is. 59:16-18; 63:1-6; Joel 3: 9-12; Zech. 14).[39]

With the independent states of Israel and Judah now shattered, holy war assumed once more a hopeful prospect for those who believed that the Israelite community could be reconstituted in institutional form. A foreign power could serve Yahweh to deliver his people from Babylon, just as a foreign power had earlier served Yahweh in crushing the false political framework that had enslaved the people. Holy war imagery

---

[35]Christensen, 160. Christensen associates Zeph. 1-2 with the reign of Josiah.

[36]See Christensen's summary of these two shifts in his conclusion, 281-283.

[37]Bernhard Anderson, *Understanding the Old Testament*, 4th ed. (Englewood Cliffs, NJ: Prentice-Hall, 1986) 620.

[38]The relationship between apocalyptic language and Yahweh as Warrior is noted in Patrick D. Miller, "God the Warrior," *Interpretation* 19 (1965): 46; "... the fusion of God's activity in the creation battle and in the historical battles of Israel is the early beginning of eschatology and apocalyptic language. In this fusion, myth and history coalesced. The singular contribution of Israel to historical thinking in viewing her history teleologically, having a goal and climax, in placing her mythological thought within that historical framework is deeply, if not ultimately, rooted in the wars of Yahweh and the language and theology that grew up about them."

[39]William Brownlee, "From Holy War to Holy Martyrdom" in *The Quest for the Kingdom of God: Essays in Honor of George Mendenhall*, ed. by H. B. Huffman, E. A. Spina, and A. W. Green (Winona Lake, IN: Eisenbrauns, 1983) 284.

could assert the prospect of Yahweh as universal divine warrior in supreme command of world history[40].

Ezekiel's prophecy concerning Gog and Magog reflects this theme of Yahweh fighting on behalf of powerless Israel:

> For in my jealousy and in my blazing wrath I declare: On that day there shall be a great shaking in the land of Israel: the fish of the sea, and the birds of the air, and the animals of the field, and all creeping things that creep on the ground, and all human beings that are on the face of the earth, shall quake at my presence, and the mountains shall be thrown down, and the cliffs shall fall, and every wall shall tumble to the ground. I will summon the sword against Gog in all my mountains, says the Lord GOD; the swords of all will be against their comrades. With pestilence and bloodshed I will enter into judgment with him; and I will pour down torrential rains and hailstones, fire and sulfur, upon him and his troops and the many peoples that are with him. (Ezek. 38:19-22)

In this text, "nearly all of the traditional motifs of holy war are together: the divine terror, the earthquake, hail from heaven, and the murderous panic among the enemies."[41] In Ezekiel's apocalyptic vision of the restoration of Israel, "God's final transformation of human history is to be effected by means of warfare,"[42] but it is warfare in which Yahweh alone fights. Haggai's vision of the new age is no different:

> Speak to Zerubbabel, governor of Judah, saying, I am about to shake the heavens and the earth, and to overthrow the throne of kingdoms; I am about to destroy the strength of the kingdoms of the nations, and overthrow the chariots and their riders; and the horses and their riders shall fall, every one by the sword of a comrade. (Hag 2:21-22)

---

[40]Norman Gottwald, "War, Holy," *IDBSup* (Nashville: Abingdon, 1976) 944.

[41]Von Rad, 111.

[42]Peter Craigie, "War, Idea of," *International Standard Bible Encyclopedia*, IV Gen. Ed. G. W. Bromiley (Grand Rapids: Eerdmans, 1988) 1020.

There is no mention in Ezekiel or Haggai of Israel's military participation. Victory is achieved by an earthquake and by the divine terror it inspires.[43]

The Book of Daniel especially emphasizes this theme. Daniel and his friends trust in Yahweh's power to deliver them. Instead of a commonly held view that the book was written to support the Maccabean revolt,[44] might not the case rather be that the book is *against* the use of force by the violent Maccabees and a call to faith in deliverance by Yahweh?[45] The book, then, sets forth an alternative to the Maccabees for resisting Greek culture.[46] The book clearly anticipates a violent conflict in which the oppressive powers are destroyed, but the "stance recommended is one of endurance and waiting ... the imagery used is that of holy war, but the elect will not participate in the final battle."[47]

Furthermore, we should note that Daniel, representing the apocalyptic genre in its epitome, places the ideology of holy war in a very different gear from that seen elsewhere in the Hebrew Scriptures. The author of Daniel apparently has little confidence in the military might of the Maccabees, but rather attempts to locate the real conflict in heaven.[48] Thus, Daniel's non-violent resistance is of the kind that does not deny the legitimacy of holy war but places it in a different realm.

The non-canonical book known as the *Testament of Moses*, or the *Assumption of Moses*, provides an example of holy war with Israel passive. Although the book comes from the Maccabean period, it proports to be instructions from Moses, similar to those of Deuteronomy 31–34, on how the children of Israel are to respond to the Antiochian persecution. The book takes the opposite view of the Maccabees. The Jews are not to fight but are to wait for the deliverance which Yahweh will bring. As in the case of Eleazar in 2 Maccabees 6, like Daniel and

---

[43]Von Rad, 112.

[44]Bernhard Anderson, 618-619, and Norman K. Gottwald, *The Hebrew Bible: A Socio-Literary Introduction* (Philadelphia: Fortress Press, 1985) 588f.

[45]See Lind, 174.

[46]John J. Collins, *The Apocalyptic Vision of the Book of Daniel* (Missoula, MT: Scholars Press, 1977) 191-215.

[47]Adela Yarbro Collins, "The Political Perspective of the Revelation to John," *Journal of Biblical Literature* 96, 2 (1977): 243. Collins agrees that the book is written in opposition to the Maccabean revolt (p. 244).

[48]Leslie Hoppe, "Religion and Politics: Paradigms from Early Judaism," *Biblical and Theological Reflections on the Challenge of Peace*, eds. John Pawlikowski and Donald Senior (Wilmington: M. Glazier, 1983) 51.

his three friends, martyrdom may come to those who trust Yahweh, but ultimately Yahweh will deliver his people. An angel (10:1) brings the downfall of Antiochus apart from human participation.[49]

On the other hand, the *Testament of Moses* does contain an element of "participation" which is absent in Daniel. In the book a certain Taxo, from the tribe of Levi, and his seven sons, submit to death rather than transgress the commands of Yahweh (9:1-7). Taxo is confident that the Lord will avenge their deaths (v. 7). This is immediately followed by the hymn in chap. 10 which points toward the belief that this avenging will take place "at once." (10:2). The innocent deaths of Taxo and his sons, then, trigger the wrath of God and "actually seem to bring about the appearance of the kingdom."[50] The chapter division, which separates the prose from the poetry, obscures this somewhat but an uninterrupted reading seems to confirm this cause/effect relationship:

> We shall fast for a three-day period and on the fourth day we shall go into a cave, which is in the open country. There let us die rather than transgress the commandments of the Lord of Lords, the God of our fathers. For if we do this, and do die, our blood will be avenged before the Lord.
> Then his kingdom will appear throughout his whole creation.
> Then the devil will have an end.
> Yea, sorrow will be led away with him.
> Then will be filled the hands of the messenger,
> who is in the highest place appointed.
> Yea, he will at once avenge them of their enemies. (*Test.* 9:6–10:2)

While the book best illustrates holy war with Israel passive militarily but active in faith, an additional element of participation is introduced, i.e., that of martyrdom which hastens the intervention of Yahweh. Even

---

[49]Hoppe, 51f.

[50]Collins, 245. David Dungan, citing George Nickelsburg, agrees. "Jesus and Violence," *Jesus, the Gospels and the Church*, ed. E. P. Sanders (Macon: Mercer, 1987) 151f. J. Priest, in the introduction to his translation of this book in *The Old Testament Pseudepigrapha*, vol. I, ed. James H. Charlesworth (Garden City, NY: Doubleday & Co., 1983) 923, cites other scholars to support the view that the death of Taxo and his sons will "compel God to exercise His vengeance." This understanding found a vivid parallel in David Koresh and his followers at the Branch Davidian compound in Waco, Texas.

here, however, the participation is not military. Yahweh alone still defeats the enemy.

## Jesus in Matthew and Mark

Whereas Luke presents Jesus in a more pacifistic light, as we shall examine later, Matthew and Mark make him more compatible with the holy war passive tradition. Not one of the three, however, depicts Jesus as summoning the Israelites to fight the occupying Roman forces. To employ our taxonomy, Jesus does not embody nor teach the holy war: active tradition. This is to say that the much-discussed thesis of S. G. F. Brandon, that Jesus sympathized with the ideals and aims of the Zealot movement, has been convincingly refuted and no longer deserves serious consideration.[51] Furthermore, one can make a good case that the zealots associated with Jesus (Lk. 6:15) are not concerned with national liberation but are modeled after Old Testament "zealots" such as Phinehas and Elijah, who were zealous to defend the Mosaic Law and whose principle opponents were Jewish apostates.[52]

If one views Jesus as declaring or predicting a holy war, to whom is it against? Is it against the Romans? unbelieving Jews? Satan and his demons? As would be expected, scholars differ on this question.

There is some evidence to support Ragnar Leivestad's view that the battle is against spiritual forces. He believes that "the enemy is not Rome, but Satan and his hosts of spirits. The dualism of Jewish apocalyptic is sharpened; the metaphysical conflict has become central to the same extent as the national redemption has been relegated to the circumference."[53]

---

[51] Almost every article in the compilation of Ernst Bammel & C. F. D. Moule, *Jesus and the Politics of His Day* (Cambridge: University Press, 1984) challenges Brandon's thesis which he developed in his *Jesus and the Zealots: A Study of the Political Factor in Primitive Christianity* (Manchester: University Press, 1967). Wolfgang Schrage comments that Brandon's thesis combines "uncritical exegesis with uncritical fantasy." *The Ethics of the New Testament* (Philadelphia: Fortress Press, 1988) 109.

[52] Stephen Charles Mott, *Biblical Ethics and Social Change* (New York: Oxford University Press, 1982) 177. Mott lists 1 Macc. 2:24, 26, 54, 58, which refer to Mattathias' killing of the Jews who had joined forces with the Seleucids and to the references to Phineas and Elijah in the justification of Mattathias' action.

[53] Ragnar Leivestad, *Christ the Conqueror* (New York: Macmillan, 1954) 40. Bruce A. Stevens agrees in "Jesus as the Divine Warrior," *The Expository Times* 94, 11 (Aug. 1983): 326-329. So also does Matthew Black in Bammel & Moule, 292.

Examples of Jesus' confronting Satan and demons abound in the Synoptic Gospels. In the temptation narrative Jesus goes into "'the desert' to confront Satan in his own house."[54] Jesus' first recorded contest with demon possession shows that the demons understood the nature of the battle: "What have you to do with us Jesus of Nazareth? Have you come to destroy us?" (Lk. 4:33/Mk. 1:24). When the disciples return from their missionary journey and relate that "the demons were subject to us in your name," Jesus responds by declaring

> I watched Satan fall from heaven like a flash of lightning. See, I have given you authority to tread on snakes and scorpions, and over all the power of the enemy; and nothing will hurt you. (Lk. 10:17-19)

Later, war terminology is used in the Beelzebub controversy where we find such words as "plundering," "attacked," "weapons," and "defeated" (Lk. 11:22/Mk. 3:27/Mt. 12:29).[55]

James Robinson views these stories as Jesus moving from his clash with Satan (in the desert) to a series of combats against the lesser demons under Satan's sway.[56] The casting out of demons and the healing of those possessed indicates that the "hope for the coming of the kingdom of God and thus for the end of the history of violence therefore already leads to specific interruptions of violence."[57] Is not Dungan also correct when he sees all the healing stories as "signs" which point "to

---

[54]Dungan, 138.

[55]The references in Luke do not contradict his basic picture of Jesus as one who is inclusive and who does not imply that violence should be directed toward humans, whether Roman or Jewish. Jesus' battle is with *spiritual* forces. If there are any holy war motifs in Luke, they convey this dimension whereas this is less clear in Matthew and Mark.

[56]James M. Robinson, *The Problem of History in Mark* (London: SCM Press, 1954) 35f. Cited in Dungan, 139. It is also important to note the sociological significance of Jesus' exorcisms. Gerd Thiessen observes regarding the huge amount of demon possession in the gospels that "while possession as such could not be class-specifically conditioned, its mass appearance could be. In a society which expresses its problems in mythical language, groups under pressure may interpret their situation as threats from demons." *The Early Miracles Stories of the Early Christian Tradition*, trans. by Francis McDonagh (Philadelphia: Fortress Press, 1983) 250. When Jesus healed the demoniac in Mk. 5:15, the man became capable of social life and communication.

[57]Klaus Wengst, *Pax Romana and the Peace of Jesus Christ*, trans. John Bowden (London: SCM Press, 1987) 68.

the unexpected eruption of eschatological Judgment into human history"?[58] Richard Horsley views these conflicts with Satan as proof that Jesus operated within the Jewish apocalyptic worldview, because "Jesus viewed individual and social life as caught up in the struggle for control between God and Satan."[59]

Similarly, William Brownlee also sees Jesus as joining the concept of the human martyr-warrior with the concept of the Divine Warrior who defeats the demonic forces and calls his people to enter a holy war where the "weapons are not carnal" (2 Cor. 10:4). By Jesus combining these concepts with the Suffering Servant motif, he produces the most dramatic development and transformation in Scripture.

We move from the holy war with its *herem* of total destruction of the enemy, to the divine-human warrior who gives his life for the salvation of the whole world, even his own enemies. Yet between the *herem* and the cross there is not simply a contrast, a radical break with the substitute of one for the other, but a theological continuity whereby in the history of the holy war the one leads to the other. [60]

Bruce Stevens concurs, seeing the themes of miracles as an expression of holy war loosely intertwined with the temporary defeat of the Warrior as Suffering Servant. Jesus was the Divine Warrior with power but did *not* use it as his opponents or Satan would have him, "but as the Father had willed, in his voluntary passion."[61]

---

[58] Dungan, 139. In a similar manner, Richard Horsley, *Jesus and the Spiral of Violence* (San Francisco: Harper, 1987) 163f., sees these mighty deeds as indicative that the Kingdom of God has come in power to liberate, establish, and protect the people in difficult historical circumstances, such as Yahweh had done at the Sea of Reeds.

[59] Horsley, 172. See also his discussion on pp. 157-160 and 186-190. In the latter section he distinguishes three closely related levels upon which occurs the struggle between God and demonic forces: (1) between God and Satan (the Prince of Light and the Angel of Darkness in the Qumran literature) (2) between divine creative forces and demonic destructive forces for control of the historical process, and (3) in the hearts of individuals. Thus, apocalypticism as understood by Jesus and his contemporaries was not alienated from history because the violent struggle between God and demonic forces was simply a symbolization of the violent social-political-religious conflict in which people were caught individually and collectively. Contrary to many interpreters, Horsley thus sees the kingdom of God not as some cataclysmic final act of God to bring history to an end, but as liberation of the people. "God was imminently and presently effecting a historical transformation." (207)

[60] Brownlee, 291.

[61] Bruce Stevens, "Jesus as the Divine Warrior," *The Expository Times* 94, 11

This understanding of the nature of Jesus' warfare would seem to lead to the logical conclusion that if holy war is declared on *spiritual* forces and they are defeated, then war against the *historical* enemies is unnecessary. That is, if the ultimate causes of evil are removed, then the human expressions of the evil forces will be either rendered inoperative or transformed. Yet there is no clear declaration of this in the texts. Indeed, this conclusion is inconsistent with other events and sayings in Matthew and Mark. For example, the cleansing of the Temple in Matthew and Mark (which Luke abbreviates and softens) is an aggressive act against an evil institution run by evil people. In addition, the cursing of the fig tree (which Luke omits) is an act of judgment against the physical realm and is apparently symbolic of judgment against those people who fail to produce the appropriate fruit. Furthermore, Jesus' statement to his disciples during his arrest in Matt. 26:53 reflects a belief found in some of our Old Testament passages.

Do you think that I cannot appeal to my Father, and he will at once send me more than twelve legions of angels? (Matt. 26:53)[62]

These resemble the angelic forces ("hosts") that accompanied the ancient Israelites in battle. It indicates that Jesus shared the long-standing and widespread belief that the heavenly hosts would accompany God and defeat the oppressive *historical and demonic* enemies at the appropriate time.[63] Matthew Black also sees in this verse the implication that a heavenly warrior host will intervene in the world, "exactly as in the apocalyptic war of the Sons of Light with the Sons of Darkness."[64] Further, shortly after his arrest, while facing the Sanhedrin, Jesus responds to the questioning by the High Priest by asserting,

---

(August, 1983): 328.

[62]Dungan, 147, asks if the rationale behind this non-retaliation is taken from the War Scroll. See the discussion in the chapter on War as Vengeance.

[63]Horsley, 173.

[64]Black, 293. Black does admit that it is impossible to tell if Jesus shared the Qumran expectation of the holy war in the last days, but he seems to think that he did. "While not a political Zealot, Jesus could perhaps be claimed as an apocalyptic Zealot, proclaiming a final impending war against Belial and all his followers in heaven and on earth."

From now on you will see the Son of Man seated at the right
hand of Power and coming on the clouds of heaven. (Matt.
26:64)

Is not Jesus telling Caiaphas and the Sanhedrin that they are being
permitted by God to abuse him but that "before long" (*ap' arti*) their
positions would be reversed and that they would stand before him, the
Son of Man, and be judged by him?[65] The "hyper-ventilated response"
by Caiaphas demands this interpretation. This type of judgment is also
the kind that accompanies the final apocalyptic battle with the forces of
evil.

Dungan's thesis is confirmed in these passages that Matthew's
portrait of Jesus is nationalistic ("the lost sheep of the house of Israel")
mentioned only in Mt. 10:6 and 5:24) and apocalyptic, portraying Jesus'
teachings and example as offering a last-minute pardon to all(Jews?)
who repent and turn to God.[66] The time factor, then, the awareness that
there is only a short time left, flavors everything in Matthew.[67]
Judgment and defeat will come to those who do not respond to his offer.
"In a word: Jesus counted on God's violence to set the limits to evil's
duration."[68] As Horsley states it, it is important to recognize that "…
even our apologetic Gospels present a Jesus whose actions as well as
perspective appear to have been revolutionary. Apparently he did not
simply protest against or resist the oppressive features of the established
order in Jewish Palestine; he articulated and acted upon his anticipation
that God was now bringing an end to that order with the coming of the
kingdom."[69]

Thus, it is hard to avoid the conclusion that Matthew and Mark
depict Jesus as one who expected Yahweh to intervene in history and
bring judgment, not only on Satan and his demons, but on the historical
order, an order characterized by brutal oppression and corruption,
Roman and Jewish. Yet, this belief is not necessarily at odds with the
view that Jesus saw this warfare as ultimately spiritual in nature.
Because these evil spiritual forces were behind the Roman and Jewish
evil structures, they helped explain why the system could be so corrupt
and oppressive. Thus, Jesus' holy war was against *both* the demonic and

---

[65]Dungan, 152. Dungan draws here on the work of John A. T. Robinson, *Jesus
and His Coming* (London: SCM Press, 1957) 43-51.
[66]Ibid., 160f.
[67]Ibid., 145.
[68]Ibid., 151.
[69]Horsley, 164.

historical forces that opposed God's kingdom. At this point Jesus is merely reflecting the basic thrust of apocalyptic literature as seen in Daniel, the *Testament of the Twelve Patriarchs*, and *1 Enoch*, confirming the observation that apocalyptic was the mother of Christian theology[70] and confirming that "what is remarkable in all this literature is that the apocalypticists move easily from the metaphorical representation of their historical enemies (the Seleucids; the corrupt priests) to demonic opponents, to cosmic powers. The political problems—involving both civil and religious authorities—will not be resolved until the demonic and cosmic powers are also brought under control (cf. Ex. 15:4-10)."[71]

None of this language suggests that peace elements are absent from Matthew or Mark. Indeed, Matthew alone contains the famous "Blessed are the Peacemakers." (5:9). The emphasis here, however, is most likely on intra-community peacemaking, because, as Mott notes, the Roman world *was* at peace.[72] Matthew's point seems to be, as Hugh Humphrey sees it, that "Christians *must* "make peace" *among themselves* so that they become an example to the world of a people enjoying the eschatological blessings, attract others and teach others that the *content* of the life they experience is qualitatively different."[73] Matthew employs the word "peace" only four times, all in chap. 10, where it describes a quality possessed by the members of the Christian community, especially the traveling missionaries.[74]

Thus, we find an emphasis in Matthew and Mark on Jesus as both peacemaker and Warrior-Christ. This tension in the texts may explain,

---

[70]E. Kasemann, "On the Subject of Primitive Christian Apocalyptic," *New Testament Questions Today* (Philadelphia: Fortress, 1969) 137.

[71]Howard Clark Kee, *Community of the New Age: Studies in Mark's Gospel* (Macon: Mercer, 1983) 71. Kee's description of apocalyptic thought is succinct: "The basic assertion of the apcalypticists was that God, having permitted the powers opposed to him to operate to human detriment in the cosmos, was about to display his sovereignty by defeating those powers and establishing his rule." (70).

[72]Mott, 175. Tacitus asserts that in Palestine "under Tiberius all was quiet," and the evidence from Josephus, Mott says, supports this.

[73]"Matthew 5:9: 'Blessed are the Peacemakers, For They Shall Be Called the Sons of God,'" in *Blessed Are the Peacemakers*, ed. by Anthony J. Tambasco (New York: Paulist Press, 1989) 74; emphases his. For a creative approach to peacemaking in the nuclear age, see Richard Bauckham, *The Bible in Politics: How to Read the Bible Politically* (Louisville: Westminster/John Knox, 1989). See especially his chapter on "The Genesis Flood" and "The Nuclear Holocaust," 131-141.

[74]Humphrey, 69.

at least partly, why the issue of Christian participation in warfare was a matter of serious debate in the early church. Most, if not all, patristic scholars recognize that pacifism was the dominant view of early Christianity. Possibly one unintended consequence of the language of the Warrior-Christ, who will conquer his enemies, was that it prevented "a unanimous and uncompromising rejection of warfare as a permissible element in [the] Christian life."[75]

## Jesus as Son of Man

Jesus' favorite self-designation, "Son of Man," is closely related to our analysis.[76] The meaning of this term has been one of the most disputed, yet oft-times neglected, elements of Christology. It is a vital part of Christology because "it embraces the total work of Jesus as almost no other idea."[77] One can trace its roots in Judaism to Dan. 7:13; the *Ethiopic Apocalypse of Enoch* 37-71 (Book II, the *Book of the Similitudes*), and *4 Ezra* 13 (The Sixth Vision).[78] In these works the Son of Man is

---

[75]Cadoux, 184.

[76]Carsten Colpe in his thorough analysis of this term in the *Theological Dictionary of the New Testament*, ed. Gerhard Friedrich, trans. and ed. by Geoffrey W. Bromiley, Vol. VIII (Grand Rapids: Eerdmans) 1972, 400-477, lists eight sayings of Jesus about the coming Son of Man which are certainly authentic(Mt. 24:27,37,39; Lk. 17:30; 18:8; 22:69; Mk .10:23; 13:26) (433-438) and lists four groups of sayings which may have become Son of Man sayings later(Lk. 22:27,48; Mk. 3:28f; Mt. 10:32f; 12:39) (438f). Colpe traces the term through Judaism back ultimately to Canaanite mythology (415-419).

[77]Oscar Cullmann, *The Christology of the New Testament*, trans. by Shirley Guthrie and Charles Hall (Philadelphia: Westminster, 1959) 137.

[78]The martial character of this son of man can best be seen in IV Ezra 13:1-13: "After seven days I dreamed a dream in the night; and behold a wind arose from the sea .... And I looked, and behold, this wind made something like the figure of a man come up out of the heart of the sea. And I looked, and behold, that man flew with the clouds of heaven; and wherever he turned his face to look, everything under his gaze trembled, and whenever his voice issued from his mouth, all who heard his voice melted as wax melts when it feels the fire. After this I looked, and behold, an innumerable multitude of men were gathered together from the four winds of heaven to make war against the man who came up out of the sea. And I looked, and behold, he carved out for himself a great mountain, and flew up upon it .... After this I looked, and behold, all who had gathered together against him, to wage war with him, were much afraid, yet dared to fight. And behold, when he saw the onrush of the approaching multitude, he neither lifted his hand nor held a spear or any weapon of war; but I

both a heavenly being who will appear *at the end of time* to judge and establish the nation of the saints, and an ideal Heavenly Man who is identical with the first man *at the beginning of time*.[79] Cullman sees Jesus' use of the term as referring to two dimensions of his work.[80] First, to his earthly work, where Jesus uniquely combines the term with "ebed Yahweh" (the Suffering Servant of Yahweh), thus fusing humiliation and exaltation.[81] Second, to the eschatological work he will fulfill in the future, especially that of judgment.[82] This judgment is in accord with the apocalyptic picture of judgment discussed above. Consequently, Jesus as Son of Man, at least in part, points to our conclusion that Matthew and Mark depict Jesus as teaching that the eschatological judgment at the end of time is none other than Yahweh's holy war against evil. The disciples will not participate in that war and, in the meantime, they are not to take up arms against the demonic religious and political structures, but are to form a community where the expression of power is diametrically opposed to that experienced in

---

saw only how he sent forth from his mouth as it were a stream of fire, and from his lips a flaming breath, and from his tongue he shot forth a storm of sparks. All these were mingled together, the stream of fire and the flaming wrath and the great storm, and fell on the onrushing multitude which was prepared to fight, and burned them all up, so that suddenly nothing was seen of the innumerable multitude but only the dust of ashes and the smell of smoke .... After this I saw the same man come down from the mountain and call to him another multitude which was peaceable. Then many people came to him, some of whom were joyful and some sorrowful; some of them were bound and some were bringing others as offerings." The interpretation of this vision is given in vv. 21-58. The man from the sea is the Son of the Most High who will destroy the evil nations by the law. Interestingly, the peaceable multitude are the ten lost tribes who will return to Israel. In Enoch 48 & 71, the Son of Man is also the Antecedent of Time.

[79]Cullmann, 150. The latter is drawn from Philo and others and does not seem to be part of Jesus' understanding. Paul, however, does make use of this aspect in his development of Christ as the Second Adam. See Cullmann, 166-177.

[80]Following Cullmann's discussion on 152-162.

[81]"Under the sign of the newly accepted personal identity of Jesus and the Son of Man the community could now consistently unite the Messianic majesty of the Son of Man with Messianic lowliness and fuse them in the kerygma of Jesus, the suffering Son of Man." Colpe, 444.

[82]Cullmann, 157f. Hoerbrt, as Cullmann notes, Jesus gives judgment a fundamentally different character by connecting it with the atoning work of the Servant of God who cancels sins and by laying the foundation for the last judgment on man's attitude toward fellowmen in whom the Son of Man is present.

society (Mk. 10:45). As Donald Senior sees it, "Mark takes a quasi-sectarian response to the issue of power, as most of early Christianity had to do. In a certain sense political structures are relativized, *their authority will be swept away at the coming of the Son of man;* their abuses will be overcome by the reality of God's reign."[83]

Finally with reference to this theme, Bruce Stevens aptly ties together the concepts found both in the Old Testament and the New Testament:

> It may be said of a myth that it never dies, it keeps coming back in new forms. The ancient Divine Warrior myth influenced the earliest portrayal of Yahweh, the ideology surrounding the monarchy and the expression of hope in later apocalyptic communities. The myth returned for a complete transformation in the early church. The historical figure of Jesus of Nazareth was identified as the Son of Man. This added a richer meaning to the abiding themes of conflict, suffering, death, and resurrection. And this is what it truly meant for Jesus to be "the King of the Jews."[84]

In sum, in the light of this analysis of Jesus in Matthew and Mark, we conclude with Gottwald that "If for himself and his immediate followers Jesus renounced direct participation in war, he asserted war's inevitability and its indispensable role in the coming of the kingdom of God."[85]

---

[83]Donald Senior, "'With Swords and Clubs'—The Setting of Mark's Community and His Critique of Abusive Power," *Biblical Theological Bulletin* 17 (1987): 19; emphasis added. This, says Senior, is a form of "subtle subversion" (18). Furthermore, Mark's community was a community in which apocalyptic theology would feel at home (18).

[84]Bruce Stevens, "Why must the Son of Man suffer: The Divine Warrior in the Gospel of Mark," *Biblische Zeitschrift* 31 (1987): 110.

[85]Norman Gottwald, "War, Holy," *IDBSup* (Nashville: Abingdon, 1976) 944.

## The Book of Revelation[86]

The last book of the Bible welds together two streams of tradition examined in our study, i.e., holy war with Israel passive (here the "new Israel," the church) and war as vengeance and annihilation of the enemy.[87] Like Israel during the period of the Judges and the exilic and post-exilic period, when the Israelites were in imminent danger of extermination, the church is beginning to feel the full force of persecution by the Roman empire.

Adela Yarbro Collins beautifully captures the thrust of the book and illustrates our thesis that Revelation carries forward the tradition that victory over the enemy will be the work of Yahweh alone, "... holy war imagery is used in such a way as to encourage a passive acceptance of suffering in the eschatological conflict ... The story does not advocate nor reinforce a program of active resistance or even self-defense, but awakens trust in the power of heaven to protect and rescue."[88]

Christ alone defeats the enemies in the final stage of the eschatological conflict: He brings the heavenly armies in 19:11-16 to defeat the beast and his allies; his angel binds Satan in 20:1-3 and the attack of Gog and Magog in crushed by fire from heaven in 20:7-10.[89]

---

[86]While issues of authorship are not generally critical factors in our study, it should be stated here that I accept the view of Raymond Brown and others that the Apocalypse was written by an unknown Christian prophet named John, but not the Son of Zebedee and probably not the same author who penned the Fourth Gospel and the three Epistles of John. Brown states that "the relationship of Revelation to the main Johannine corpus remains puzzling." *Community of the Beloved Disciple* (New York: Paulist Press, 1979) 6. For our purposes, Brown observes that the bitter tone toward Rome in the Apocalypse is absent in the Gospel, indicating that the setting for the two books is substantially different (65). The traditional dating, first attested by Irenaeus, which assigns the book to the latter part of Domitian's reign (90-96 C.E.) is accepted here. See A. Y. Collins, 246.

[87]The book will be discussed more fully in the chapter on "Holy War as Vengeance."

[88]A. Y. Collins, 247.

[89]Collins admits that 17:14 ("but the Lamb is the Lord of lords and Kings of kings, he will defeat them and they will be defeated by his followers, the called, the chosen, the faithful") hints that the followers of the Lamb might have an active role in the final battle. This verse, along with 14:4, shows "that the author was aware of the tradition that the elect would fight in the last battle. But they are just glimpses of such an idea and are not at all emphasized. The dominant

The book does, however, contain an interesting variation on our theme. The opening of the fifth seal in 6:9-11 points to a belief that the end cannot arrive until a fixed number of martyrs has met their death. Thus, the role of the elect is not entirely passive; "rather there is the possibility of a kind of synergism. Each martyr's death brings the eschaton closer."[90]

In conclusion, from the most ancient Old Testament literature to the end of the New Testament period, we find a tradition of faith that survived all the exigencies of Israel's experiences. The belief persisted in some quarters that war was Yahweh's business and that Israel's responsibility consisted not in careful martial preparation, but in trusting in Yahweh to deliver them from the hands of the enemy.[91] This theme was carried over into the New Testament especially in the gospels of Matthew and Mark and in the book of Revelation. There, however, the theme was substantially transformed, although it exhibits a strong continuity with other motifs in the Hebrew Scripture, most notably its combination with the suffering servant and Son of Man motifs.

---

conception of the final holy war is similar to that of Daniel, where the people will participate in the new order brought about by the eschatological battle but not in the battle itself" (247f.).

[90]A. Y. Collins, 249. But this "synergism" is entirely different from the kind seen in holy war: Israel active. There is an active cooperation and participation in what God is doing, but not a participation in the killing of the enemy.

[91]Efraim Inbar notes that rabbinical Judaism struggled with this concept, but in the end rejected it because "the biblical world view was in general more open to the notion of miracles than the Talmudic world view, which is rather more rationalistic and less inclined to accept miraculous intervention." "War in Jewish Tradition," *The Jerusalem Journal of International Relations* 9, 2 (June 1987): 94.

# Chapter Four

# WAR AS VENGEFUL
# AND TOTAL

Without question the most difficult dimension of biblical warfare to modern readers, both religious and non-religious, is found in those passages where the tone goes beyond a matter-of-fact statement of war, but where the biblical text states that Yahweh ordered (or apparently approved) the wholesale slaughter of people, and where there is obvious delight in the killing of the enemy. The language and imagery used in these passages was one of the principle factors why some early Christians, most notably Marcion, rejected the Old Testament as Christian Scripture.[1]

This attitude toward war, which was positive to those engaged in it, but negative to a sensitive reader of the text, can be found throughout most parts of the Old Testament, although it is concentrated in the Joshua/Judges era and in the exilic and post-exilic prophets. This concentration is not surprising, since during these two periods Israel engaged in a life and death struggle for its very existence. We also find later expressions most vividly in the *War Scroll* of Qumran and in the Book of Revelation.

An early example of this occurs under Moses in Exodus 32. Following the creation of the golden calf and the idolatrous orgy which followed, Moses orders his loyalists to destroy the unfaithful:

> He said to them, "Thus says the LORD, the God of Israel, 'put your sword on your side, each of you! Go back and forth from gate to gate throughout the camp, and each of you kill your brother your friend, and your neighbor.'" The sons of Levi did as Moses commanded, and about three thousand of the people fell on that day. (Exod. 32:27-28)

---

[1]Patrick D. Miller, Jr., "God the Warrior," *Interpretation* 19 (1965): 41. Kenneth L. Latourette, *A History of Christianity* (New York: Harper & Bros., 1953) 126. Justo L. Gonzalez, *A History of Christian Thought*, vol. 1 (Nashville: Abingdon Press, 1970) 140-144.

In spite of the serious religious failure indicated by the people's demand for an idol, one has to wonder if the punishment fit the crime.

Under Moses, Israel engages in its first experiences of battle as a "nation" and of annihilation of the enemy. Consequently, we discover here the genesis of Israel's holy war tradition. The first battle listed following the deliverance at the Sea of Reeds was with the Amalekites in Exod. 17:8-16 where Yahweh promises Moses that He "will utterly blot out the remembrance of Amalek from under heaven" (v.14).[2] Another example of extermination of the enemy is found in Numbers 31. Following a victory over a coalition of Midianite kings, the Israelites burned the towns but captured women and children and confiscated booty. The incompleteness of destruction infuriates Moses and he orders the death of all women and children, with the exception of virgins (v. 18). Later, Moses led the people to victories over Sihon, king of Heshbon and Og king of Bashan. In both cases, there were no survivors (Deut. 2:34; 3:3). During the conquest under Moses' successor Joshua, the inhabitants of the following cities are said to have been completely destroyed: Jericho (Josh. 6:21), Ai (8:26, 28), and Hazor (11:14).

The Judges era differed from the conquest era in that the Israelites were not generally conquering new cities but were defending themselves against invading enemy forces. Consequently, the relevant issue of what to do with women and children did not arise. The issue was whether or not to take prisoners. For the most part the policy seemed to be to kill all enemy soldiers, apparently even those who might try to surrender.[3]

The book begins with a narrative describing the defeat of a Canaanite king, Adoni-zedek. The Israelites "gave him a dose of his

---

[2]This story is attributed to the Elohistic(E) source. The Amalekites lived further north so the events may reflect hostilities of a later date. Amalek is said to be the grandson of Esau (Gen. 36:12, 16) the Amalekites remain a persistent enemy of Israel up to the time of David. They are mentioned in 1 Chr. 4:43 and Ps. 83:7 so they survived long into Israel's history. See note on Exod. 17:8 in the *Jerusalem Bible* (New York: Doubleday & Co., 1966) 99.

[3]This is reminiscent of how the allies pursued Iraqi forces when they were retreating from Kuwait on "the road of death." Apparently the air forces wanted to test previously unused weapons and did so on the fleeing Iraqis. The result was massive destruction of men and equipment. Some observers who supported the war effort questioned this use of force. Even wars which are defended as just wars inevitably result in activities which clearly fall outside the guidelines of traditional just war theory.

own medicine," as it were, by cutting off his thumbs and toes, as he had done to his victims (Judg. 1:7-8). Ehud's pursuit and destruction of the Moabites (Judg. 3:28-30), and Barak's similar policy with Sisera's army (Judg. 4:15, 16) seem to be the standard practice of the time.

During Gideon's war with the Midianites, two Midianite chieftains were beheaded by Gideon's men who brought the heads as trophies to Gideon (Judg. 7:25). Gideon himself summarily executed two Midian kings. Moreover, he killed the men of the Israelite city of Succoth due to their failure to feed his soldiers during the conflict (Judg. 8:13-21). Gideon's son Abimelech, who had ambitions to be a king in contrast to his father who turned down an opportunity to reign as king (Judg. 8:22-27), murdered his seventy brothers in order to solidify his claim to kingship, and then brutally put down a revolt by slaughtering the one thousand inhabitants of Migdal-Shechem and even sowed the town with salt to assure barrenness of the soil (Judg. 9:42-49). Jephthah inflicted a "very severe defeat" on the Ammonites and humbled them but he apparently did not engage in a total annihilation policy (Judg. 11:33).

Virtually all the narratives about Samson have to do with his single-handed ability to inflict death and destruction to the Philistines, who exercised political control over Israel during his lifetime (Judg. 14:19; 15:5, 8,16; 16:27,30), and who brought "a rude barbaric energy ... as well as exotic culture of Mycenaean type"[4] to the land of Canaan. In spite of this pervasive climate of violence, the gruesome killing and dismemberment of a Levite's concubine (Judg. 19:22-30) shocked even the jaded sensibilities of the besieged Israelites as they declared that "never had such a thing been done or been seen since the Israelites came out of the land of Egypt" (v. 30).

The book of Judges gives the impression that when the Israelites were not engaging foreign invaders, they were fighting against each other with an equal amount of resolve and brutality. Holy war (*herem*) is declared against the tribe of Benjamin (Judg. 21:11) after bloody encounters leave 18,000 Israelites and 25,100 Benjamites dead (Judg. 20:25,35). The Israelites spare the tribe of Benjamin from extinction by securing brides for the remaining men through a most unorthodox and shameless method (Judg. 21:15-24).

In sum, the people of Israel faced some formidable foes during the period of the Judges and suffered many casualties. For example, an important city like Bethel was destroyed four times from B.C.E. 1200-

---

[4]W. F. Albright, *From the Stone Age to Christianity* (Baltimore: Johns Hopkins, 1940) 219.

1000, so "one can hardly be surprised if under such conditions Israel became martially minded."[5]

The book of 1 Samuel continues the story of Israel's struggle to become politically and militarily secure in the Promised Land. The movement toward a monarchy relates directly to warfare because whereas previous wars had been fought by the peasant militia under the leadership of a charismatic warrior, the people were asking for a king who would be their leader and "fight (their) battles" (1 Sam. 8:20). One tradition in the complex narrative clearly views this request as a rejection of Yahweh as King, who had previously led them into battle and who had given them victory over often superior forces (e.g., 1 Sam. 8:10-22).

A critical passage relating holy war to Saul's reign as king[6] is found in 1 Sam. 15:1-35. This passage is discussed in some detail in chap. 2. The stark statement in 15:33: "Then Samuel butchered Agag before Yahweh at Gilgal" (Jerusalem Bible), illustrates that holy war was to be carried on without mercy. The writer introduces the element of vengeance with poetic elegance: "As your sword has made women childless, so shall your mother be made childless among women" (v. 33).[7]

The reign of the incomparable king David, a man of many talents and gifts, is marked by a relentless focus on his military skills. He is "a warrior king par excellence."[8] On three occasions in 1 Sam. 18:7; 21:12; 29:5, songs celebrate his exploits: "Saul has killed his thousands, and David his tens of thousands." David exhibits some of the elements of the earlier deliverers by consulting Yahweh regarding attack plans (1

---

[5]Ibid., 219. As was noted in the Introduction, this is equivalent to the city of Philadelphia being destroyed four times since the Declaration of Independence.

[6]Saul's tenure as king is so different from the traditional trappings surrounding monarchs that some scholars prefer to call him a "commander" or "prince" rather than a king. He imposed no taxes, had a headquarters rather than a capital, did not conscript soldiers, etc. David will function as Israel's first full-fledged king but Saul was more than the deliverers depicted in the book of Judges. Therefore, Saul can be seen as the key transition figure from the amphictyony to a monarchy. See Norman Gottwald, *The Hebrew Bible: A Socio-Literary Introduction* (Philadelphia: Fortress Press, 1985) 320, and Bernhard W. Anderson, *Understanding the Old Testament*, 4th Edition (Englewood Cliffs, NJ: Prentice-Hall, 1986) 214-216.

[7]The idea of "payback time" has already been noted earlier in the story of Adoni-zedek in Judg. 1.

[8]Keith W. Whitelam, *The Just King: Monarchical Judicial Authority in Ancient Israel* (Sheffield: JSOT Press, 1979) 166.

Sam. 30:6-10), but appears more and more to reflect the common practices of monarchs by engaging in war for expansionist purposes (1 Kings 8:1-14) and by brutalizing some of the conquered nations (2 Sam. 8:3-7, 13-14; 1 Kings 11:14-16).

Waldemar Janzen gives a good summary of what we have seen to this point, "even sly murder can be praised when committed against an enemy (Judg. 3:15ff; 4:18ff). Cunning deceit and violence can bring honor when committed against national enemies (1 Sam. 27:8-12). Merciless warfare is generally accepted (2 Sam. 8:2; 11:1; 1 Kings 11:15f; 2 Kings 3:25), even though it is true that certain excesses of cruelty, such as mutilation of enemies, are the rare exception in Israel."[9]

The classical prophets, beginning with Amos, Hosea, Isaiah, and Micah in the eighth century, contain the oft-quoted passages extolling peace and peacemaking activities. References to warfare are often warnings and judgments directed *against* Israel and Judah because of the deep religious and moral decay of both the leaders and people of the land. On the other hand, these prophets are not hesitant to denounce the cruel and oppressive foreign powers and often describe judgment on them in most vivid terms. Isaiah's oracle against Babylon is a prime example.

> I will punish the world for its evil, and the wicked for their iniquity; I will put an end to the pride of the arrogant, and lay low the insolence of tyrants. I will make mortals more rare than fine gold, and humans than the gold of Ophir. Whoever is found will be thrust through, and whoever is caught will fall by the sword. Their infants will be dashed to pieces before their eyes; their houses will be plundered, and their wives ravished. See, I am stirring up the Medes against them, who have no regard for silver and do not delight in gold. Their bows will slaughter the young men; they will have no mercy on the fruit of the womb; their eyes will not pity children. (Isa. 13:11-12, 15-18)

Isaiah pronounces a similar judgment on Assyria (10:5-15).

The book of Nahum denounces Assyria, possibly the most brutal empire in the history of the ancient Near East, in unusually scathing terms. "Nahum (is) almost shrill in his hymn of jubilation at the

---

[9]Waldemar Janzen, "War in the Old Testament," *Mennonite Quarterly Review* 46 (1972): 159.

destruction of Nineveh."[10] The collections of the oracles against the nations in Isaiah 13-23; Jeremiah 46-51; and Ezekiel 25-32 often describe harsh outcries for vengeance against these nations which have brutalized Israel.[11] Joel 4:10 calls for Israel to beat their plowshares back into swords, thus reversing the earlier call of Isaiah 2:4 and Micah 4:3.

Paul Hanson traces the tragic development in Israel's vision of war and peace in the post-exilic and apocalyptic period.[12] After discussing the brilliant contributions of Second Isaiah to the concept of peace, Hanson notes that the justice and equality which characterized the early Yahwistic and prophetic notion of community began to collapse. Harsh vindictiveness replaces the vision of inclusive peace. Isaiah 66:1-6 depicts Yahweh's garments as dripping with the blood of Israel's enemies. This vision of the future overwhelmed the earlier vision of imminent universal peace. Hanson laments: "The subsequent unholy history of the genre in later additions to the books of Isaiah, Jeremiah, and Ezekiel is one which most students of the Bible would be glad to forget."[13]

This negative vision, Hanson observes, leads directly to the apocalyptic vision of the whole world becoming the object of God's fierce wrath. The peace of Yahweh is no longer a responsibility or call which Israel must declare in history. It is something which only Yahweh will bring after destroying Israel's enemies. "Vanished is the magnanimity of spirit which prodded Second Isaiah into hitherto uncharted territory."[14]

The prophet Ezekiel condemns the blood-thirsty Israelites who "shed blood" and who "depend on [their] swords" (33:25f). Or, as H. L. Ellison translates it, "[they] live by violence."[15] Ezekiel warns these who are

---

[10]Richard J. Sklba, "A Covenant of Peace," *The Bible Today* (May 1983): 153.
[11]Ibid., 153.
[12]This paragraph summarizes Hanson's analysis in "War and Peace in the Hebrew Bible, *Interpretation* 38, 4 (Oct 1984): 359-361.
[13]Hanson, 360. Yahweh's shalom, he notes, was engulfed by images of war in such places as Zech. 12:2-3; 14:1-2; Ezek. 39:1-6.
[14]Ibid., 361.
[15]Cited in John B. Taylor, *Ezekiel: An Introduction and Commentary* (Downes Grove, IL: Inter-varsity Press, 1969) 217. V. 26 ("you depend on your swords" NRSV) is difficult to translate. D. M. G. Stalker amends it to read, "You stand upon your waste places." *Ezekiel: An Introduction and Commentary* (London: SCM Press, 1968) 240. At any rate, Ezekiel condemns the savage violence of the Israelites.

confident of possessing the land that this kind of behavior leads not to victory and security but to destruction (vv. 27-29).

Other exilic or post-exilic literature reflects the bitter vindictiveness and the desire for revenge of a vanquished, crushed people.[16] The entire book of Obadiah celebrates the coming destruction of the Edomites, who took advantage of Judah's helplessness after the Babylonian invasion. A psalmist voices the all too human feelings of those who have been herded like cattle for miles into oppressive concentration camps where basic needs are ignored:

> O daughter Babylon, you devastator! Happy shall they be who pay you back what you have done to us! Happy shall they be who take your little ones and dash them against the rock! (Ps. 137:8-9)

The book of Esther has often been cited as an example of a vengeful attitude. C. A. Moore calls the book "vengeful, blood-thirsty, and chauvinistic in spirit."[17] He renders this verdict essentially on the basis of 8:11: "By these letters the king allowed the Jews who were in every city to assemble and defend their lives, to destroy, to kill, and to annihilate any armed force of any people or province that might attack them, with their children and women, and to plunder their goods."

Robert Gordis examines thoroughly this verse and concludes with his own translation and comment: "By these letters the king permitted the Jews in every city to gather and defend themselves, to destroy, kill, and wipe out every armed force of a people or a province attacking 'them, their children and their wives, with their goods as booty.'" The last five words in the Hebrew text are not a *paraphrase* of 3:13, giving the Jews permission to retaliate in precisely the manner planned by Hamam, but a *citation* of Haman's original edict, against which his intended victims may now protect themselves. In accordance with modern usage the citation should be placed in quotation marks. The book, therefore, underscores that, while the Jews were now empowered to fight against those who 'sought to do them harm' (9:2), their only goal was to repulse those who might attack them, their wives, and their children."[18]

---

[16] Millar Burrows, *An Outline of Biblical Theology* (Philadelphia: Westminster, 1946) 317. See also the appendix on "War Songs."

[17] C. A. Moore, *Esther* (Garden City, NY: Doubleday, 1971) 80.

[18] Robert Gordis, "Studies in the Esther Narrative," *Journal of Biblical Literature* 95 (1976): 51f.

Thus, some of the harshness of the book is softened by the recognition that while the book is antagonistic toward the enemies of the Jews, it is hostile only toward Haman and his supporters, not toward the king, his court, or to the general population. It is not, Gordis maintains, anti-Gentile in spirit.[19]

It has long been noted that one emotion necessary to fuel an intense military campaign is hatred of the enemy. This is accomplished by dehumanizing them.[20] It is much harder to sustain a costly and bloody campaign if a nation views the enemy as "people like us" who also have a legitimate claim. This dynamic was at work to some extent in ancient Israel. To be sure, warfare could be viewed abstractly as taking possession of the land promised to them by Yahweh, or as defending their borders from attack by outsiders. However, in prolonged conflicts, these motives alone cannot maintain the necessary fervency. One must view the enemy as less than human and deserving of destruction.

T. R. Hobbs has examined this phenomenon in some detail. Hobbs describes the "strangers" in ancient Israel as those who were outside the group and who possessed no group privileges or responsibilities, but who were to be treated well.[21] Unfortunately, however, the stranger became dehumanized. The enemy is "pregnant with wickedness" (Ps. 12:14), a dangerous animal (Ps. 17:12: lion; Ps. 22:13: bull and lion; Ps. 91:13: lions, adders, and dragons), chaff (Ps. 35:5), and dust and mud to be trampled with impunity (Ps. 18:37-42). In Psalm 144:7, 11, the enemy is seen as a perpetual liar and utterly corrupt. As Hobbs observes, these are stereotypes which are the stuff of propaganda.[22] Hobbs notes also that the bureaucratic record of battles, whether Israelite or neighboring nations, is always one-sided and listed on a scoreboard with a kind of detachment common to administrators. It was the hallmark of imperial

---

[19]Gordis, 52.

[20]One of the saddest dimensions of the Israeli-Palestinian conflict is that many Jews, whose relatives were so brutally dehumanized by the Nazis in the Holocaust, now exhibit the same attitude toward the Palestinians. Haim Gordon, an Israeli peace activist, describes the attitudes toward, and the statements about, Palestinians in the Israeli media, in the large majority of the Knesset members, by government officials, and by the average man and women in the streets, as "depraved jingoism." *Struggle: A Newsletter on Israeli Democracy*, March 1991.

[21]T. R. Hobbs, *A Time for War: A Study of Warfare in the Old Testament* (Wilmington, DE: Michael Glazier, 1989) 190. He cites Gen. 31:15; Ex. 21:8; Deut. 14:21; 17:15; Jer. 5:19.

[22]Ibid., 191.

battle reporting in Assyria and Egypt not to list or picture their own dead.[23]

Thus, Israel reflected a common and understandable attitude toward their long-standing enemies. To their credit, however, and in contrast to their surrounding cultures, the element of redemption at times accompanied this hatred. For example, even though Isaiah dehumanizes the Egyptians in chapter 19, he affirms, "though Yahweh has struck the Egyptians harshly, he will heal them" (v. 22). The despised and brutal Assyrians will also share in this healing[24] (vv. 23-25). In the prophets' best moments, revenge and destruction were not the last words.

As Miller has observed, these wars and the Israelite attitude toward the enemy, pose serious historical, theological, and apologetic problems.[25] What kind of God would order the wholesale slaughter of groups of people? To answer that the slaughter of the enemy was only rarely carried out is historically questionable and begs the question. How does one reconcile these wars with the basic aspects of the Christian faith? It is not the purpose of this chapter to try to provide an answer. The purpose here is to examine the texts as they are, not as we might wish they were.

## The Dead Sea Scrolls

No where is this understanding of war better exhibited than in the writings of the Dead Sea Scrolls. Although these scrolls are not a part of Scripture, and thus fall outside the specific purpose of this study, we must examine them because apparently they reflect attitudes which existed in the New Testament era and because the Essenes[26] may be

---

[23]Ibid., 192. Note that the "body bag" count and television pictures of American dead were a big factor in fueling the antiwar movement during the Viet Nam conflict. The fact that the government learned its lesson well was seen during the Persian Gulf War when cameras were not allowed in the battle zones. Though the stated reason was not to allow the Iraqis to observe battle strategy, the real reason was probably to guarantee that the Allied public would not see pictures of their own dead and wounded. Nothing can change the public's attitude toward war quicker than dead and mutilated bodies of their sons and daughters.

[24]The book of Jonah vividly extends Yahweh's mercy to the Assyrians. See chapter 5.

[25]Miller, 41.

[26]G. Ernest Wright sees the Essenes as an example of a basic shift in

said to have embodied the motifs seen in the above mentioned sections of the Old Testament. The historical setting for the Essenes is similar to that which produced the vicious imagery noted above. That is, Israel was under occupation by an empire bent on keeping them militarily, politically, and economically, subjugated.[27]

The Essene community reflects several holy war motifs examined in this study. For example, the *Scroll of the Rule* contains passages demanding a strategy of strict nonretaliation upon all members of the sect.[28]

These are the norms of conduct for the man of understanding in these times, concerning what he must love and how he must hate. Everlasting hatred for all men of the Pit in a spirit of concealment. He shall surrender his property to them and the wages of the work of his hands, as a slave to his master and as a poor man in the presence of his overlord. But he shall be a man full of zeal for the Commandment, whose time is the Day of Vengeance. To no man will I render the reward of evil, with goodness will I pursue each one: for the judgment of all the living is with God, and He it is who will pay to each man his reward. As for the multitude of the men of the Pit, I will not lay hands on them until the Day of Judgment. But I will not

---

metaphysical and cosmological views which took place in Judaism between the fourth and second centuries B.C.E. These views provided a metaphysical background for the continual warfare against evil on earth. The rebellion in heaven by Satan has been crushed but skirmishes continue on earth. The polarization of good and evil is now given cosmic dimensions and even geographical location. The war between God and his historical enemies on earth can now be understood as actually the final destruction of Satan and his armies. Wright thinks that this view provides the backdrop for Jesus' teaching on the Kingdom of God. *The Old Testament and Theology* (New York: Harper & Row, 1969) 141-143.

[27]Whether the *War Scroll*, to be examined below, was written during the Ptolemaic/Seleucid occupation, or during the Maccabean period, or during the Roman period, is not a critical factor here. In each of these periods Israelite existence and way of life were severely threatened and are capable of providing the backdrop for the kind of material found in the Scroll. For a brief treatment of dating see Theodore Gaster, *The Dead Sea Scriptures* (Garden City, NY: Doubleday, 1957) 277f.

[28]The next few paragraphs follow closely the discussion of David Dungan, "Jesus and Violence," *Jesus, the Gospels and the Church*, ed. E. P. Sanders (Macon: Mercer University Press, 1987) 141f.

withdraw my anger from perverse men nor will I be content until He begins the Judgment! (*1QS* IX. 21-23; X. 18-20).

The rationale for the counsel against retaliation is the belief that the Day of Vengeance is approaching. Non-retaliation is "grounded in the eschatological intensity of 'the everlasting hatred towards the men of the Pit.'"[29] The purpose for the "spirit of concealment" of hatred for the enemies is to guarantee that the enemy is not "tipped off" about the soon-coming judgment. Evidently, the Essenes, as Dungan observes, viewed themselves as an "... army outpost in a condition of 'red alert,' that is, full battle-readiness .... In this context of battle-readiness, nonretaliation for day-to-day insults or injuries would have been an important *interim strategy* whose essential purpose was to keep the full contours of the main Essene fighting force from being spotted by the Enemy (human and supernatural). It was a part of a 'total blackout' that would be thrown off as soon as the fighting began."[30]

There is also the intriguing question as to whether this understanding of the rationale behind nonretaliation found in the *War Scroll* was the background of Jesus' statement in Matthew 26:51-54.

Put your sword back into its place; for all who take the sword will perish by the sword. Do you think that I cannot appeal to my Father, and he will at once send me more than twelve legions of angels? But how then would the scriptures be fulfilled, which say it must happen in this way?

This passage, along with Jesus' statement threatening Caiaphas with divine retribution (Matt. 26:64), leads us to posit that Matthew is intent

---

[29]Krister Stendahl, "Hate, Non-Retaliation, and Love" *Harvard Theological Review* 55 (1962): 343.

[30]Dungan, 142. Emphasis his. Stendahl, 349, notes that this "spirit of concealment" is made more explicit in 2 Macc. 16:12ff.: "Now I urge those who read this book not to be depressed by such calamities, but to recognize that these punishments were designed not to destroy but to discipline our people. In fact, not to let the impious alone for long, but to punish them immediately, is a sign of great kindness. For in the case of the other nations the Lord waits patiently to punish them until they have reached the full measure of their sins; but he does not deal in this way with us, in order that he may not take vengeance on us afterward when or sins have reached their height." Thus, only Israel is warned by chastisement and hardships but the other nations run unwarned to their condemnation.

on depicting "Jesus' death [as] anything but that of a weak, unarmed, impotent man. On the contrary, Matthew repeatedly stresses that Jesus was fully aware of being part of a larger divine plan. As the designated Ruler of Israel in the Age to Come, his present nonresistance and nonretaliation was purposeful, voluntary and, above all, temporary."[31]

Several quotes from the *War Scroll*[32] highlight the element of vengeance and total annihilation of the enemy reflected in the earlier biblical passages:

> Wickedness will thus be humbled and left without remnant, and no survivor shall remain of the Sons of Darkness (1:6, 7).

> The marshalled squadron of God are able to wreak His angry vengeance upon all the Sons of Darkness (3:6)

> God's anger is vented in fury against Belial .... (4:1, 2)

> ... they shall write upon their standards: Right Hand of God, Battle-Array of God, Tumult of God, Slain of God ... War of God, Vengeance of God, Feud of God; Requital of God; Strength of God; Recompense of God; Might of God; Annihilation by God of all vain nations. (4:12)

---

[31]Dungan, 147. Interestingly, Dungan relates this concept to what he sees as Gandhi's view of nonretaliation and nonviolence. He says that Gandhi eventually came to the conclusion that "nonviolence was the most moral form of resistance *only if the capacity for violent retribution is truly there as well*" (148, emphasis his). Dungan cites statements from Gandhi which seem to teach that nonviolence was a morally acceptable *strategy* (as over against, I assume, an ideology) only if it could be expected to awaken the conscience of the oppressors. Presumably, if the strategy couldn't or didn't work, then violence was a morally acceptable alternative. He also believes that Dr. King (for whom nonviolence was not only a strategy but a deeply held ideological belief) was able to achieve so much from his nonviolent techniques because of the threat of violence from Malcolm X, the Black Muslims, and the Black Panthers (149f). Note also that Mt. 26:24 fits into the Holy War: Passive tradition examined in chap. 3

[32]The translations are from Gaster. Other good translations are A. Dupont-Sommer's, *The Essene Writings From Qumran*, trans. by G. Vermes (New York: World Publishing Co., 1962); Geza Vermes, *The Dead Sea Scrolls in English* (Sheffield, 1995 [4th ed]; .and Florentino Garciá Martínez, *The Dead Sea Scrolls Translated: The Qumran Texts in English* (Leiden and Grand Rapids: Brill and Eerdmans, 1996 [2nd ed.]).

And on the second javelin they shall write: Spurtings of blood,
causing men to fall slain through the anger of God. (6:3)

... these shall pursue the enemy to annihilate him in the battle
of God unto his eternal extinction. (9:5, 6)

It is also evident from some of these passages that these elaborate
descriptions of the final battles are deeply rooted in the tradition of holy
war with Israel active. Indeed, the battle plans are drawn up, as Yigael
Yadin has pointed out, so that they conform to the standard Roman
patterns of military organization, procedure, and strategy.[33] However,
as noted in the holy war: active chapter, vigorous fighting is still
accompanied by a belief that victory is ultimately from Yahweh. After
carefully describing the battle strategy and outcome, the *War Scroll*
erupts into a doxology:

[To none] but Thee belong the [issues of] war, and it is by the
strength of Thy hand that their corpses have been flung forth,
with none to bury them .... Thine is the battle; from Thee comes
the power; and it is not ours. It is not our strength nor the might
of our hands that achieveth this valor, but it cometh through
Thy strength and through Thy great valorous might .... Thou
hast related unto us the warlike triumphs of Thy hand—how
Thou hast waged battle against our foes and caused the troops
of Belial—the seven vain nations—to fall into the hands of the
pauper fold whom Thou didn't redeem by wondrous might
[and set] in [safe]ty and peace. (11:1-9)

Thus, the concept of "synergism," discussed in chapter 2, is
confirmed by the mention of the "armies of angels" who will
accompany Israel in battle.

Thou wilt muster an army of [these] Thine elect, in their
thousands and tens of thousands, side by side with Thine holy
beings and Thine angels, and that they shall prevail in battle
and, along with the heavenly [be triumphant] .... Warrior

---

[33]Cited in Gaster, 277. Examples cited include: troops drawn up in three lines
(the Roman triplex acies) the soldiers hurl javelins seven times, the attack is
launched by a united war-cry destined to strike terror in the foe, the high priests
exhort the troops before they go into action, the inscriptions on the standards, etc.

angels are in our muster, and He that is Mighty in War is in our throng. The army of His spirits marches beside us. (13:4, 5)

The *War Scroll*, then, exhibits a strong belief that "though powerful angels will fight on both sides, God will, in his good time, decide the issue in favor of the light."[34] As Frank M. Cross describes it, "The Essenes marshaled their communities in battle array and wrote liturgies of the Holy War of Armageddon, living for the day of the Second Conquest when they would march with their Messianic leader to Zion. Meanwhile they kept the laws of purity laid down in Scripture for soldiers in holy war, an ascetic regimen while at the same time they anticipated life with the holy angels before the throne of God, a situation requiring similar purity."[35]

Alongside these passages the document recalls the events at the Sea of Reeds and moreover recalls that Yahweh declared that "Assyria shall fall by the sword of no human being, and the sword of no man shall devour him" (12:11). This concept is holy war with Israel passive and not participating in the fighting. It seems to illustrate that these war traditions were often juxtaposed and related to each other and were not necessarily seen to be contradictory.

In summary, the *War Scroll* is a remarkable document which draws on several strands of holy war tradition noted in the Hebrew Bible. Conspicuously absent is any sense of a redemptive dimension to these final holy war battles. Gone completely is the restraint seen in some of the prophets. Forgotten or not learned is the truth that a just cause does not make all means just. Israel alone is the object of God's mercy. The nations will not be redeemed, they will be totally destroyed. This destruction will come about as a result of the "synergism" of Yahweh's angels fighting alongside the meticulously prepared Israelite soldiers.[36]

---

[34]James C. Vanderkam, "The Dead Sea Scrolls and Early Christianity," *Bible Review* 8, 1 (Feb 1992): 23.

[35]Frank Moore Cross, *Canaanite Myth and Hebrew Epic* (Cambridge: Harvard, 1973) 333f.

[36]Though not much is known about them, the Sicarii, or "dagger men," which emerged as a group in the fifties C.E., may have shared much in common with the Essenes, but there is little evidence of religious motivations from this group which "inaugurated a program of assassination and kidnapping against key, symbolic figures of the Jewish ruling circles who were collaborating with Roman rule. Then, after joining other groups who were battling against Jewish aristocratic leaders and Roman troops in Jerusalem at the outset of the great revolt in the summer of 66, they withdrew from the hostilities when their fellow

Furthermore, the *War Scroll* both reflected and influenced the religious and socio-political climate of Jesus' day. Scholars have long noted that apocalyptic thought, to one degree or another, filled the air in first-century Palestine. This was examined in the *Holy War: Passive* chapter but is mentioned here to set the stage for an examination of the book of Revelation and to note, with John J. Collins, that the Qumran literature represented a distinctive shift in Jewish apocalyptic because it was strongly influenced by Persian dualism's cosmic emphasis on the antithesis of light and darkness. This shift, Collins believed, was a mixed blessing, because "By providing a criterion other than national for the identity of a religious group, it potentially opened the way for a universalistic religion. On the other hand its rigid dichotomy of light and darkness must be seen as a gross oversimplification of the human condition and potentially open to bigotry and intolerance which have always been as typical of sectarianism as they have been of nationalism."[37] This "mixed blessing" will be amply demonstrated in the Book of Revelation.

## The Book of Revelation

The Apocalypse of John was mentioned briefly in chapter three because it reflects the tradition of holy war with Israel passive. However, the element of vengeance is even more strongly reflected in the pages of this fascinating book. The stream of imagery noted in several sections of Scripture "became a flood in the Revelation of John."[38] Contrary to Klassen who insists that in the events symbolized in the book "the purpose is always to bring men to repentance through the tragedies of history,"[39] the book seems much closer to the spirit of the War Scroll[40] than to First and Second Isaiah. The possibility of

---

Jewish insurgents turned on them—and sat out the rest of the revolt atop Masada." Richard A. Horsely & John S. Hanson, *Bandits, Prophets, and Messiahs* (Minneapolis: Winston Press, 1985) 248.

[37]John J. Collins, "The Mythology of Holy War in Daniel and the Qumran War Scroll: A Point of Transition in Jewish Apocalyptic," *Vetus Testamentum* 25, 3 (July 1975): 612.

[38]Bruce A. Stevens, "Jesus as the Divine Warrior," *The Expository Times* 94, 11 (Aug 1983): 328.

[39]William Klassen, "Vengeance in the Apocalypse of John," *Catholic Biblical Quarterly* 27 (1966): 304.

[40]Matthew Black calls it "a kind of 'War Scroll' of Christianity." "Not Peace but a Sword: Matt. 10:34ff.; Luke 12:51ff.," in *Jesus and the Politics of His Day,*

redemption for the enemy appears to be totally out of the question.[41] Revelation 22:11 summarizes this, "Let the evildoer still do evil, and the filthy still be filthy, and the righteous still do right, and the holy still be holy."

For our purposes, Richard Bauckham ably summarizes what gave rise to John's attitude, "John never forgets that Rome's power is founded on war and conquest .... The satanic, antichristian nature of Roman power, as exercised in John's time, was demonstrated most obviously by the Roman state religion, in which the power of the state was deified and its worship required of all subjects .... He knows that the *Pax Romana* was, in Tacitus' phrase, 'peace with bloodshed,' established by violent conquests, maintained by continual war on the frontiers, and requiring repression of dissent."[42]

Furthermore, the destruction of even the natural order is inevitable because the social order represented by Rome has brought incorrigible wickedness to God's creation so that the only option is to destroy it and create a new heaven and earth.[43]

In addition, the book seems to present the final eschatological battle as "an act of divine vengeance for the blood of the martyrs."[44] Even a casual reader will be struck by the strong emphasis on martyrdom in the book, but what purpose does it accomplish? Collins is probably right in her assessment, "It has been noted that the desire for vengeance on enemies and for a special reward are important elements of the idea of martyrdom in Revelation. Such natural human desires are not particularly admirable in themselves. But in the overall context they do serve the worthy purpose of making allegiance to transcendent values psychologically possible in difficult circumstances."[45]

Thus, the book is a manual for encouragement for those who will inevitably suffer and likely die for their devotion to the Lamb. Furthermore, it is written to convince them that they cannot and/or

---

eds. Ernst Bammel & C. F. D. Moule (Cambridge: University Press, 1984) 293.

[41] Adela Yarbro Collins cites 11:13 as the one possible exception to this. "The Political Perspective of the Revelation to John", *Journal of Biblical Literature* 96, 2 (1977): 250.

[42] Richard Bauckham, *The Bible in Politics: How to Read the Bible Politically* (Louisville: Westminster/John Knox, 1989) 88, 100. The Tacitus quote is from his *Annals* I, 10,4.

[43] See Collins, 254f. for a good discussion of this.

[44] Ibid., 250.

[45] Ibid., 254.

should not resist the state violently. Instead the suffering and dying saints can "stay the course" because divine retribution is coming.

Robert Jewett's fascinating book, *The Captain America Complex*, which attempts a biblical and theological analysis of American foreign policy, sees the book of Revelation as having the single greatest religious impact on American policy because it

> [S]tands triumphantly at the end of the canon, submerging the strand of Prophetic Realism — including the message of Jesus — under a grandiose flood of zealous images and ideas. It pictures the plot of world history as a battle between God and his enemies. Over and over again it promises total victory to the saints. It urges them to keep themselves pure and undefiled while God annihilates their opponents, who are stereotyped as bestial and irredeemable. Perhaps the most insidious aspect in terms of its impact of later generations is the coalescence of the humane tradition of the Fatherhood of God and the zealous tradition of the annihilation of the enemy. For example, the idea of God's word defined in Is. 11:3ff. and in the early Christian tradition as the redemptive force which would come to replace warfare as a means of adjudicating differences is transposed in Rev. 19:11ff. into an image of annihilation.[46]

Jewett views the glorifying of violence in the book of Revelation as a culmination of a development of radical stereotyping which began in Israel's Deuteronomic writings. Noting that the early phases of biblical history did not manifest a tendency toward stereotyping of the enemy,[47] Deuteronomy 7 calls for the extermination of the foreigners, stereotyping them as the source of corruption.

---

[46]Robert Jewett, *The Captain America Complex* (Philadelphia: Westminster, 1973) 24f. In our terms, Jewett is illustrating how the holy war tradition (his "Zealous Nationalism") has competed with the pacifist and just war traditions (his "Prophetic Realism") during the course of American history. Holy war won, but the others exerted an influence. Jewett's brilliant analysis of America's love affair with violence--its roots and its fruits--has been confirmed in the nearly twenty-five years since it was written.

[47]He notes the favorable treatment of Uriah the Hittite and Ruth the Moabite, along with the fact that in the Song of Deborah (Judg. 5) enemies retained their essential humanity (p. 143).

> When the LORD your God brings you into the land that you
> are about to enter and occupy, and he clears away many
> nations before you—the Hittites, the Girgashites, the Amorites,
> the Canaanites, the Perizzites, the Hivites, and the Jebusites,
> seven nations mightier and more numerous than you—and
> when the LORD your God gives them over to you and you
> defeat them, then you must utterly destroy them. Make no
> covenant with them and show them no mercy. (Deut. 7:1-2)

This theme decisively shaped subsequent religious trends and
culminated in the books of Daniel and Revelation, "where the saints are
entirely pure and their antagonists entirely corrupt."[48] When one's
political enemies are seen as "beasts for whom wanton destruction is
natural, there is no hope except for their annihilation."[49]

This tendency to view one's enemies as the enemies of God, a theme
which draws strong support from Psalm 79, is vividly illustrated in Sam
Keen's *Faces of the Enemy*[50] where he gathers scores of cartoons,
pictures, and quotes which demonstrate how nations have
dehumanized and demonized the enemy throughout history. Projecting
the tone of Revelation on to modern times, he asserts that "God and
country may be quite separable in theory, but in day-to-day politics
and religion they are fused. God sanctifies *our* social order, *our* way of
life, *our* values, *our* territory. Thus, warfare is applied theology. Probe
the rhetoric used to justify war, and you will find that every war is a
"just" war, a crusade, a battle between the forces of good and evil.
Warfare is a religio-political ritual in which the sacred blood of our
heroes is sacrificed to hallow our ground and to destroy the enemies of
God. Battle is the corporate ordeal through which the heroic nation
justifies its claim, and refutes its enemies claim, to be the chosen people
of God, the bearers of an historical destiny, the representatives of the

---

[48]Jewett, 145. He lists a sixfold pattern of contemporary stereotyping of
people into "Good Guys and Bad Guys" derived from Daniel and Revelation:
(1) The identification of the person or movement with one side of the cosmic
struggle between good and evil; (2) The Good Guys are marked by a defensive
stance the Bad Guys by an offensive stance; (3) The behavior of the Good Guys is
clean while that of the Bad Guys is dirty. (4) One is law-abiding, the other
incorrigibly lawless; (5) One is faithful, the other refuses to repent; (6) The Good
Guy must maintain his humility even in the face of the arrogance of his
antagonist (pp. 150-153).
[49]Jewett, 147.
[50]Keen, *Faces of the Enemy* (San Francisco: Harper & Row, 1986).

sacred.[51] "Ernest Becker concurs, saying "If there is one thing that the tragic wars of our time have taught us, it is that the enemy has a ritual role to play by means of which evil is redeemed. All wars are conducted as 'holy' wars in the double sense then--as a revelation of fate, a testing of divine favor, and as a means of purging evil from the world."[52]

This attitude toward the enemy is undoubtedly a major factor in the rise and development of the principle of discrimination in the just war theory, because it distinguishes moral sensitivity from insensitivity. Joseph Allen rightly observes that "here it is revealed what the coercer thinks of those coerced—whether one considers the wrongdoer as a fellow member of God's inclusive covenant or only as an evil to be stamped out or obstruction to be overcome, and whether one views bystanders as fellows human beings with their own rights or only as potential devices to be used against the enemy."[53]

William Klassen makes a valiant effort to rescue the book of Revelation from this damning indictment by so many scholars. From Nietzsche, who described the book as "the most obscene of all the written outbursts which has revenge on its conscience," to biblical scholars, who see the writer as "living from a high pitch of hatred" and displaying a "virtuosity of hatred," a long list can be compiled of those who recoil from the apparent teachings of the book.[54] Even C. G. Jung, from a psychological perspective, saw the book as a hateful explosion of an old man at the end of his life who had spoken about love so much that he repressed all feelings of hatred. Klassen, in contrast, sees the message of the book, "to be that those who follow the power of love rather than the love of power will conquer. But only those who follow the Lamb in serving others unto death will share in that victory. It may well be that in the Apocalypse of John the symbol of sacrifice is taken

---

[51]Ibid., 27; emphasis his. He cites Martin Luther's famous statement against the peasant revolt in 1525: "Therefore let everyone who can, smite, slay, and stab, secretly or openly, remembering that nothing can be more poisonous, hurtful, or devilish than a rebel. These are strange times when a prince can win heaven with bloodshed better than other men with prayer."

[52]From Beckers' *Escape From Evil*, cited in Keen, 28.

[53]Joseph L. Allen, *Love and Conflict: A Covenantal Model of Christian Ethics* (Nashville: Abingdon, 1984) 212.

[54]These observations are taken from "Love Your Enemies: Some Reflection on the Current Status of Research," in *The Love of Enemy and Nonretalilation in the New Testament*, ed. Willard Swartley (Louisville: Westminster/John Knox, 1992) 18.

over by a small beleaguered community and is transformed into a
victory symbol .... It is still possible that given the apocalyptic world of
symbolism we are here in the presence of the profoundest effort of the
early Christian community to use the suffering Lamb Christology to
defuse all desire of participating in vengeance against the strongest
enemy the church has seen."[55]

Furthermore, Klassen notes that the war of the Lamb is a defensive
war and that God is never described as going out to war and that the
verb *polemeo* ("going out to war") is used of Christ only two times
(19:11; 2:16).[56] In addition, he makes a strong case for differentiating
between the wrath of God and human desire for vengeance, insisting
that the book represents a genuine Christian response to a serious
violation of justice.[57]

Possibly the reaction against Revelation has been too strong,
allowing the book's violent imagery to override the important message
that God is still in control of an incredibly evil world and that, in spite
of the violent chaos in the world, good will win out in the end. Maybe
the writer of this book would be shocked to see how people in
subsequent history have used it to justify gross stereotypes and savage
treatment of enemies.[58] At any rate, whatever the author's intentions,
the legacy of the book carries enormous negative baggage, contributing
to some of the saddest chapters in history.

---

[55]Klassen, in, Swartley, 19.

[56]Klassen *CBQ*, 305.

[57]Klassen, *CBQ*, 304. He further points out that the ultimate destiny of the
world is determined not by men's violence but by the Lamb who overcame
violence by his own sacrifice. Furtermore, the emphasis in the book is not on
delight with the suffering of the unrighteous but on the sevenfold "blessing" (1:3;
14:13; 16:15; 19:9; 20:6; 22:7; 22:14) (310f.).

[58]Not to mention the irresponsibility of those who supported the Cold War in
the hopes that a nuclear exchange between the U.S. and the Soviet Union would
usher in the parousia. Hans K. LaRondelle points out that this is a misuse of the
book of Revelation because the book "brings a fundamentally different concept
of Armageddon by continually stressing the religious-moral nature and the
cosmic dimension of this universal war." "The Biblical Concept of
Armageddon," *Journal of the Evangelical Theological Society* 28, 1 (March 1985):
22.

# Chapter Five

# WAR AS REDEMPTIVE
# AND INCLUSIVE

It is easy for the reader to be overwhelmed by the sheer volume of material referred to in the previous chapter. Although the Hebrew faith did not glorify war and warriors as did the surrounding nations, nonetheless the amount of bloodshed linked to Yahweh's work in history and the glee over the enemy's destruction is disturbing to most people.

However, there is another focus in the Biblical text that is equally powerful. A number of passages face the brutalities of war in the light of the ultimate redemption that Yahweh will bring out of it. That is, they view wars as a brutal and evil fact of life, as "emergency measures evoked by human sin,"[1] out of which Yahweh will bring good. The focus is not on the war itself, but on the instrumental "value" of it. That is, the wars were not ends in themselves, but were to bring about the fulfillment of God's promises to His people.[2] These promises included the possession of a land, but the ultimate good coming from them would mean blessings upon all people (Gen. 12:1-3). It is an unfortunate means which results in a good end. It is Rom. 8:28 applied to war.

> We know that all things work together for good for those who love God, who are called according to his purpose.

This understanding of Yahweh's work through war explains why the prophets could insist that Yahweh was at work through the invasions by Assyria and later Babylon. The goal was for Israel to repent from moral and social evil and to order life in the community reflective of God's nature. The pleas and warnings of the prophets had gone unheeded. Hosea, through his own painful experience with his

---

[1]Waldemar Janzen, "War in the Old Testament," *Mennonite Quarterly Review* 46 (1972): 165.

[2]George L. Carey, "Biblical-Theological Perspectives on War and Peace," *The Evangelical Quarterly* 57, 2 (April 1985): 165.

wife Gomer, perceived how Yahweh felt about His unfaithful bride, Israel. Yahweh's pain was almost unbearable (Hos. 6:4-6; 11:8,9). Since Yahweh's agonizing pleas had gone unheeded, he used the pagan nations to do what words did not do.[3] However the warrior language was never intended to glorify warfare, whether Israel's or the nation's Yahweh used for His purposes. It was a means to convey Yahweh's sovereign control, and, furthermore, the goal of his activity in war was peace and justice.[4] Here is a God "whose moral purpose is consistently bent on delivering the oppressed and punishing the oppressor. Justice and mercy are to be demonstrated in the military metaphors for God, not heroism or glory."[5]

Although the clearest expressions of Yahweh's ultimate goals would be found in later writings, hints of the ultimate redemption of even Israel's bitterest enemies can be found in a remarkable passage in Isaiah 19. Yahweh will redeem both Egypt and Assyria.[6]

> On that day Israel will be the third with Egypt and Assyria, a blessing in the midst of the earth, whom the LORD of hosts has blessed, saying, "Blessed be Egypt my people, and Assyria the work of my hands, and Israel my heritage."'(Isa. 19:24-24)

Isaiah also includes a similar concern for Moab, a longtime enemy of Israel in 15:5 and 16:9.

> My heart cries out for Moab; his fugitives flee to Zoar, to Eglath-shelishiyah. For at the ascent of Luhith they go up weeping; on the road to Horonaim they raise a cry of destruction ... (Isa. 15:5)

---

[3] It is not necessary to interpret literally the statements that Yahweh raised up the Assyrians, Babylonians, or Persians for the express purpose of punishing Israel. The Hebrews did not make the philosophical distinctions between ultimate and the penultimate causes, between God's active or permissive will. God hardening Pharaoh's heart, sending an evil spirit to Saul, etc., were expressions of God's ultimate sovereignty and control over human history.

[4] Janzen, 161.

[5] Ibid., 162f.

[6] This was to be a genuine reconciliation with their long-time enemies, not the kind of "forgiveness" seen in the statement: "We should forgive our enemies but only after they have been taken out and shot." Enemies were to become neighbors.

Therefore, I weep with the weeping of Jazer for the vines of Sibmah; I drench you with my tears, O Heshbon and Elealeh; for the shout over your fruit harvest and your grain harvest has ceased. (Isa. 16:9)[7']

In Isa. 2:2-4 and 11:1-9, the redemption of Israel's long-standing enemies is stated in such a way that must have shocked Isaiah's contemporaries as it shocks the modern reader. Here natural enemies in the world of nature will be reconciled as will the nations who have warred against each other. Furthermore, this will be accomplished not by force but by the Torah of Yahweh which the nations willingly accept.[8] Isaiah 2 sees Jerusalem as breaking from the power politics of Egypt and Assyria, but as Lind observes, it "... was not intended to isolate the city in a political ghetto, but was occasioned because Jerusalem was to lead the nations in a new international politics of voluntary obedience to Yahwistic torah, a politics which would render obsolete the sword and military college."[9]

We should also note that the Isaiah 2 passage seems to support the view that warlike behavior is *learned* behavior. "This view of human nature is an implicit repudiation of the modern theory that war is a consequence of innate human aggression."[10] Part of the work of redemption, then, is the learning of new patterns of relationships. Or, more accurately, it is the unlearning of the old patterns of hatred, exclusion, and conflict and replacing them with creative and inclusive ones.

Second Isaiah possesses the clearest vision of how Yahweh worked to bring ultimate good out of the unmitigated evil of warfare. His words

---

[7]Cited in F. Derek Kidner, "Old Testament Perspectives on War," *Evangelical Quarterly* 57, 2 (April 1985): 111. Kidner also cites the amazing passage in Amos 9:7: "Are not you like the Ethiopians to me, O people of Israel? says the Lord. Did I not bring Israel up from the land of Egypt, and the Philistines from Kir?" Israel, Amos implies, misunderstood her calling and election. Her purpose was to be Yahweh's vessel to gather all nations to redemption.

[8]Moshe Weinfeld, "Zion and Jerusalem as Religious and Political Capital: Ideology and Utopia," in *The Poet and the Historian: Essays in Literary and Historical Biblical Criticism*, ed. by Richard E. Friedman (Chico, CA: Scholars Press, 1983) 113.

[9]Millard Lind, "Perspectives on War and Peace in the Hebrew Scriptures," *Monotheism, Power, Justice: Collected Old Testament Essays* (Elkhart, IN: Institute of Mennonite Studies, 1990) 176.

[10]Irving M. Zeitlin, *Ancient Judaism: Biblical Criticism from Max Weber to the Present* (Cambridge, Eng: Polity Press, 1984) 227.

begin with the beautiful message of comfort for the war torn and devastated people of God (40:1-2). Jerusalem was a heap of rubble and the nation was in chaos, but Yahweh was not finished with his people.

> For a brief moment I abandoned you, but with great compassion I will gather you. In overflowing wrath for a moment I hid my face from you, but with everlasting love I will have compassion on you, says the LORD, your Redeemer. (Isa. 54:7-8)

In chap. 52:7-10 the prophet bursts forth with promises of Israel's rebirth "with a freshness reminiscent of Ex. 15."[11,]

> How beautiful upon the mountains are the feet of the messenger who announces peace, who brings good news, who announces salvation, who says to Zion, "Your God reigns." Listen! Your sentinels lift up their voices, together they sing for joy; for in plain sight they see the return of the LORD to Zion. Break forth together into singing you ruins of Jerusalem; for the LORD has comforted his people, he has redeemed Jerusalem. The LORD has bared his holy arm before the eyes of all the nations; and all the ends of the earth shall see the salvation of our God. (Isa. 52:7-10)

> Awake, awake, put on strength, O arm of the LORD! Awake, as in days of old, the generations of long ago! Was it not you who cut Rahab in pieces, who pierced the dragon? Was it not you who dried up the sea, the waters of the great deep who made the depths of the sea a way for the redeemed to cross over? So the ransomed of the LORD shall return, and come to Zion with singing; everlasting joy shall be upon their heads; they shall obtain joy and gladness, and sorrow and sighing shall flee away. (Isa. 51:9-11)

Paul Hanson concludes that "where Yahweh reigned, the order of shalom prevailed over all which threatened to disrupt or diminish life:

---

[11] Paul Hanson, "War and Peace in the Hebrew Bible," *Interpretation* 38, 4 (Oct 1984): 357. See also his commentary on *Isaiah 40-66*, Interpretation (Louisville: Westminster/John Knox, 1995) 145-47.

Chaos was overcome, war ended, sorrow ceased, and the harmony of the redeemed world found its truest expression in worship."[12]

Second Isaiah's emphasis on the universal dimensions of Yahweh's redemption is striking. The prophet sought to lead the people beyond the self-pity brought on by a total defeat in war and beyond the tendency toward exclusiveness when referring to God's salvation. Again, Hanson states it poignantly, "This extension is a very profound one, for until all nations were brought into the healing orbit of God's peace, war would continue to rage, and chaos would continue to open its ugly maw to devour Israel. Second Isaiah's universalism thus solves a hitherto unresolved conflict within Yahwism, that between the inner community and the outside world. God's reign of peace was intended for all, and to this task Israel was now called by the Word of God through Second Isaiah."[13]

We see Second Isaiah's belief that Yahweh's holy warfare would ultimately lead to universal redemption also in 52:10:

> The Lord has bared his holy arm before the eyes of all the nations;'and all the ends of the earth shall see the salvation of our God.

As Yahweh used his "strong arm" to rescue Israel, so he would again display His power, but this time the results would be even more dramatic. The whole world would see (i.e., experience) Yahweh's salvation.

Second Isaiah displays the fundamental tension between universalism and particularism that is so characteristic of post-exilic Judaism. The particularism and separatism exhibited by Nehemiah and Ezra, which was necessary for the survival and maintaining of Judah's identity, is countered by the beautiful stories in Jonah, Ruth, and Judith. The book of Ruth reminds the children of Israel that an ancestor of the great King David was none other than a woman from the hated Moabites. The book of Jonah has the audacity to insist that God's care and redemption reach even to the despised and brutal Assyrians. The book of Judith, although containing some holy war nationalism, sounds some universalistic tones by noting that the safety of Jerusalem is assured at Bethulia, in that very Samaria so hated by all right-minded Jews. Furthermore, Achior the Ammonite displays significant religious

---

[12]Ibid., 357.
[13]Ibid., 358.

insight in his speech in 5:5-21, and in 14:5-10 he is actually converted to Judaism. These separatist and inclusivist themes indicate the tension and complexity within Jewish thought, which, as Donahue notes, will extend well into the New Testament period.[14]

A. Trocme describes Jewish universalism as "asymmetrical" and very different from other forms of universalism. He asserts that "the universalism of Greece or Rome, whether rational or scientific, all suffer from the same infirmity: they lack dynamism. They are too well balanced, too symmetrical to inspire action. The universalism which grows out of Judaism is, on the contrary, asymmetrical. It contains a creative impulse that enables it to last for centuries while continuously renewing itself."[15]

What made Judaism asymmetrical was the combination of three ideas: (1) the idea of being a chosen people, an idea that activates the belief in a redemptive mission; (2) the belief in the individual's moral responsibility in the midst of history as over against oriental and Greek beliefs that humankind is an irresponsible victim of a fate it did not choose; and (3) the requirements of an inexorable justice, but a justice that is redemptive because God's punishment is borne by God himself (Isa. 52 & 53).[16] Thus, Judaism's universalism was unique and laid the foundation for the kind of universalism developed in the New Testament.

Trocme's reference to Isaiah 52-53 points to that which is particularly striking about the redemption brought about by Yahweh in Second Isaiah, i.e., redemption comes through suffering, the kind developed in the Suffering Servant passages.[17] "There the *use* of violence does not bring redemption; rather the *receipt* of violence accomplishes redemption."[18] Ultimate redemption is achieved by willingly accepting and absorbing the violence which so characterizes human history.

Another exilic prophet, Ezekiel, seeks to instruct a community in chaos on acceptable attitudes towards enemies. Commenting on Ezek.

---

[14]John R. Donahue, "Who is my Enemy? The Parable of the Good Samaritan and the Love of Enemies," in *The Love of Enemy and Nonretaliation in the New Testament*, ed. by Willard M. Swartley (Louisville: Westminster/John Knox, 1992) 140.

[15]A. Trocme, *Jesus and the Nonviolent Revolution*, trans. by Michael Shank & Marlin Miller (Scottsdale: Herald, 1973) 20.

[16]Trocme, 21-26.

[17]See to the discussion in the chapter on Pacifism.

[18]Peter Craigie, *The Problem of War in the Old Testament* (Grand Rapids:'Eerdmans, 1978) 99.

33:23-29, Millar Burrows observes that "when nations that have committed aggression against others have been restrained, the victorious powers must rigidly observe the difference between just and necessary discipline and unbridled revenge or selfish exploitation. The spirit of pride and self-aggrandizement at the expense of the vanquished may be symbolized by the 'eating of the blood' for which Ezekiel denounced those who had taken possession of the waste places of devastated Palestine in the time of the exile."[19]

All of these passages illustrate why in 1903 Hugo Winckler began the German debate on the prophets and politics by proposing that all the great Israelite prophets were in the employ of the enemy![20] It has always been so that those who suggest that the enemy possesses rights and that God loves them also, will be subjected to charges of treason. The prophets, of course, were not introducing new ideas but were highlighting what was already embedded in their tradition in such passages as Exod. 23:4-6:

> When you come upon your enemy's ox or donkey going astray, you shall bring it back. When you see the donkey of one who hates you lying under its burden and you would hold back from setting it free, you must help to set it free. You shall not pervert the justice due to your poor in their lawsuits.

To be sure, the theme of love of one's enemies was not central to the Yahwistic faith.[21] Nonetheless, it was a natural outgrowth of the faith's basic tenets. In addition, the boldness and courage of these ancient prophets at this point provide us with perhaps their most enduring and relevant contributions to the modern international political scene.

---

[19] Millar Burrows, *An Outline of Biblical Theology* (Philadelphia: Westminster Press, 1946) 321.

[20] Cited in Lind, "Perspectives," 174.

[21] Walter Zimmerli, *The Old Testament and the World*, trans. by John J. Scullion (Atlanta: John Knox, 1976) 65.

# Chapter Six

# PACIFISM

While moderns are quick to take offense at the violence and warmaking in the Old Testament, they are prone to overlook the surprising number of instances in the text where the Israelites handled conflict in non-violent ways. Along with the familiar passages extolling peace, these accounts demonstrate a strong pacifist orientation that thrived throughout Israelite history.

## Before Babylon

The Patriarchal Period is especially instructive. In comparison to other ancient near eastern literature, Genesis leaves its reader struck by the lengths to which the patriarchs went to avoid violent conflict. The oft-quoted observation by Julius Wellhausen highlights this phenomenon: "it is remarkable that the heroes of Israelite legend show so little taste for war, and in this point they seem to be scarcely a true reflection of the character of the Israelites as known from their history."[1]

Genesis 13:5-17 records Abraham's refusal to fight with Lot over disputed land used for the sustaining of their flocks. Abraham was very wealthy (13:2) and could have hired warriors to drive Lot away, but instead he offered Lot the first choice of land:

> Then Abram said to Lot, "Let there be no strife between you and me, and between your herders and my herders; for we are kindred. Is not the whole land before you? Separate yourself from me. If you take the left hand, then I will go to the right; or

---

[1]Julius Wellhausen, *Prolegomena to the History of Ancient Israel* (New York: Meridian Books, 1957) 320f. Cited in Lind and elsewhere. Several references cited in this chapter are taken from Millard C. Lind's, *Yahweh is a Warrior* (Scottdale, PA: Herald Press, 1980). Lind is from a Mennonite pacifist tradition and his thesis is that the essence of the concept of holy war in Israel was that Yahweh alone fought the battles while Israel believed and observed God's deliverance.

it you take the right hand, then I will go to the left." (Gen. 13:8-9)

It may also be possible to interpret the insertion of Gen. 21:32 by a later redactor as a call for peacemaking activities. The verse reads: "Abraham stayed for a long while in the land of the Philistines," but, of course, the Philistines would not arrive in Canaan for centuries. This verse follows on the heel of Abraham's covenant with Abimelech (21:22-33) which points to the laudable practice of peaceful coexistence with the inhabitants of Canaan, rather than the policy of exterminating them.[2]

Isaac displayed a similar attitude (Gen. 26:15-22) when he refused to fight over water rights, first with the Philistines and then in two separate instances with the shepherds of Gerar. He does this even though he was more powerful than his disputants (v. 16). For both Abraham and Isaac, might did not make right.[3]

Genesis 32-33 provides a lengthy account of Jacob's return to Canaan following his long stay in Paddan-aram. According to 27:41-45, Jacob had fled Canaan because Esau was plotting to kill him as the result of the latest of Jacob's deceptions. The drama intensifies as Jacob returns to his homeland. Jacob was certain that Esau had not forgotten! The report that Esau had four hundred men with him (32:6) confirms Jacob's fear that conflict is inevitable. But Jacob's experience with the angel at the Jabbok River and Esau's inexplicable change of heart point to a better way. Yahweh had prepared the way for a peaceful reconciliation. Jacob offers himself as a vassal instead of asserting his status as rightful heir. The peace initiative works. Jacob obtains land and lives at peace.

The Joseph narrative climaxes with an emphasis on peace and reconciliation when everything points to vengeance and bloodshed. Joseph has attained a position of considerable power and could unleash his revenge upon his brothers without fear of reprisal.[4] Instead he

---

[2]Following the suggestion of Roland Bainton, *Christian Attitudes Toward War and Peace* (Nashville: Abingdon Press, 1990) 27.

[3]Genesis 48:22 seems to be the only exception to this non-violent approach to conflict resolution with regard to land. The Jerusalem Bible notes that "this is an isolated piece of tradition dealing with Jacob's apportionment of Canaan and an armed conquest of Shechem, where, according to 33:19, Jacob had done no more than buy a field." *The Jerusalem Bible* (Garden City, NY: Doubleday & Co., 1966) 73.

[4]Joseph does, however, prolong the agony of his family by resorting to questionable tactics in order to make his point. The long trips back from Egypt to

chooses the way of peace, not of retaliation.[5] The Joseph narratives illustrate that "once more the Bible takes sides with the victim .... The victim will figure at the center of the reconciliation process. That is, the relations between the persecuting, murderous community and the victim are reversed. It is no longer the violent behavior of the community that brings peace. It is the shrewdness and purity of the victim that will finally and completely uproot the violence from the midst of this sibling group."[6]

In addition to these positive examples of peacemaking, Genesis also illustrates the negative results of violence. Simeon and Levi responded to the rape of their sister Dinah with vengeance upon the Shechemites (34:1-31). They rejected a peaceful settlement to this wrongdoing (vv. 8-10), and even after a rebuke from their father Jacob, remained unrepentant (vv. 30,31). As a result, both forfeited their territorial claims (Gen. 49:5-7).

These early portrayals of the ancestors of the Israelite nation support Lind's conclusion that "most of these traditions are pacifistic; they delineate a particular self-identity and a way of relating to the Canaanite city-states by a people who had no political standing .... Developed in a period of weakness, this "politics of promise" with its concomitant way of life in relation to the eponymous ancestors of Moab,

---

an aging Jacob (always with one son short!) remove some of the glow from Joseph's halo. In a popular article a case is made by Maurice Samuel that Joseph was indeed "an insufferable brat" in "Joseph--The Brilliant Failure," *Bible Review* 2, 1 (Spring, 1986): 40. But in the end he does act nobly.

[5]Note also that Judah (44:18-34) is put in a favorable light by his willingness to sacrifice his freedom for the sake of Benjamin and Jacob. This act seemed to trigger Joseph's decision to be reconciled to his brothers (45:1: *then* Joseph could not control his feelings ...). Is the author implying that this is the kind of leadership that should come from the descendants of Judah instead of what was occurring in his day? Cf. Lind, 42. Dominique Barbé sees this event as the first appearance in the Bible of a "lamb of God," one "who, in freedom and innocence, guilty neither in his own conscience nor in the eyes of public opinion, offers his life in exchange for that of the accused." Dominique Barbé *A Theology of Conflict* (Maryknoll: Orbis Books, 1989) 34.

[6]Barbé, 34. Joseph's purity is seen in his not taking revenge or using his power to force his brothers' contrition and his shrewdness is displayed in his dramatically placing Benjamin under the threat of punishment by way of example. "It is not enough to forgive. The brothers must feel in their flesh what it is to be a scapegoat (through the person of Benjamin) in order definitely to reject the sacrificial logic."

Ammon, and Edom, to the Philistines, and to intertribal strife, was promoted by J in a time of Israel's political strength."[7]

Lind's view is bolstered by the observation of other scholars that "the P-narrative of the Pentateuch has absolutely no mention of violence, or at least of war .... Even JE is relatively noncommittal about God's war; the glorification of war comes from Josiah's propaganda effort to reclaim the Northern Kingdom for Yahweh, which lies at the basis of the Deuteronomic Landnahme. Chronicles also surprisingly knows nothing of any "war" to take Canaan."[8]

Using J. H. Yoder's typology, these examples of Abraham, Isaac, and Jacob appear to illustrate "the pacifism of the very long view" (non-violence will lead to greater justice in the long term) or "the pacifism of programmatic political alternatives"(offering a feasible solution for problems which violence and war will not solve).[9]

The Exodus events, although discussed in more detail elsewhere,[10] contain elements of traditional pacifism. For one thing the account seems to go out of its way not to place the Egyptians as a whole in a bad light. Some Egyptians actually accompany the children of Israel while others donate items to them (Exod. 12:35,38). The Egyptians are not the object of hostile expressions in the book--all the hostility seems to be directed toward the Pharaoh[11] who alone embodies the evil of rejecting Yahweh and oppressing the helpless Israelites. In addition, the people of Israel initially reject Moses as leader because he has killed an Egyptian guard (Exod. 2:11-15), indicating that a violent leader is unacceptable. Dominique Barbé comments on this episode and points to a non-violent strategy by noting that "[Violence] is not the way to the people's liberation and departure from Egypt. Genuine liberation does not consist in taking freedom by storm, by a frontal assault. Genuine liberation occurs when agitation and disturbance become so annoying

---

[7]Lind, 45.

[8]Robert North, S.J., "Violence and the Bible: The Girard Connection," *The Catholic Biblical Quarterly* 47 (1985); 15. North cites Schwager and Lohfink as supporting this view. The priests did participate in war, but apparently only in ceremonial ways such as carrying the ark. One might conclude from this that if Israel was to be a "kingdom of priests" (Exod. 19:6) then ideally no one should participate in warfare.

[9]John H. Yoder, *Nevertheless: Varieties of Religious Pacifism*, revised and expanded edition (Scottdale, PA: Herald Press, 1992) 38-42, 118f.

[10]See the chapter on "War: Israel Passive."

[11]John L McKenzie, *The Old Testament Without Illusions* (Chicago: Thomas More Press, 1979) 256.

that the dominant society itself is led to rid itself of the trouble-makers."[12]

The Sinai covenant contains a strong pacifist element. It is especially noteworthy that the Ten Commandments, the heart of the covenant, lists no specifications relating to warfare. In fact, as Lind reminds us, the non-martial character of the Ten Commandments has long been noted.[13]

Although the book of Joshua pictures the settlement of Canaan as a result of a series of swift military campaigns, some scholars have argued that the texts indicate that there were other methods used to accomplish the settlement.[14] Apparently Joshua secured the city of Shechem without warfare. Possibly the Shechemites identified with Israel because of the tradition which places Jacob in that area (Gen. 33:18-20; 34:1-31), and they simply welcomed the Israelites as kinsmen.[15] Israel's treaty with the Gibeonites in Josh. 9 may well be an example of other similar treaties which facilitated the Israelite foothold in the land. The fact that the Gibeonites tricked the Israelites into a treaty had no bearing on the outcome; Israel was bound by the terms of the treaty (v .19).

During the ninth century BCE a cluster of events surrounding the prophet Elisha are remarkable for their emphasis on non-violent conflict resolution and peace initiatives. The healing of the Syrian general Naaman is fraught with peace implications. The statement that "through him Yahweh had granted victory to the Aramaeans" is so "pro-Syrian" that it must have been scandalous to many Israelites. It implies that Yahweh, the God of the nations, guides the destiny of Aram as he guides Israel.[16] This parabolic deed illustrates Yoder's

---

[12]Barbé, 35.

[13]Lind, "Paradigm of Holy War in the Old Testament," *Monotheism, Power, Justice: Collected Old Testament Essays* (Elkhart, IN: Institute of Mennonite Studies, 1990) 187. Referred to hereafter as *Monotheism*.

[14] See Norman Gottwald, *The Hebrew Bible: A Socio-Literary Introduction* (Philadelphia: Fortress Press, 1985) 261-88 for a good summary of the three major models (conquest, immigration, social revolution). See also Bergant in *Reflections*, 22. Some of the methods were non-violent while others, whether peasant revolt or use of mercenary troops, involved the use of force.

[15]This "welcome" would explain Joshua's appeal to them in his famous speech in chap. 24. "Choose you this day whom you will serve" would have more meaning to those who lived in Canaanite Baal territory than to those who had apparently adopted Yahwism at Mt. Sinai.

[16]The sociologist Max Weber views Elisha as representing a group of "free Nebiim (who) had no national Israelite character. Under given conditions they made their services also available to non-Israelites." *Ancient Judaism*, trans. by

category of "the pacifism of prophetic protest."[17] Jesus notes the inclusive and radical nature of this event when he enrages the synagogue worshippers by asserting that "in the prophet Elisha's time there were many lepers in Israel, but none of these was cured, except the Syrian, Naaman" (Luke 4:27f).

In 2 Kings 6:8-23, Elisha captures an armed band of Aramaeans through the help of Yahweh and delivers them to the king. Instead of imprisoning or killing them, the king follows Elisha's instructions to feed them and send them home. 2 Kings 6:23 dramatically states the result of this peace initiative: "[H]e sent them off and they returned to their master. *Aramaean raiding parties never invaded the territory of Israel again.*" This event fits nicely into Yoder's category of the "pacifism of the honest study of cases."[18]

Sometime during the ministry of Elisha the Syrians invaded Israel and placed the capital, Samaria, under siege (2 Kings 6:24-7:20).[19] The story includes elements of a holy war as the Syrians "hear a noise of chariots and horses, the noise of a great army" (7:6) and consequently withdraw. As a result of this action by Yahweh, there were no casualties on either side. Peace came when war was expected. Deliverance came not as a result of violence and death, but was accomplished without bloodshed.

One can discern pragmatic reasons for the inclusion of these stories describing periods of peace between Israel and Syria. Irving Zeitlin has noted this, saying that "the emergence of the class divisions was closely connected with the long and frightening wars with Aram. From 884-754, they exhausted and impoverished the people. To pay their debts, many were not only compelled to sell their land and houses, but even themselves and their children into servitude. [This] led to the greatest

---

Hans Garth and Don Martindale (Glencoe, IL: Free Press, 1952) 102. Weber thinks that kings such as Ahab had both Baal and Yahweh prophets who "lived off the royal table"(102). But there was also a group, represented by Elisha, who "shunned any exploitation of ecstatic charisma for profit"(102).

[17]Yoder, 56-61.

[18]Ibid, 22-28.

[19]The chronology of this and surrounding events is uncertain. The Syrian king is possibly Ben-hadad III. The Deuteronomic editor(s) does not appear concerned that these stories be told in chronological order. See the *Jerusalem Bible*, note on 2 Kings 6:24.

evil of the "proletariatization" of large numbers of people and the corruption and oppression of the privileged classes."[20]

That is, during this time the prophets observed the horrible domestic consequences of warfare and thus initiated peacemaking activities. War not only *must* be averted, but it *could* be averted by bold initiatives.

Second Chronicles 28:9-15 records a remarkable story about the peacemaking initiatives of an obscure prophet named Oded. This version of the Syro-Ephraimite war is quite different from the one recorded in 2 Kings 16. Oded confronts the troops returning to Samaria following a victory over Judah by challenging the standard practice of enslaving the captured women and children. Oded employs the threat of Yahweh's anger on the Samaritans as the motivating factor for them to release the captives. The result is striking:

> So the warriors left the captives and the booty before the officials and all the assembly. Then those who were mentioned by name got up and took the captives, and with the booty they clothed all that were naked among them; they clothed them, gave them sandals, provided them with food and drink, and anointed them; and carrying all the feeble among them on donkeys they brought them to their kindred at Jericho, the city of palm trees. Then they returned to Samaria. (2 Chr. 28:14-15)

The Chronicler, by putting the Samaritans in such a favorable light, anticipates Jesus' parable of the Good Samaritan (Lk. 10:29-37).

In the eighth century prophecy of Isaiah (2:2-4; 9:5; and 11:1-9) we see remarkable visions of peace that come about not as a result of force and warfare but as a result of the Torah of Yahweh going forth to the nations.

> In days to come the mountain of the LORD's house shall be established as the highest of the mountains, and shall be raised above the hills; all the nations shall stream to it. Many peoples shall come and say, "Come, let us go up to the mountain of the LORD, to the house of the God of Jacob; that he may teach us his ways and that we may walk in his paths." For out of Zion shall go forth instruction, and the word of the LORD from Jerusalem. He shall judge between the nations, and shall arbitrate for

---

[20]Irving M. Zeitlin, *Ancient Judaism: Biblical Criticism from Max Weber to the Present* (Cambridge: Polity Press, 1984) 215. This event is an example of Yoder's "pacifism of non-violent social change" (52-55).

many peoples; they shall beat their swords into plowshares, and their spears into pruning hooks; nation shall not lift up sword against nation, neither shall they learn war any more. (Isa. 2:2-4)

A shoot shall come out from the stump of Jesse, and a branch shall grow out of his roots. The spirit of the LORD shall rest on him, the spirit of wisdom and understanding, the spirit of counsel and might, the spirit of knowledge and the fear of the LORD. His delight shall be in the fear of the LORD. He shall not judge by what his eyes see, or decide by what his ears hear; but with righteousness he shall judge the poor, and decide with equity for the meek of the earth; he shall strike the earth with the rod of his mouth, and with the breath of his lips he shall kill the wicked. Righteousness shall be the belt around his waist, and faithfulness the belt around his loins. The wolf shall live with the lamb, the leopard shall lie down with the kid, the calf and the lion and the fatling together, and a little child shall lead them. The cow and the bear shall graze, their young shall lie down together; and the lion shall eat straw like the ox. The nursing child shall play over the hole of the asp, and the weaned child shall put its hand on the adder's den. They will not hurt or destroy on all my holy mountain; for the earth will be full of the knowledge of the LORD as the waters cover the sea. (Isa. 11:1-9)

Isaiah's vision of peace is contrasted with Micah's vision by Moshe Weinfeld in an extended passage:

In contrast to the prophecy of Micah in which the king imposes peace on the nations in the aftermath of his victory (5:4), in Isaiah 11 the peace results from the cosmic harmony depicted as the end of enmity not just among men, but even among the beasts (vv. 6-8). In addition, in contrast to the prophecy of Micah in which the people's wealth is consecrated after their subjugation (4:13), in Isaiah 11 the nations comes of their own accord to seek the stem of Jesse and to honor it (v. 9). The metamorphosis of the court ideology in Isaiah attains its highest pitch in the idea of striking "with the staff of his mouth" (v. 4), which articulates an express contrast to striking "with an iron staff" (Ps. 2:9), and to the crushing of the enemy with the sword (Mic. 5:5). This spirituality in the vision of the ideal king is characteristic of Isaiah and especially conspicuous when one compares Isaiah's with Micah's vision.[21]

The foregoing comparison in no way diminishes Micah's powerful contribution to the vision of Yahweh's reign of peace. Micah 4:1-7 is a key passage.

> In days to come the mountain of the LORD's house shall be established as the highest of the mountains, and shall be raised up above the hills. Peoples shall stream to it, and many nations shall come and say: "Come, let us go up to the mountain of the LORD, to the house of the God of Jacob; that he may teach us his ways and that we may walk in his paths." For out of Zion shall go forth instruction, and the word of the LORD from Jerusalem. He shall judge between many peoples, and shall arbitrate between strong nations far away; they shall beat their swords into plowshares, and their spears into pruning hooks; nation shall not lift up sword against nation, neither shall they learn war any more; but they shall all sit under their own vines and under their own fig trees, and no one shall make them afraid; for the mouth of the LORD of hosts has spoken. For all the peoples walk, each in the name of its god, but we will walk in the name of the LORD our God forever and ever. In that day,

---

[21] Moshe Weinfeld, "Zion and Jerusalem as Religious and Political Capital: Ideology and Utopia," in *The Poet and the Historian: Essays in Literary and Historical Biblical Criticism*, ed. by Richard E. Friedman (Chico, CA: Scholars Press, 1983) 104. An interesting application of this biblical emphasis on non-violence is given by Barbé in his summary of Amos, Isaiah, and Jeremiah. "The prophets mince no words, then, in their condemnation of sacrificial rite. The scapegoat mechanism, ritual or real, will have to be rejected. But now a serious problem arises. In case of serious, violent social crisis, how will society be able to cope? We must make every effort to grasp all the consequences of the prophet's rejection of human sacrifice as part of the social relationship. That rejection is tantamount to the assertion that no human being, not even the most wicked, is totally responsible for the violence of the group. The violence is the community's as well. To cast the whole blame on one individual, even a guilty one, is a mystification and will not eliminate the evil. To slay Hitler or Somoza is not enough! No human being, whatever the degree of his or her responsibility for the prevailing evil, may be sacrificed for the good of all as if that individual were the only one responsible. We must ever recall that the 'person responsible' is responsible only in a qualified way, only 'in moderation.' The community must maintain a consciousness of its own guilt--the blame that lies with itself" (p. 41).

says the LORD, I will assemble the lame and gather those who have been driven away, and those whom I have afflicted. The lame I will make the remnant, and those who were cast off, a strong nation; and the LORD will reign over them in Mount Zion now and forevermore.

Micah employs agrarian images to set forth concretely what the reign of peace will look like. Economic priorities will be shifted from weapons to human uses (v. 3); security will result from just economic distribution (v. 4); and social compassion will be the order of the day (vv. 6,7). Peter Kjeseth observes that this passage illustrates the widespread belief in the Old Testament that peace and justice are inseparably related.[22]

Another eighth-century prophet, Hosea, attacks the mystique of violence that seemed to have engulfed the northern kingdom. Although Hosea may not have been a "pure pacifist," his scathing denunciation of militarism and violence is unmistakable.[23] For one thing, he sees a cause and effect relationship between the mystique of violence and social disintegration.

You have plowed wickedness, you have reaped injustice, you have eaten the fruit of lies. Because you have trusted in your power and in the multitude of your warriors, therefore the tumult of war shall rise against your people, and all your fortresses shall be destroyed, as Shalman destroyed Beth-arbel on the day of battle when mothers were dashed in pieces with their children. (Hos. 10:13-14)

Furthermore, he sets forth the interrelation of ecological decay, destructive personal behavior, and the popularization of crime and brutality:

Hear the word of the LORD, O people of Israel; for the LORD has an indictment against the inhabitants of the land. There is no faithfulness or loyalty, and no knowledge of God in the

---

[22]Peter Kjeseth, "Biblical Paths to Peacemaking," *Peace Ways*, ed. by Charles P. Lutz and Jerry Polk (Minneapolis: Augsburg Pub. House, 1983) 110. Is. 32:16, 17 is one of many passages which relate peace to justice.

[23]The following analysis of Hosea draws on Robert Jewett's *The Captain American Complex* (Philadelphia: Westminster, 1973) 196-209. His application of these themes to modern American policy is sobering.

land. Swearing, lying, and murder, and stealing and adultery break out; bloodshed follows bloodshed. therefore the land mourns, and all who live in it languish; together with the wild animals and the birds of the air, even the fish of the sea are perishing. (Hos. 4:1-3)

Finally, this mystique of violence leads to the militarization of foreign policy, as seen in 10:13 (cited above) and 12:1.

Ephraim herds the wind, and pursues the east wind all day long; they multiply falsehood and violence; they make a treaty with Assyria, and oil is carried to Egypt. (Hos. 12:1)

These are standard themes found in many varieties of pacifist literature throughout history.

## The Exile and After

Millard Lind views Deutero-Isaiah's emphasis on monotheism as closely related to the question of violent Enlil power so characteristic of the religion of Babylon and Persia.[24] Although Cyrus has become a representative for Yahweh in history, he does not become Yahweh's "king of justice," which would be expected of any Near East conqueror. Rather, Yahweh's Torah displaces Cyrus' violent power as the basis for the peace of the international community.

Turn to me and be saved, all the ends of the earth! For I am God, and there is no other. By myself I have sworn, from my mouth has gone forth in righteousness a word that shall not return: "To me every knee shall bow, every tongue shall swear." (Isa. 45:22-23)

Isaiah here reflects a tradition which is based upon a corporate religious experience found in the Torah and the prophets and summarized by Lind as "trust in God which excludes both reliance upon armaments and integration into the power community. This trust is that obedience to the word of Yahweh rather than self-interest backed by violent power

---

[24]Millard Lind, "Perspectives on War and Peace in the Hebrew Scriptures," *Monotheism*, 178.

will pacify the nations, and will provide the base for a new system of justice."[25]

Near the end of Judah's independence Jeremiah, who was Yahweh's prophetic warrior,[26] spoke against the court prophets who proclaimed peace when there was no peace (Jer. 6:14). To Jeremiah, "the claim of justice is prior to that of peace, because there can be no genuine peace without justice."[27] Consequently, the way of peace, Jeremiah insisted, was for unjust Judah to submit to Babylon (Jer. 21:8f; 38:17). It would seem that if ever military resistance was justified against any nation, it was justified against the Babylonians. Yet, Jeremiah proclaimed that it was offensive to Yahweh.[28] He viewed the Judean dynasty so corrupt that it was preferable that the pagan Babylonians rule his beloved country. Norman Gottwald places Jeremiah in the "co-existence party" which favored submission to Babylon and disagreed with the "autonomy party" which sought independence from Babylon with the aid of Egypt.[29] Jeremiah was certainly no visionary or idealist. The way to achieve a pragmatic peace with Babylon was to submit to them. Resisting a far superior army would be futile. Jerusalem and the temple would be spared and possibly leaders would emerge who would listen to the word of Yahweh. So, unlike Isaiah of Jerusalem, Jeremiah did not advocate a foreign policy of complete independence from the foreign powers, but like Isaiah and Hosea, he opposed integration into a Western political power block.[30]

Furthermore, Jeremiah's form of pacifism, which is a call to surrender to a much superior army, is also intimately related to the holy war tradition. However, he reverses the older tradition, which counted on Yahweh's help in battle, by turning the tradition *against* Judah. As Duane Christensen states, "the ideology of holy war was formative in the prophet's self-understanding. His call and confirmation

---

[25]Ibid., 179. This is compatible with Yoder's "pacifism of programmatic political alternatives," but could fit into other varieties of pacifism as well.

[26]Edgar W. Conrad, *Fear Not Warrior: A Study of 'al tira' Pericopae in the Hebrew Scripture* (Chico, CA: Scholars Press, 1985) 38-51. See the discussion in chap. 2.

[27]Stephen C. Mott, *Biblical Ethics and Social Change* (New York: Oxford University Press, 1982) 168.

[28]John L. McKenzie, *The Old Testament Without Illusions* (Chicago: Thomas More Press, 1979) 215.

[29]Norman K. Gottwald, *The Hebrew Bible: A Socio-Literary Introduction* (Philadelphia: Fortress, 1985) 403.

[30]Lind, "Perspectives," 177.

into the prophetic office, his trust in Yahweh, his rejection of trust in human resources, his prophetic intercession, his rejection of the inviolabililty of Zion, his relation to the false prophets, his "pacifism" must all be understood in light of the fact that Jeremiah understood himself primarily as the herald of the Divine Warrior, proclaiming holy war against Judah and Jerusalem, and by extension, to foreign nations as well."[31]

As is the case with Amos, who combines the holy war tradition with just war motifs,[32] Jeremiah unites the holy war tradition with elements of pacifism. This joining together illustrates that these understanding about war were not always viewed as mutually exclusive, but in some sense compatible with the shalom Yahweh was seeking to accomplish in history.

Visions of universal peace, righteousness, and justice reach their high water mark in Second Isaiah. Jerusalem and Judah lay in waste, having been devastated in its war with Babylon. Second Isaiah, following the other great prophets, saw this devastation as Yahweh's judgment upon an evil people. Nevertheless, out of this chaos of confusion and destruction, Yahweh was to bring peace and justice. Yahweh the redeemer would restore Israel (54:7-8) and make them instruments of peace (52:7-10). This would have universal dimensions:

> he says, "It is too light a thing that you should be my servant to raise up the tribes of Jacob and to restore the survivors of Israel; I will give you as a light to the nations, that my salvation may reach to the end of the earth." (Isa. 49:6)

Israel would welcome those nations who had previously been at war with them (55:3b-5). Paul Hanson notes that "this extension is a very profound one, for until all nations were brought into the healing orbit of God's peace, war would continue to rage, and chaos would continue to open its ugly maw to devour Israel. Second Isaiah's universalism thus solves a hitherto unresolved conflict within Yahwism, that between the inner community and the outside world. God's reign of peace was intended for all, and to this task Israel was now called by the Word of God through Second Isaiah."[33]

---

[31]Duane L. Christensen, *Transformation of the War Oracle in Old Testament Prophecy* (Missoula, MT: Scholars Press, 1975) 193.

[32]See chap. 7 on Just War.

[33]Paul D. Hanson, "War and Peace in the Hebrew Bible," *Interpretation* 38, 4 (Oct 1984) 358.

However, the Servant songs in Second Isaiah pointed to a puzzling phenomenon. How would this peace be brought about? It would be accomplished through suffering. Once again Hanson describes this vividly: "God's shalom entered the human family not through the unsheathing of Yahweh's terrible sword from heaven, but through the obedient suffering of the Servant, a suffering at first unnoticed, but ultimately recognized as the 'sin offering' that makes 'many to be accounted righteous.'" (Is. 53:10-11)[34]

This is an astonishing and unexpected element in peacemaking. The suffering and death of this "suffering mediator"[35] somehow have redemptive significance for the whole world. Is the prophet insisting that peace comes about only through undeserved suffering? The prophet seems to imply that "whereas the old kingdom was established by the *use* of violence, the new kingdom ... (is) established by the *receipt* of violence."[36] The early church, which applied these passages to Jesus, apparently understood him in this way. The life and work of Gandhi and Martin Luther King, Jr. are examples of those whose suffering and death brought about a measure of reconciliation and peace. These passages and the lives of these people point to the reality that peacemaking is a dangerous occupation. Those who embark on this course, at whatever level, can expect similar treatment. In Yoder's terms, this is the "pacifism of redemptive personalism, .... It makes a new start at its own expense. The redemptive personalist will refuse to cooperate in evil, will break the chain of evil causes and effects, and will take the resultant suffering upon oneself. This is an expression of respect for the person of the adversary."[37]

Examples of the pacifism of redemptive personalism can be found in the intertestamental period. Although 2 Maccabees primarily reflects a holy war ideology where Israel is active, chapters 6 and 7 contain the moving accounts of those who refused to obey the decrees of Antiochus. Ninety-year-old Eleazar, against the advice of all those around him, remained faithful to Yahweh and submitted to the death penalty (6:18-30), earning him high praise in v. 31.

---

[34]Hanson, 358.

[35]Gerhard von Rad, *Old Testament Theology*, Vol. II (London: Oliver and Boyd, 1962) 259. See also the discussion by Randall T. Ruble, "The Gift of Shalom in the Old Testament," in *Peace, War, and God's Justice*, ed. by Thomas D. Parker and Brian J. Fraser (Toronto: United Church Pub. House, 1989) 13.

[36]Peter Craigie, *The Problem of War in the Old Testament* (Grand Rapids: Eerdmans, 1978) 99. Emphasis his.

[37]Yoder, 92f.

So in this way he died, leaving in his death an example of nobility and a memorial of courage, not only to the young but to the great body of his nation. (2 Macc. 6:31)

In contrast to Eleazar, whose faithfulness to Yahweh resulted in death, the book of Daniel records how Daniel and his three friends were willing to accept martyrdom but Yahweh miraculously delivered them from the jaws of death. The promise of resurrection in 12:1-3 provides Daniel with the confidence that even if death does result from refusal to obey Antiochus' decrees, ultimate victory is achieved in the afterlife. This is a "pacifism of the very long view."[38]

A fascinating attempt to ground pacifism in Old Testament theology is seen in Daniel Smith's *The Religion of the Landless*. Smith rejects the paradigms of the Exodus, King David, etc., in favor of the Exile of the Israelites after the destruction of Judah by Babylon in 586 BCE. Employing a sociological analysis, Smith focuses on four modern cases and relates his findings to the biblical era of the Exile.[39] He concludes

---

[38]*Ibid.*, 118f.

[39]Daniel L. Smith, *The Religion of the Landless* (Bloomington, IN: Meyer, Stone, and Co., 1989). The four cases are the Japanese-American internment in World War II, black slavery societies and religious responses in the New World, South African Bantustans and the Zionist religious responses to segregated living, and the movement of the residents of Bikini Island (the Marshall Islands) by the United States. Smith selects four behavioral patterns or mechanisms for survival seen in these groups: (1) Structural adaptation, i.e., combining traditional structures with innovations and new leadership to provide a combination of continuity and flexibility. (2) The rise of new leadership in crisis and the typical split in strategic theories expressed by leaders in dominated situations. The split is between those leaders who argue for total, often violent, resistance and those who call for social and nonviolent resistance, with more of an ideological and cultural strategy of group boundary maintenance. This is seen in Jeremiah and Hananiah's conflict where Jeremiah calls for an abandonment of a holy war against the Babylonians which had been inspired by Hananiah's false promise that God would crush Babylon and bring home the exiles in a short time. (3) The role of ritual behavior as a means of protecting social boundaries and thus a creative mechanism. The reforms of Ezra and Nehemiah, along with the laws cited in Lev. 11, are cited as revealing a prevailing concern for maintenance of separation from the unclean. (4) Folklore innovations can be illustrated in the rise of new hero stories to illustrate models of behavior. The diaspora stories (Daniel, Esther) illustrate the pious, clever hero who overcomes the physically more powerful members of the dominant group.

that "Exodus is the road to nationalism and power. But there is another biblical paradigm. It is a warning against Exodus theology. In the place of Joshua the revolutionary conqueror, it points to Jeremiah the prophet of subversive righteousness and Ezra the priest of a radically alternative community. In the place of David the emperor, it points to Daniel the wise. In the place of Solomon's great Temple, it points to the perseverance of singing the Lord's song in a foreign land. It is a religion of the landless, the faith of those who dwell in Babylon."[40]

Smith believes that early Christians, because of their relationship with Roman authorities, understood this paradigm. Their refusal to serve in the military or to commit murder in any form was not couched so much in the language of the "sacredness of human life" or in an ancient "pacifism," but rather from a disengagement from an allegiance to the rule of "Babylon."[41] In Smith's view, much of subsequent Christian history has sought to develop a theology of power. He emphatically rejects this theme which developed from Augustine to Reinhold Niebuhr as a form of what Yoder calls "Neo-Constantianianism."

As Smith understands the Old Testament, to live as exiles is to renounce violence. But Hebraic nonviolence is not "passive-ism." Jeremiah was an activist who counseled those in exile to live and to be effective, to be the constantly present, living critique.

This is why the early Christians, though nonviolent, were otherwise decidedly "militaristic" in language, in social persistence, and in the realization that living in exile meant a kind of constant state of "mobilization" and identification with the cause of those who suffer.[42]

Those familiar with H. Richard Niebuhr's *Christ and Culture* will recognize that Smith is working out of the "Christ Against Culture" model which Niebuhr viewed as extremist and out of the mainline of Christian thought. In rejecting Niebuhr's typology, Smith represents a growing number of scholars, the best known being John Howard Yoder

---

The Messiah figures and the Suffering Servant are also types of the diaspora hero. Chapter nine, pp. 201-216, provides a good summary of the conclusions reached in his study.

[40]Ibid., 205. He cites the work of two moderns to illustrate how this theology is relevant: the Jewish historian Simon Dubnow and the Mennonite theologian John H. Yoder.

[41]Ibid., 209. Smith's views are compatible with Yoder's categories of "the pacifism of prophetic protest," "the pacifism of proclamation," and especially, "the pacifism of consistent nonconformity." Yoder, 56-67,102-106.

[42]Ibid., 210.

and Stanley Hauerwas, who are seeking to show that this model best expresses the Biblical materials and represents the only hope for a world caught up in the spiral of violence. A newer category of pacifism in Yoder's revised work is "the pacifism of Rabbinic monotheism"[43] and this seems to fit neatly into Smith's scheme.

Following Bainton's categorization, the type of pacifism seen in these examples is not the legalistic and eschatological type of Tertullian, nor the Gnostic type of repugnance of the physical held by Marcion, but rather the pragmatic and redemptive type as represented by Origen.[44] Notice also that the different examples cited in this chapter point to the various ways that peace came about. At times non-violent initiatives led to peace (e.g., Elisha's cure of Naaman, the story of Oded, etc.). At other times the threat of violence forced the aggressor to pursue or accept a non-violent resolution to the conflict (e.g., 2 Kings 6:24-7:20). However peace triumphed, the patriarchs and prophets often pointed to a more excellent way of dealing with conflicts than the well-worn pattern of violence and vengeance. Lind confesses that there is much in Israel's history and theology which contradicts this tradition of pacifism in the Old Testament. What is remarkable is that the tradition survived at all.[45]

## Jesus in Luke's Gospel

Luke brings together in the life and ministry of Jesus of Nazareth these threads of pacifism that run throughout the entire Old Testament

---

[43]Yoder, 122-125. He lists six underlying axioms of this type: (1) Radical Monotheism. We are not in charge of the world. Good will triumph in God's own time and by his doing. (2) Disillusionment with Royalty. Israel gave the kingship model of its neighbors a good test but it failed. Since Jeremiah on a world scale and since Bar Kochba even in the former land of Israel, nonviolence is the normative Jewish moral vision. (3) Minority Survival. It is possible to survive among political oppressors. (4) Avoiding Idolatry. Every Gentile army is held together by idolatry. (5) God's covenant law. The first social sin in Genesis (chap. 4) was fratricide; God condemned the sin but saved the killer's life. The only social demand of the covenant with Noah (chap. 9) was to abstain from bloodshed. (6) One God Reigns. Other people and their governments have a place in God's plan. Yoder notes that all of these characteristics were present in the first century of our era and were taken over unquestioningly by the first Christians. None of them, however, is specific to Christian faith.

[44]Bainton, 81ff. Expanding on Bainton's typology, Yoder discusses twenty-nine varieties of pacifism in *Nevertheless*.

[45]Lind, "Paradigm," 190.

period. There are numerous indications in Luke's gospel to substantiate David Dungan's statement that "we can easily see the author methodically shaping a narrative about a peace-loving Lord,"[46] concurring with Josephine Ford that "it is very possible that Luke wrote to persuade his readers that violence was not the way in which the kingdom of God could be established."[47] Luke reveals Jesus to be a reconciliatory person who greets those who deserted him with a peace greeting (24:36).[48]

To be sure, the infancy narratives exhibit a militant tone as seen in the mention of Gabriel, a war angel; the naming of Jesus after Joshua, the "paradigmatic warrior in the Deuteronomic history;"[49] and the martial imagery of the Magnificat and Benedictus, which bear the marks of holy war songs.[50] Ford believes that Luke purposefully included this material in order to portray the revolutionary atmosphere of Jesus' time and "to show that Jesus had inaugurated an *entirely new* age, and this is thrown into higher relief by contrasting material in the infancy narratives."[51] Ford further states that "From now on in his Gospel, Luke will take almost every opportunity offered him to show

---

[46]David Dungan, "Jesus and Violence," *Jesus, the Gospels and the Church*, ed. by E. P. Sanders (Macon: Mercer, 1987) 154.

[47]Josephine M. Ford, *My Enemy is My Guest* (Maryknoll: Orbis, 1984) 22.

[48]Paul Dyck, "Peter Stuhlmacher's Contributions to a Biblical Theology of the New Testament," *Essays on War and Peace: Bible and Early Church*, ed. Willard M. Swartley (Elkhart, IN: Institute of Mennonite Studies, 1986) 87. Elsewhere Swartley deftly analyzes, from a peace perspective, the approaches to Luke by Conzelmann, Cassidy, and Yoder. He finds in Luke support for all three views but concludes that the portrait of Jesus as a social, economic, and political revolutionary by Cassidy and Yoder is more consistent with the overall picture in Luke. But, "it is important to remember that Luke's *eirene* does not serve an ideology or apologetic that either consistently courts or condemns the state and political leaders, though both critical and favorable comments may appear, as Conzelmann and Cassidy have shown. The *eirene* of the Gospel has its own mind and mission. It will not be seduced into either the Pietist or Sadducee-Zealot perversions. It creates its own agenda, seeking to find more "children of peace" and to testify to all people about "the things that make for peace." "Politics and Peace in Luke's Gospel," in *Political Issues in Luke-Acts*, ed. by Richard J. Cassidy and Philip J. Scharper (Maryknoll, MD: Orbis Books, 1983) 18-37.

[49]Edgar W. Conrad, *Fear Not Warrior: A Study of 'al tira' Pericopes in the Hebrew Scripture* (Chico, CA: Scholars Press, 1985) 53.

[50]Ford, 13-28. See for a discussion of each of these.

[51]Ibid., 28, emphasis hers.

that Jesus, contrary to all expectations as seen in the infancy narratives, is a preacher with an urgent message to his generation and to the generations to come, the powerful message of nonviolent resistance and, more strikingly, loving one's enemy in word and deed."[52]

Luke's treatment of the material from the Sermon on the Mount (or "plain" in Luke) is selective. He teaches against retaliation and condemnation of the enemy and insists that his followers be doers of this teaching, not just hearers. Indeed, he puts nonretaliation at the very top of the list of Jesus' teachings.[53] In explaining what love of the enemy means, Luke speaks of "doing good," "praying for," and "blessing" one's enemy. These, according to Schottroff, are terms more intelligible to the Hellenistic world and included an appeal for a missionary attitude towards one's persecutors that brings out the universal all-embracing claim of the salvation offered by Christianity.[54]

The charge to the missionaries in 9:2-5 and 10:2-16 contains peace motifs. The instruction in 9:3 not to carry a staff is significant because it leaves the disciples totally defenseless. In Palestine a staff functions not only for support in walking but "it also served as a poor man's weapon against robbers and wild animals. Also swift escape while barefoot was impossible. Thus the renunciation of staff and sandals led to defense-lessness and entailed nonviolence; it had to become a demonstrative signal of absolute readiness for peace."[55]

Luke's insistence on including several references to the hated Samaritans[56], who Matthew and Mark fail to mention and who John cites only twice, is a strong indication that he depicts a Jesus who reaches out redemptively to the enemy. Indeed, Jesus' "unconditional acceptance of the outcasts was at the root of the conflict between Jesus

---

[52]Ibid., 36.

[53]Dungan, 155.

[54]Luise Schottroff, "Non-violence and the Love of One's Enemies," *Essays on the Love Commandment*, ed. & translated by R. H. & I. Fuller (Philadelphia: Westminster, 1978) 23. Robert J. Daly concurs that this commandment is meant to convert the persecutors and bring them into the Christian fold. "The Love Command and the Call to Non-violence," in *Christian Biblical Ethics*, ed. by Robert J. Daly (New York: Paulist Press, 1984) 216.

[55]Gerhard Lohfink, *Jesus and Community* (Philadelphia: Fortress, 1984) 53f. See also his brief discussion on the early church and war, 168-170.

[56]For a good, brief background on the Samaritans, see John R. Donahue, "Who is My Enemy: The Parable of the Good Samaritan and the Love of Enemies, *Nonretaliation and Love of Enemy*, ed. W. Swartley (see footnote 58).

and the establishment."[57] For example, Jesus refused to bring judgment on an inhospitable Samaritan village (9:51-56), sent out his messengers into this area (10:1-16), which, ironically, is geographically the place of Joshua's first battles against the Canaanites, and tells the story of the Good Samaritan (10:29-37). By so doing Luke provides a "powerful link to and transformation of Israel's conquest tradition .... But now, rather than eradicating the enemy, the new strategy eradicates the enmity. The Samaritans receive the peace of the kingdom of God. Instead of killing people to get rid of idolatry, the attack through the gospel is upon Satan directly. Instead of razing high places, Satan is blown off his throne! Hence the root of idolatry is plucked from its source."[58]

Nowhere is Luke's universalistic vision dramatized any more than in the parable of the Good Samaritan. John Dominic Crossan relates the parable to the inbreaking of the kingdom of God because the story illustrates that "the kingdom of God break(s) abruptly into human consciousness and demand(s) the overturn of prior values, closed options, set judgments and established conclusions .... The hearer struggling with the contradictory dualism of Good/Samaritan is actually experiencing in and through this the inbreaking of the kingdom of God."[59]

The hearer, then, sees that "the world with its sure arrangement of insiders and outsiders is no longer an adequate model for predicting the kingdom.[60] In sum, Luke demonstrates that the Christian's "exclusive faith centering in the finality of salvation in Christ had an inclusive focus—no one was excluded."[61] Or as Richard Baukham states, "Jesus'

---

[57]Dyck, 84.

[58]Willard M. Swartley, "Luke's Transformation of Tradition: Eirene and Love of Enemy," *The Love of Enemy and Nonretaliation in the New Testament*. ed. by Willard Swartley (Louisville: Westminster/John Knox, 1992) 167. Hereafter referred to as *Love of Enemy*.

[59]J. Dominic Crossan, *Parables: The Challenge of the Historical Jesus* (New York: Harper & Row, 1973) 65-66.

[60]Bernard Brandon Scott, *Hear Then the Parable: A Commentary on the Parables of Jesus* (Minneapolis: Fortress, 1989) 202.

[61]George L. Carey, "Biblical-Theological Perspectives on War and Peace," *The Evangelical Quarterly* 57,2 (April 1985): 166. He views the concept of the Kingdom of God functioning in this way because "it enabled the Jesus-people of the New Testament to rise above the narrow nationalism of their day to embrace a unity which is eager to draw all mankind into the love of God." The effort to exclude certain people from God's concern may be behind Jesus' strong statements against those who could not "interpret the times"(Lk. 12:56; 19:44;

vision of the Kingdom of God, provisionally present in a fragmentary way throughout his ministry, was of a society without the privilege and status which favour some and exclude others."[62]

In addition, Luke is also careful to point out later in 17:11-19, where Jesus cures ten lepers, that only a Samaritan returns to thank Him. The concept of inclusiveness would be most evident to Jewish listeners because "to be healed was to be cultically cleansed and to find one's way back into the community" (i.e., by showing oneself to the priest).[63] This story, juxtaposed with the parable of the Good Samaritan provides a powerful illustration of what Jewish teachers at the time of Jesus defined as the two fundamental religious obligations, e.g., worship of God and love of neighbor. Thus,

The Samaritan leper who twice gives glory to God embodies the first of these fundamental dispositions, while the Good Samaritan is a model of love of neighbor. Luke forcefully says that those who are called enemy and scorned as outsiders are fulfilling fundamental religious attitudes expected of Jews and followers of Jesus.[64]

In sum, the Samaritans play a crucial role in Luke's purpose to show that Jesus taught and practiced love for the enemy. Or, as Swartley states it, "by casting Samaritans in paradigmatic roles Luke converts stock strands of enmity, from Jewish perspectives, and thus shows concretely what love for the enemy entails in socio-ethnic terms."[65]

A cluster of passages in chapters 13 and 14 highlight Jesus' pacifist stance.[66] When Jesus hears about the Galileans who are killed by Pilate (13:1-5), Jesus does not respond with criticism of the Roman authorities, but instead uses it to call his listeners to repentance. Luke omits the cursing of the fig tree in Mt. 21:19-20, which shows Jesus in a hard light, and instead tells a parable of the barren fig tree (13:6-9), which focuses

---

Mt. 16:3 uses the "signs of the time") i.e., against those who engaged in speculation about the end of time. Those who did this "rejoiced in thinking of the salvation of a chosen few and the destruction of their enemies. Such hopes were self-serving and nourished a type of nationalism our Lord opposed." Dale W. Brown, *Biblical Pacifism* (Elgin, IL: Brethren Press, 1986) 81.

[62]Richard Bauckham, *The Bible in Politics: How to Read the Bible Politically* (Louisville: Westminster/John Knox, 1989) 146.

[63]David P. Reid, "Peace and Praise in Luke," in *Blessed Are The Peacemakers*, ed. by Anthony J. Tambasco (New York: Paulist Press, 1989) 85.

[64]Donahue, in *Love of Enemy*, 147

[65]Swartley in *Love of Enemy*, 171.

[66]Following Ford, 89-107.

on the patience of the vineyard owner.[67] These stories point to a Jesus whose teaching strikes at the root of religious fanaticism of the first century, which was ready to punish and exact revenge without mercy.[68] In addition, the story of table etiquette in 14:1-14 enhances the universalistic and inclusive emphases so dominant in Luke's gospel.

The parable of the Great Banquet is especially instructive. John Donahue connects the three excuses given (i.e., bought a piece of land, bought five yoke of oxen, just married a wife) with the three deferments from holy war given in Deut. 20:5-7 (i.e., built a new house, planted a vineyard, engaged to a woman).[69] Is this not Luke's way of demonstrating that Jesus does not call his people into holy war but into a banquet that includes all? Or, as Ford reads the thrust of Jesus' saying, "You waived these dispensations in your holy war but you offer them as excuses when an invitation to the (nonviolent) banquet of the kingdom of God is offered to you."[70]

Furthermore, Donahue reminds us that the apocalyptic vision of the final intervention of God into history was one always inaugurated by violence. Not surprisingly, Luke here, as he does elsewhere in his gospel, omits the violent elements (e.g., Mt. 22:7) normally associated with the eschatological banquet.[71] In addition, Jesus invites as substitute guests the poor, the crippled, and the lame—the very ones who are excluded by the Qumran literature from the messianic banquet.[72] This emphasis is a stunning way to highlight the inclusiveness of the messianic banquet. The banquet is for *all* who will respond to the invitation.

The final week as seen in Luke's gospel contains a number of significant differences with the other gospels, almost all of which point to a more pacifistic position.[73] Ford lists five differences in Luke's account of the triumphal entry: (1) Jesus tells the parable of the pounds to mitigate the disciples expectation in 19:11 that the kingdom of God was to appear immediately, thus avoiding a political interpretation of

---

[67]*Jerusalem Bible*, note on Lk. 13:6.

[68]Ford, 101.

[69]John R. Donahue, *The Gospel in Parable* (Philadelphia: Fortress Press, 1988) 141.

[70]Ford, 104. Luke, she says, has "turned the tables" and used holy war principles in the cause of the kingdom.

[71]Donahue, 142. Ford also notes that the host in Matthew, unlike in Luke, is a warlike king, 103.

[72]Donahue, 144, cites 1QM 7:4-6 and 1QSa. 2:6-10.

[73]Following Ford, 108-35.

the coming events; (2) Luke has only the disciples, not the crowd, acclaiming Jesus King; (3) Luke omits the mention of the branches because of their association with the Maccabees (1 Macc. 13:52; 2 Macc. 10:1-9; (4) Luke avoids the mention of "Son of David' (Mt. 21:9; Mk. 11:10) because of the inevitable political/military connotations; and (5) Luke alone records the request of the Pharisees for Jesus to rebuke his disciples and Jesus' response that the stones will cry out, signifying that even inanimate nature reacts to the rejection of a peaceful king.[74]

Possibly on the same day when the Roman troops arrived in Jerusalem led by the governor with all the trappings of imperial power, Jesus entered the city from the east in a radically different way. As Borg sees it, "his entry was a planned political demonstration, an appeal to Jerusalem to follow the path of peace, even as it proclaimed that his movement was the peace party in a generation headed for war. It also implied that the alternative of peace was still open."[75] Furthermore, if Zech. 9:9f is implied in Luke's account, it adds an additional non-military point.

As noted earlier, a significant omission by Luke is the cursing of the fig tree; instead, he describes Jesus weeping over Jerusalem (19:41-48), signifying that "he is not the agent of destruction but one who shows deep sympathy."[76] Ford notes in this passage that the concepts "peace" and "visitation," which echo the infancy narratives, have undergone a radical change. Peace involves acceptance of Jesus's message. Visitation refers now to political disaster, not political victory, for Israel, in direct opposition to the nationalistic expectations of the infancy narratives.

Luke's account of the cleansing of the temple is restrained and abbreviated, "too ambiguous for Luke's irenic theme."[77] There is no mention of the animals, the buyers, or to the overturning of the tables or chairs. For Luke, "Jesus must not appear to be like a destructive zealot."[78] Borg sees the event as a prophetic act which attacked "the

---

[74]Ford, 109f.

[75]Marcus Borg, *Jesus: A New Vision* (San Francisco: Harper, 1987) 174. He views the Jesus movement as the peace party within Palestine (137-140).

[76]Ford, 110. Swaim also cites 19:41 as an indication that Jesus favors Jeremiah's view of submitting to Babylon rather than fighting a futile war. J. Carter Swaim, *War, Peace and the Bible* (Maryknoll: Orbis, 1982) 77.

[77]Dungan, 155.

[78]Ford, 112. Furthermore, as Gerard Sloyan notes: "To extrapolate from that one outburst of Jesus to a mentality of armed resistance to the Romans is...perverse." *Jesus in Focus: A Life in its Setting* (Mystic, CT: Twenty-Third Publications, 1984) 15.

politics of holiness," the common view of these "ecclesiastical merchants" who embodied exclusiveness and who manifested the clear-cut distinction between sacred and profane, pure and impure, holy nation and impure nation.[79]

Luke's inclusion of the dispute among the disciples about who was the greatest carries an implication of the rejection of violence. The phrase "lord it over them" points to the fact that the social and political order was based upon domination and violence (or at least on the threat of violence). Thus, this is an example of how Luke depicts Jesus as "consistently reprimanding (the disciples) for their ambition and their inclination to violence."[80]

The statement about the two swords in Luke 22:35-38 is problematic and merits examination.

> He said to them, "When I sent you out without a purse, bag, or sandals, did you lack anything?" They said, "No, not a thing." He said to them, 'But now, the one who has a purse must take it, and likewise a bag. And the one who has no sword must sell his cloak and buy one. For I tell you, this scripture must be fulfilled in me, 'And he was counted among the lawless'; and indeed what is written about me is being fulfilled." They said, "Lord, look, here are two swords." He replied, "It is enough."

G. W. H. Lampe connects this passage with vv. 49-51 which describe one of Jesus' "followers" (apparently one of the twelve) cutting off the right ear of the high priest's servant.[81] This connection, along with

---

[79]Borg, 175. He notes that the act could not have been intended as a takeover or occupation of the temple area, as Brandon has argued, because the Romans, whose garrison overlooked the temple courts, would have immediately intervened. Borg's approach is in agreement with that of Edward Schillebeeckx, *Jesus: An Experiment in Christology* (New York: Crossroads, 1981) 243-245. Or, according to Schrage "a truly revolutionary action, which would also have attacked the prevailing economic system because the money-changers of the temple were also bankers, would certainly have provoked the intervention of the temple police and the Roman garrison." Wolfgang Schrage, *The Ethics of the New Testament* (Philadelphia: Fortress Press, 1988) 111.

[80]Richard J. Cassidy, *Jesus, Politics, and Society* (Maryknoll: Orbis, 1978) 24.

[81]G. W. H. Lampe, "The Two Swords (Luke 22:35-38)," *Jesus and the Politics of His Day*, ed. Ernst Bammel & C. F. D. Moule (Cambridge: University Press, 1984) 345. Lampe sees Mark's account of this incident as symbolic of the high priest being disqualified from holding office because his men laid hands on Jesus. Also, since Luke alone mentions that it was the *right* ear (the high priest's

Luke's insertion of Isa. 53:12, where Jesus is "reckoned with the transgressors," points to Luke's desire to show that, even though the high priest may have been worthy of contempt and rejection, the armed assault on his representative was lawless aggression on the part of the "transgressors."[82] Jesus' statement in v. 51, "Leave off! That will do!" shows that he immediately dissociates himself from his disciples' lawlessness. Furthermore, a number of commentators concur with the RSV translation of v. 38, "Enough of this!" which expresses Jesus' frustration with his disciples' lack of comprehension and his desire to break off the discussion.[83] In addition, Luke alone records that Jesus not only stopped the violence, but healed the ear of the servant.

This explanation, while helping to place the passage in a context of Jesus' rejection of violence, doesn't yet explain Jesus' admonition to buy a sword in v. 36. S. G. F. Brandon interprets this verse literally and cites it as further proof that Jesus was a Zealot.[84] In somewhat of a similar manner, Lamar Williamson cites several scholars (Cullmann, Walaskay, et al.) who take it literally, but think that Jesus "intended the use of the arms to be far more restrained than the Zealots would have liked."[85] Other interpreters, such as Hans-Werner Bartsch, see the words as referring to the Zealot revolt of 66-70 CE. which instruct Jesus' followers to join the armed forces of the Zealots because they could no longer flee the battle area.[86] This, then, is Luke's way of showing Jesus' solidarity with the revolutionary "have-nots" without justifying their

---

right ear was ceremonially smeared with the blood of the ram of concentration in Lev. 8:23f) he may have seen the act not only as symbolic of the disqualification of the high priest but also of his deconsecration and being rendered unclean.

[82]"Jesus' teaching on this occasion has the maximum significance--namely, that the members of violent resistance movements are to be numbered with transgressors." Ford, 116. Ford draws heavily on a brief article by Paul Minear, "A Note on Luke 22:36," *Novum Testamentum* 7 (1964) 129-134.

[83]Cited in Cassidy, 45.

[84]S. G. F. Brandon, *Jesus and the Zealots* (Manchester: University Press, 1967) 340f.

[85] Lamar Williamson, "Jesus and the Gospels and the Christian Vision of Shalom," *Horizons in Biblical Theology* 6, 2 (Dec. 1984) 56. He is indebted to Paul Walaskay (73) for the categories of interpretation. Williamson (65) mistakenly says that Matthew is more pacifistic than Luke.

[86]Hans-Werner Bartsch, "The Sword—Word of Jesus," *Brethren Life and Thought* 19 (Summer 1974) 151. Bartsch also thinks that Jesus is referring to the "sword" of the last great battle between the children of light and the children of darkness and placing his own execution by the Romans into that battle (153).

use of violence against powerful Rome. For Jesus it is impossible to be neutral in the revolt; one must take sides with the revolutionaries or the Romans. One cannot "stay aside in order to avoid the sinful business of the sword."[87] Other interpreters, however, see Jesus' words as symbolic of the disciples' mission in a hostile world which the disciples mistakenly take literally. The difficult response of Jesus, "that is enough!" means that Jesus abruptly closes the issue because, as had so often been the case, the disciples misunderstood him.[88] It is not possible to resolve the problem to the satisfaction of all, but, for our purposes, it does not of necessity contradict Luke's general effort to place Jesus in a non-violent light. Furthermore, a basic hermeneutic principle is that clear passages interpret obscure ones and not vice versa. Or, at least, an obscure one, such as the saying here, should not be used as a basis for establishing doctrinal truths.

In the account of Jesus' arrest Luke significantly reduces the violence of the scene.[89] For example, he omits the violent seizure of Jesus and does not mention the condemnation of Judas (Mt. 26:45-46; Mk. 14:41f), but rather inserts an expression of grief toward Judas, in line with Luke's emphasis of love for the enemy. Luke shows the disciples, not Jesus, responding with aggression and, significantly, Jesus' rebuke omits Matthew's statement about the twelve legions of angels at Jesus' disposal. Furthermore, only Luke reports that Jesus healed the ear of the servant, providing a concrete illustration of what it means to love one's enemies and to do good to them who hate. Also, Jesus strongly rebukes the crowd for arresting him as a teacher of violence and rebellion. Luke alone inserts Jesus saying that "this is your hour and the power of darkness" (22:53), implying that armed resistance belongs to the realm of supernatural evil. After the arrest Jesus is mocked, but Luke omits accusations of treason found in Matthew and Mark. Rather, Jesus is accused of a religious offense.

The account of the trial of Jesus contains a number of elements peculiar to Luke.[90] Drawing on the work of P. W. Walaskay, Ford notes that Luke poses two questions—a political and a religious one--to

---

[87]Ibid., 153.

[88]Robert J. Karris, "Luke," *The New Jerome Bible Commentary*, eds. Raymond Brown, Joseph Fitzmyer, & Roland Murphy (Englewood Cliffs: Prentice Hall, 1990) 716f. Lampe (341f) seems also to hold this view although he sees v. 38 and the insertion of the Isaiah passage as a later composition of Luke which created major difficulties in interpretation.

[89]Following Ford, 120-122.

[90]Ibid., 123-128.

Jesus before the Sanhedrin. Jesus replies affirmatively to the question as to whether he was the Son of God, but gives an obscure answer, certainly not a confession, to the political question regarding Messiahship. At any rate, Luke reports that the trial by Pilate acquits Jesus of all political charges with Pilate taking extreme measures to have Jesus released. Furthermore, "Luke wishes Barabbas ("Son of a Father"), a revolutionary, to be the complete antithesis to Jesus, the Son of God, a champion of nonresistance .... The total picture in Luke is that of a nonviolent, innocent man condemned to a revolutionary's death and the release of a man who all recognized to be guilty of sedition and murder."[91]

While on the cross Jesus (unlike the Maccabean martyrs in 2 Macc. 7) forgives his enemies (23:34)[92] as well as the repentant criminal (Luke alone records this conversation). Ford concludes, that "Luke has proclaimed Jesus innocent six times; by Pilate (three times), by Herod, by the criminal, and by the centurion—innocent of being a violent, revolutionary person. It was important to point out that Christians were not to be revolutionaries who resisted Rome. This was all the more necessary as Christianity moved into more educated and wealthier circles in the Greco-Roman world .... Thus Luke's account of the crucifixion and death of Jesus brings to a climax his portrayal of Jesus as one who taught and lived an ethic that was completely dissimilar to the militant ideology of the Maccabees, the Hasmoneans, and the revolutionary groups of the first century CE."[93]

---

[91]Ibid., 128. Gerhard Schneider concurs. "Luke 23:2 relies ... on the material in Mark which Luke has edited in order to reconstruct a specifically detailed charge from the Jewish side before Pilate. That the evangelist has thereby grasped in its essence the historically true position can be indirectly confirmed from the Jewish tradition about Jesus, a tradition which see in Jesus one who led the people astray." "The Political Charge Against Jesus (Luke 23:2)," *Jesus and the Politics of His Day*, eds. E. Brammel & C. F. D. Moule (Cambridge: Cambridge University, 1984) 403-414.

[92]Most likely the Romans according to David Daube, "For They Know Not What They Do, Lk. 23:34," *TU (Studia Patristica)* 79 (1961) 58-70.

[93]Ford, 135. Furthermore, Luke seems to be the only gospel writer to use the word "peace" to refer to the absence of war (11:21; 14:32; 19:42). "Perhaps he was influenced by the OT idea of *shalom*, or perhaps the pervasive *pax Romana* of the Augustan age had left an impressive image on his mind. Was the peace associated with the coming of Jesus meant to stand in contrast to the peace of the Augustan age?" Edwin D. Freed, *The New Testament: A Critical Introduction* (Belmont, CA: Wadsworth, 1991) 92.

In summary, the picture of Jesus in Luke's gospel is one of a pacifist whose life reflects the tradition of pacifism seen already in the Old Testament as well as mirroring the martyrdom motif prominent in the Greco-Roman world.[94] This is not to say, however, that Jesus was complacent about existing social and political conditions. Because, while Luke indicates that Jesus rejected the use of violence against persons, he also indicates that Jesus frequently challenged and contravened the social patterns that the Romans and their allies maintained.[95]

Jesus, like the prophets of old, recognized the ambiguity of power and insisted on the accountability of power. Rulers were "neither divinized nor demonized (but) called to account."[96] For Luke's Jesus, the "powers that be" could be challenged head-on without violence.

To be sure, there are some exceptions to this picture of Jesus in Luke,[97] but the overwhelming impression is one that is in stark contrast to Matthew and Mark, and, to a lesser degree, to John's gospel.[98]

## "Love Your Enemies" and "Resist Not"

Of course, a major issue regarding Jesus' teachings concerning the use of violence revolves around the interpretation of the famous "love your enemy" passages in Matthew 5 and Luke 6.[99] There are several crucial points, the interpretation of which determine where one comes out on this matter.

1. Who are the enemies? Richard Horsley has argued vigorously that the enemies here are not external, political enemies, and that the cluster of sayings around these verses does not pertain to the question of

---

[94]Dungan, building on the work of Charles Talbert and Isadore Levy, believes that Luke worked within the framework of the Pythagorean bios-tradition and not in the Jewish apocalyptic framework found in Matthew. See his discussion on pp. 156-160.

[95] Cassidy, 84

[96]Allen Verhey, *The Great Reversal: Ethics and the New Testament* (Grand Rapids: Eerdmans, 1984) 31.

[97]For example, see Swartley in *Love of Enemy*, 168-170, for his discussion of 19:11-27.

[98]Yoder would probably insist that Luke embodies the category of "the pacifism of the Messianic community," which, we must add, is Yoder's position.

[99]It is not without significance that Klassen, citing H. Koester, observes that "love your enemies" was the most frequently cited saying of Jesus in the second century. William Klassen, *Love of Enemies* (Philadelphia: Fortress, 1984) 107. It obviously stirred up much controversy then as it does today.

non-violence or non-resistance.[100] The basic thrust of his argument is twofold: (1) The modern scholarly assumption that Jesus is speaking these words in conscious opposition to the Zealots, who advocated violence against the Romans, is a scholarly fiction because the Zealots did not come into existence until long after Jesus' ministry; and (2) The enemies throughout Matthew and Luke are not national or domestic enemies but rather local adversaries. Horsley examines carefully the socio-economic background of the times and concludes that Jesus' sayings call for the "imitation of the mercy of God in dealing with precisely those 'squabbles of day-to-day life' which were integrally related to the struggle for supreme values and which took place in circumstances where people had "their backs to the wall."[101]

Horsley's analysis has much to commend itself but Mt. 5:38-42 depicts enemies as being more than merely fellow peasants, especially v.41 which describes an enemy as a Roman soldier who compels a Jew to carry his baggage. Furthermore, his insistence on translating Matthew's term *antistenai* ("resist not") as "protest" or "testify against"[102] is refuted by Walter Wink's assessment that the term is a military term that literally refers to armed resistance.[103]

---

[100]Richard A. Horsley, "Ethics and Exegesis: 'Love Your Enemies' and the Doctrine of Non-violence," *Journal of the American Academy of Religion* 54 (1986) 3-31. He also deals with these passages in his *Jesus and the Spiral of Violence* (San Francisco: Harper & Row, 1987) 259-275. Horsley says that by religious conviction he is a pacifist, but he is critical of the presuppositions and exegesis of Yoder and others who seek to articulate and absolutist pacifist position from these synoptic texts.

[101]Ibid., 23. Mott agrees with the view that these passages cannot be used to answer questions about military violence and non-violence because these cases are *bilateral* (concerned with the relationship between the subject and one other person) whereas the very thorny questions are *multilateral*, in which the subject's duty is not only to a second person but also to a third person or party for whom one bears responsibility. (p.173)

[102]Stuart D. Currie agrees with Horsley that this is a litigation text, believing, against Wink, that Matthew saw Jesus as providing an alternative to the *lex talionis*, and, in effect, saying, "But I tell you, do not protest against the wrongdoer. Don't file a complaint; don't make a court case of it, don't seek damages." "Matthew 5:39a—Resistance or Protest?" *Harvard Theological Review* 57, 2 (April 1964) 145.

[103]Walter Wink, "Neither Passivity nor Violence: Jesus's Third Way," *Society of Biblical Literature 1988 Seminar Papers*, ed. David J. Lull (Atlanta: Scholars Press, 1988) 220-222. Since the saying was part of the public message of Jesus, "the most natural understanding of his words would be a reference to the

The addition of "hate your enemy" in Mt. 5:43 has, of course, raised a serious question as to the source of this statement. Since the other maxims quoted by Matthew are gathered directly from the Mosaic Law, it is hard to accept the suggestion that it was a popular saying based on 2 Sam. 19:6 or that it was a bit of exegesis added by Jesus or that it was a later redaction to indicate the popular (mis)understanding of "You shall love your neighbor" (Lev. 19:18).[104] The fact that Jesus said, "you have *heard* ..." has given rise to the suggestion that it had a synagogue setting where a targum used in Galilee in Jesus' day had glossed the words "you shall love your neighbor" with the words "and hate your enemy."[105] Morton Smith concludes that this interpretation is possible because the statement is not incompatible with the spirit of orthodox Judaism,[106] but he is more impressed by the striking parallels in the Dead Sea Scrolls,[107] implying an Essene influence that would be widely felt in Jesus' day. Maybe it is more an inference from Old Testament *practice* where many Jews recognized the duty of compassion only when they were dealing with fellow-Jews or proselytes.[108]

2. What is the literary genre of these passages? Robert Tannehill has contributed to our understanding of Mt. 5:39-42 by positing that these forms of material are to be understood as "focal instances" characterized by specificness and extremeness. "Extremeness means that it stands in deliberate tension with ordinary human behavior. Specificness means that there is a surprising narrowness of focus due to the desire to present an extreme instance .... The open-ended series of focal instances has none of the ... characteristics of the legal rule .... It is not manageable in its literal sense. It does not deal explicitly with a general area of human behavior. It does not permit clear deduction as to the

---

national enemies of Israel, who at that time were the Roman occupying forces." O. J. F. Seitz, "Love Your Enemies," *New Testament Studies* 16 (1969, 70): 52. Krister Stendahl prefers to see the "enemy" as any outsider (non-Christian); these are "the enemies of God and of his Messiah." "Hate, Non-retaliation, and Love," *Harvard Theological Review* 55 (1962): 345.

[104] The latter is favored by Seitz, 51. Both of these suggestions are rejected by Morton Smith, "Mt. 5:43: 'Hate Thine Enemy," *Harvard Theological Review* 45 (Jan 1952): 71.

[105] Smith, 72. See also Seitz, 52.

[106] citing several sources such as Maimonides and the Midrash, 72.

[107] Smith, 73.

[108] L. H. Marshall, *The Challenge of New Testament Ethics* (London, Macmillan & Co., 1960) 119. Marshall sites Ecclus. 12:6, 7 as an example of an attitude which would promote this practice: "For the most High hateth sinners and will repay vengeance to the ungodly. Give to the good, help not the sinner."

range of its applications... The source of the great hermeneutical potential of such language (is) its power to speak again and again to new situations .... It helps not by giving a clear indication of what he is to do but by throwing a strong light on the situation from one direction, forcefully calling to his attention one factor in his situation .... It starts him thinking in a definite direction .... The focal instance serves as an illuminator of the hearer's situation. The hearer is invited to lay the saying alongside his own situation and, through the imaginative shock produced, to see that situation in a new way."[109]

Tannehill's analysis coincides with David Tracy's analysis of the nature and function of Jesus parables. Tracy calls the parables an example of "limit language," language which stretches the limits of credulity and jars listeners out of lethargy and demands that they look at reality from a different perspective.[110] The function of the parables, then, is not to demand specific types of behavior, but to challenge one's overall perspective and outlook on life and to offer a new and better one.[111] Jesus' examples of turning the other cheek, handing over one's underwear to a creditor, and carrying baggage an extra mile are meant, then, not to be viewed legalistically, but to provide shocking examples of what it means to love one's enemies.

3. What, if anything, are these passages teaching about non-violence and/or non-resistance? Scholars have often interpreted these passages as commanding that one submit to any and every indecency and to reject

---

[109]Robert C. Tannehill, "The 'Focal Instance' as a Form of New Testament Speech: A Study of Matthew 5:39b-42," *Journal of Religion* 50 (1970) 380-383. He cites Mt. 8:21f and 23:8-10 as other examples of "focal instances."

[110]David Tracy, *Blessed Rage for Order* (New York: Seabury Press, 1975) 126-136. John Dominic Crossan likes Tannehill's contrast of focal instance with legal rule but thinks the examples here are best described as a satiric parody of case law rather than focal instance. The logia are characteristically ridiculous, containing a certain sensation of nonsense. Crossan's analysis seems more of an extension or qualification of Tannehill's position. See Crossan's insightful analysis in "Jesus and Pacifism," *No Famine in the Land*, (FS: J. L. McKenzie) eds. J. L. Flanagan & A. W. Robinson (Missoula, MT: Scholars Press, 1975) 195-208.

[111]A good example is the shocking parable of the laborers in the vineyard in Mt 20:1-16, where the one-hour worker is paid the same as a full-day worker. This is obviously not an attempt to establish a radical economic program but a striking way to make the point that God deals with all people the way the owner of the vineyard dealt with the one-hour worker, i.e., on the basis of grace not of works. What an unforgettable way of teaching an abstract truth! Parables often, according to Tracy, paint a picture that is unbelievable and thus, capable of shocking the listener into a totally different way of looking at reality.

retaliation of any kind. A better way of viewing them is to see the examples given by Jesus as encouraging what Wink calls "subversive assertiveness." and "Jesus' Third Way."[112] Wink generally prefers Matthew's account because he believes that Luke has altered the sayings by mistakenly seeing them as a response to armed robbery when, in fact, we have a set of unequal relations in which retaliation would be suicidal. Wink interprets the core sayings in the following manner: "(1) Matthew alone mentions the "right cheek" because the issue is a backhanded slap from a superior to an inferior. Instead of counseling people to stifle their inner rage at such an indignity, Jesus tells them to turn the other cheek because it will rob the oppressor of the power to humiliate. The person is in effect saying, "Try again. Your first blow failed to achieve its intended effect. I deny you the power to humiliate me. I am a human being just like you. Your status (gender, race, age, wealth) does not alter that fact. You cannot demean me." The saying is not, then, an "attack on our natural tendency to put self-protection first,"[113] but a way to channel the justified rage at being dehumanized.

(2) Because of the serious socio-economic conditions in Palestine in the time of Jesus, most notably the high indebtedness of many, it was not uncommon for the rich to sue the poor for their outer garment. Jesus' shocking counsel is for the debtor to give the credit or not only the outer garment but the undergarment as well, which meant that the debtor would march out of the court stark naked! Wink eloquently states that, "there stands the creditor, beet-red with embarrassment, your outer garment in one hand, your underwear in the other. You have suddenly turned the tables on him. You had no hope of winning the case; the law was entirely in his favor. But you have transcended his attempt to humiliate you. You have risen above shame. At the same time you have registered a stunning protest against a system that spawns such debt. You have said in effect, "You want my robe? Here, take everything! Now you've got all I have except my body. Is that what you'll take next?"[114]

This creditor is now not a respected moneylender because he has caused nakedness, which is taboo in Judaism. This deft lampooning of The Powers That Be has unmasked the essential cruelty of the system.

---

[112]Wink, 222. The following is a summary of the most salient points in his article, 210-224.
[113]Tannehill, 380.
[114]Wink, 215.

(3) Jesus employs the example of how to respond to the forced labor (*angareia*) which Roman soldiers could demand of subjects. The question here, as in the other two, is how to recover the initiative and assert human dignity when change in the system is not possible at the present time. When the person offers to carry the pack another mile, the soldier has to wonder what this means. Is this an insult, a provocation, a plan to file a complaint, etc.?

From a situation of servile impressment, you have once more seized the initiative. You have taken back the power of choice. The soldier is thrown off-balance by being deprived of the predictability of your response .... You have forced him into making a decision for which nothing in his previous experience has prepared him. If he has enjoyed feeling superior to the vanquished, he will not enjoy it today. Imagine the hilarious situation of Roman infantryman pleading with a Jew, "Aw, come on, please give me back my pack!" The humor of this scene may escape those who picture it through sanctimonious eyes, but it could scarcely have been lost on Jesus' hearers, who must have regaled at the prospect of thus discomfiting their oppressors.[115]

Jesus thus offers a realistic, not a utopian or apocalyptic, solution to those who have had to bow and scrape before their oppressors. They can now liberate themselves from both servile actions and a servile mentality, thus laying the foundation for a social revolution.

Wink thinks that the reason for the widespread misunderstanding of these passages has to do, in part, with Matthew's framing of the saying in the context of the *lex talionis*. Wink insists that Jesus is not talking about revenge or reparations, so that the misreading of this as passive acquiescence is an unintended consequence of Matthew's attempt to distance Jesus from Judaism by means of the antitheses.[116] Jesus'

---

[115]Ibid., 218.

[116]Ibid., 223. Scholars have long noted that Matthew, in an effort to show Jesus as the "New Moses," builds this section of the Sermon on the Mount around six antitheses, comparing Jesus' new law with Moses' old law. See Donald Senior, Jesus' Most Scandalous Teaching," *Biblical and Theological Reflections on 'The Challenge of Peace,*" (Wilmington, DE: Michael Glazier, 1983) 57. In the section under discussion this paradigm "backfired," according to Wink, because it skewed the focus of Jesus' saying. In addition, in keeping with the discussion earlier about Luke's more pacifistic portrayal of Jesus, Victor Furnish notes that "Whereas in Matthew the teaching on nonretaliation assumes a polemical form in opposition to Jewish practices, in Luke the teaching is presented as a further positive example of what is involved in loving one's enemies. Love means forgoing the luxury of spiteful vengeance or calculated

examples do illustrate Mt. 5:39b, "do not resist evil (violently)," by showing a new way of being in the world that "at last breaks the spiral of violence. A way of fighting evil with all one's power, power without being transformed into the very evil we fight. A way of not becoming what we hate. Do not counter evil in kind – this insight is the distilled essence state with sublime simplicity, of the experience of those Jews who had, in Jesus' very lifetime, so courageously and effectively practiced nonviolent direct action against Rome."[117]

Thus, contrary to Horsley, these passages *do* deal with the issue of non-violence. They do not counsel passivity nor violence, but rather a creative way of actively attacking and lampooning the forces of oppression.

4. What is the motive and goal of these actions? If Wink's analysis is correct, then certain commonly attributed goals and motives are called into question. An effort by Dungan to place these sayings into the equivalent of our category of holy war: passive, where the focus is on passive acceptance of injustice because God will exact vengeance in the future,[118] seems inaccurate. Wink's interpretation, however, is compatible with Donald Senior's view that the behavior cited in Jesus' examples is not meant to win the enemy's favor or to produce superior virtue, but it is done because such actions reflect God's way of loving.[119] The God of Israel is a God of compassion for all but this compassion and love of enemy does not contradict God's active stance on the behalf of outcasts which Jesus embodied. Identification with the poor and oppressed will often lead one "to unmask the powers that be." Senior, in a somewhat different focus than Wink, sees the love of enemy command as an example of the tension between "the now and the not yet" which characterizes much within the New Testament.

Jesus' command is neither an impossible ideal, unsuitable for the "real world," nor is it a law so tyrannically demanding that it leaves us no possibility but failure. Jesus' teaching on love of enemies and, in

---

retaliation. It busies itself only with doing good." *The Love Commandment in the New Testament* (Nashville: Abingdon, 1972) 56.

[117]Wink, 223. I. Howard Marshall, who tends to take the view which Wink is refuting, cites an example of a poor widow which lends itself to Wink's approach. "New Testament Perspectives on War," *Evangelical Quarterly* 57, 2 (April 1985) 123.

[118]David Dungan, "Jesus and Violence," *Jesus, the Gospels, and the Church*, ed. E. P. Sanders (Macon: Mercer University Press, 1987) 136.

[119] Donald Senior, "Enemy Love: The Challenge of Peace," *The Bible Today* (May 1983) 165.

fact, the entire Gospel comes to us an impelling invitation to seek a way of life that is both "already" and "not yet."[120]

This tension is heightened in Wink's approach because one must lampoon the powers that be without dehumanizing the individual oppressors, without resorting to the same attitude and violent behavior of the enemies.

The goal, then, of Jesus' teachings here appears to be in harmony with the kind of pacifism usually described as "pacifism as a strategy," as over against "pacifism as obedient witness."[121] That is, it is the kind of nonviolence which Richard Gregg characterizes as "moral jui-jitsu" because it puts at a disadvantage the other person who is expecting violence.[122] This element of surprise, as Martin Luther King Jr. noted from his experience, can evoke a more positive response which leads to a better peace and often has a strong appeal to the uncommitted bystander.[123] L. H. Marshall describes it as "the energy of a steadfast will bent on creating fellowship."[124]

5. Although it is not a crucial point of interpretation, it is interesting to note the question regarding the *source* of this love of enemies and resist not command. A comparable saying of the Stoic Seneca is often quoted: "If you want to imitate the gods, do favours even to the ungrateful; for the sun rises even over the wicked, and the sea is open even to pirates."[125] Similar quotations are found in Marcus Aurelius and others. On this basis, William Klassen traces the commandment to Greek wisdom but also sees the roots of it in Judaism.[126] On the other hand, John Piper regards the command as being derived directly from

---

[120]Ibid., 168.

[121]For a good critical discussion of this distinction see Joseph L. Allen, *Love and Conflict: A Covenantal Model of Christian Ethics* (Nashville: Abingdon, 1984) 191-198.

[122]Richard B. Gregg, *The Power of Nonviolence*, 2nd rev. ed. (New York: Schocken Books, 1966) 43ff. Or, to use Yoder's typology, this is the pacifism of nonviolent social change(52-55) or the pacifism of redemptive personalism (92-95).

[123]Martin Luther King, Jr., *Stride Toward Freedom* (New York: Harper & Bros., 1958) 102.

[124]L. H. Marshall, *The Challenge of New Testament Ethics*, 120.

[125]Cited in Rudolf Schnackenburg, *The Moral Teaching of the New Testament* (New York: Herder & Herder, 1966) 104.

[126]Klassen, 12-42.

Jesus and as a radical departure from Judaism.[127] On the basis of the Old Testament passages cited in this chapter and those examined in the chapter on "holy war as redemptive," Klassen's view is preferred. One can make the case that Jesus' understanding was unique, but it seems to go too far to insist that he arrived at this understanding apart from his Jewish background.[128]

Thus, we conclude that the "love your enemies" and "resist not" passages are not only referring to local disputes but primarily to the economic and political Powers That Be and that Jesus employs a sort of "shock language" to illustrate that it is possible in these circumstances to imitate God's love while at the same time maintaining self-respect and integrity in an oppressive socio-political climate.

In sum, in spite of the extensive interest in the Bible on holy war—related in part to Israel's strategic location and to the cultures which surrounded them—it is remarkable to find both narratives and teachings in both Testaments which expressed so unmistakably the desire for, and possibility of, peace. A strong belief persisted throughout the biblical period that violence and war should and can be resisted and replaced by a better way.

---

[127]John Piper, *'Love Your Enemies: Jesus' Love Command in the Synoptic Gospels and in the Early Christian Paranesis* (SNTSMS 38; Cambridge: Cambridge University, 1979) 56-65.

[128]For a discussion of this see Schnackenburg, 90-98. Victor P. Furnish sees Jesus' broadening of the concept of "neighbor" to include those outside one's ethnic, social, and even religious group, and the radicalization of the command to include one's enemies as being "quite unprecedented." "War and Peace in the New Testament," *Interpretation* 38, 4 (1984): 368.

# Chapter Seven

# JUST WAR MOTIFS

While the holy war tradition is the most striking and most dominant view of war in the Old Testament (but found to a lesser extent in the New Testament), and while a strong pacifist tradition can be seen in most all periods of biblical history, concepts resembling the medieval and modern doctrine of a just war can also be found.[1] That is to say that in some instances a war is justified not on the basis of a perceived direct command of God or on the basis of some unique Israelite theological principle, but on the basis of a universal sense of justice. Or, as Robert Good calls it, a jural or legal understanding of war.[2] In the instances to be cited, the speaker or writer justifying war sounds very much like a lawyer in court. In a court of law, appeals must be made to commonly accepted principles of law and justice. Appeals cannot be made to mere personal interest or to peculiar religious beliefs. A lawyer seeks to persuade a judge or jury by drawing on universal principles which apply to all like cases. The concept of mutual rights and obligations and a consistent application of these provide the basis of a just decision.[3] As Yahweh is depicted in the Old Testament as a Warrior, so also is he depicted as a judge, and in his role as a judge, he makes judgments according to universal standards of justice, not on the basis that he alone is sovereign or that his might makes right. To state it differently, it is not right because Yahweh says it, Yahweh says it because it is true and right.

---

[1]The criteria of a just war are generally listed as: (1) Just cause (defensive wars only). (2) Just intention (secure a just peace). (3) Last resort (all negotiations have failed). (4) Formal declaration (governments only). (5) Limited objectives (total destruction unwarranted). (6) Proportionate means (use only what is necessary to repel aggression and secure a just peace). (7) Noncombatant immunity (civilians, POWs, and casualties are immune).

[2]Robert M. Good, "The Just War in Ancient Israel," *JBL* 104 (1985): 385-400. This article is a major source for many ideas presented in this chapter.

[3]See Good, 388.

It is noteworthy that the Deuteronomic historians[4], so often accused of being the foremost proponents of holy war, cite instances and concepts which are compatible with just war teachings.

> Once again Jephthah sent messengers to the king of the Ammonites and said to him: "Thus says Jephthah: Israel did not take away the land of Moab or the land of the Ammonites, but when they came up from Egypt, Israel went through the wilderness to the Red Sea and came to Kadesh. Israel then sent messengers to the king of Edom, saying, 'Let us pass through your land'; but the king of Edom would not listen. They also sent to the king of Moab, but he would not consent. So Israel remained at Kadesh. Then they journeyed through the wilderness, went around the land of Edom and the land of Moab, and camped on the other side of the Arnon. They did not enter the territory of Moab, for the Arnon was the boundary of Moab. Israel then sent messengers to King Sihon of the Amorites, king of Heshbon; and Israel said to him, 'Let us pass through your territory; so Sihon gathered all his people together, and encamped at Jahaz, and fought with Israel. Then the LORD, the God of Israel, gave Sihon and all his people into the hand of Israel, and they defeated them; so Israel occupied all the land of the Amorites, who inhabited that country. They occupied all the territory of the Amorites from the Arnon to the Jabbok and from the wilderness to the Jordan. So now the LORD, the God of Israel, has conquered the Amorites for the benefit of his people Israel. Do you intend to take their place? Should you not possess what your god Chemosh gives you to possess? And should we not be the ones to possess everything that the LORD our God has conquered for our benefit? Now are you any better than King Balak son of Zippor of Moab? Did he ever enter into conflict with Israel, or did he ever go to war with them? While Israel lived in Heshbon and its villages, and in Aroer and its villages, and in all the towns that are along the Arnon, three hundred years, why did you not recover them within that time? It is not I who have sinner against you, but you are the one who does me wrong by making war on me. Let

---

[4]The view that the D document underwent several redactions is accepted here. See Alexander Rofe, who identifies four strata, D1, D2, DS, & DP, in "The Laws of Warfare in the Book of Deuteronomy: Their Origins, Intent, and Positivity." *JSOT* 32 (1985): 23-44.

the Lord, who is judge, decide today for the Israelites or for the Ammonites. (Judges 11:14-27)

This speech of Jephthah has a remarkable courtroom ring to it. He challenges the Ammonite king's right of ownership of the land and describes how Israel rightly owns it. Referring back to the Mosaic period when Israel was marching toward the promised land, Jephthah reminds the "court" that the Israelites requested permission to pass through Ammonite land but were unjustly refused passage and were forced to defend themselves from an attack by Sihon, the Ammonite king. Israel, Jephthah insists, has legal "title" to the land. His argument is bolstered by appeal to the fact that Israel occupied several transjordan towns for 300 years without legitimately being challenged.[5] Good observes that "Jephthah's entire missive is predicated on the existence of standards for judgment that would apply in all similar cases. We are, in short, justified in speaking here of a preexilic concept of war as an expression of divine legal judgment."[6]

Jephthah asks Yahweh to judge the issue, not on the basis that Israel is God's chosen people, but on the merits of the case based on the reciprocal rights and obligations of the disputants. Jephthah assumes that the Ammonites accept the logic of his case because they too accept the universal justice principles which apply to this situation.

Psalm 82 contains some remarkable concepts which relate to our discussion.

God has taken his place in the divine council; in the midst of the gods he holds judgment: "How long will you judge unjustly and show partiality to the wicked? Give justice to the weak and the orphan; maintain the right of the lowly and the destitute. Rescue the weak and the needy; deliver them from the hand of the wicked." They have neither knowledge nor understanding, they walk around in darkness; all the foundations of the earth are shaken. I say, "You are gods, children of the Most High, all of you; nevertheless, you shall die like mortals, and fall like any prince." Rise up, O God, judge the earth; for all the nations belong to you!

---

[5]This statement by Jephthah points to a later editing of the story by one of the D historians because the number of years between the Sihon story and the Jephthah story is considerably less than three hundred years.

[6]Good, 395.

The "gods" referred to here apparently make up the divine council referred to in Deuteronomy 32:43 and Job 1, although it may be possible to interpret them as earthly rulers. But for our purposes the key element is that the norms of justice and compassion transcend the rule of the gods. Paul Hanson describes this Psalm as judging "the gods on the basis of the universal norm of compassionate justice. There is thus a higher authority in heaven than the patron god of each nation and its corresponding king. Though stemming from divine pedigree, the gods are no longer the source of right and wrong, nor the final court of appeal. They are rather subject to judgment against a norm to which all are held responsible."[7]

Israel's surrounding cultures viewed truth as based on divine royal power and prerogative, but truth in Israel was grounded on impartial justice. Even the patriarch Abraham experienced this in his "debate" with Yahweh over the destruction of Sodom when God answered his objections by asking, "Will the judge of the whole earth not administer justice?" (Gen. 18:25 JB).

The classical prophets often viewed war as a righteous judgment of God against evil, whether against the nations or against Israel itself. Amos' oracles against the nations in chapters 1 and 2 follow a set pattern[8] which includes the messenger formula ("This is what Yahweh has said'), the indictment ("because of three crimes ...."), and the pronouncement of punishment ("I will send fire ...."). His oracle against Syria in 1:3-5 is typical of the logic he uses in the first two chapters in justifying wars against evil nations.

> Thus says the LORD: For three transgressions of Damascus, and for four, I will not revoke the punishment; because they have threshed Gilead with threshing sledges of iron. So I will send a fire on the house of Hazael, and it shall devour the strongholds of Ben-hadad. I will break the gate bars of Damascus, and cut off the inhabitants from the Valley of Aven, and the one who holds the scepter from Beth-eden; and the people of Aram shall go into exile to Kir, says the LORD. (Amos 1:3-5)

Because of the brutal treatment of Gilead,[9] Damascus will suffer defeat in war.[10] Once again, war will be waged on Syria, not because

---

[7]Paul Hanson, "War, Peace, and Justice in Early Israel," *Bible Review* (Fall 1987): 40.

[8]James L. Mays, *Amos: A Commentary* (Philadelphia: Westminster, 1969) 23.

[9]"The pregnant women of Gilead" in the Greek text, see v. 13.

of specific religious reasons, but because Syria has violated commonly accepted norms of justice. "Fire" (war) is coming to the other nations, e.g., Philistia (1:6-8), Phoenicia (1:9-10), Edom (1:11-12), Ammon (1:13-15), Moab (2:1-3), even Judah (2:4-5) and Israel (2:6-16), because of universally recognized moral evils such as deportation (1:6), brutal slavery (1:6, 9), killing of non-combatants (1:13), and exploitation of the poor (2:6-7). These passages are not unlike a courtroom indictment and do not refer to evils peculiar to Israel's faith; many others share these fundamental principles.[11] Only Judah is condemned for what might be called special theological reasons, i.e., rejecting Yahweh's law[12] and idolatry (2:4-5). Without specifically condemning war as such, Amos condemns the kinds of practices which are common during war. His judgment appears to be based not on any specific biblical revelation, but on the belief that all human beings are valued by God.[13] Or as Walter Houston states, "In Amos 1-2 we find Amos taking it for granted that his hearers will assent to the idea that there are moral standards to be observed in warfare, standards which all people ought to be expected to recognize."[14]

To be sure, Amos' oracles also contain "explicit battle imagery reminiscent of Israel's holy war tradition."[15] But Amos has transformed the older war oracle from a tactical element in military strategy into a literary mode of prophetic judgment speech against both military foes

---

[10]Amos employs the metaphor of "fire" to describe war. This is a common metaphor depicting warfare in ancient near eastern literature. Cf. Moshe Weinfeld, "Divine Intervention in War in Ancient Israel and in the Ancient Near East," in *History, Historiography and Interpretation: Studies in biblical and cuneiform literature.* Ed. by Hayim Tadmore and Moshe Weinfeld (Jerusalem: The Magnes Press, 1986) 131-136.

[11]For example see the Laws of Eshnuana, the Code of Hammurabi, and the Mesopotamian Legal Documents in James Pritchard, *The Ancient Near East,* Vol. 1 (Princeton: Princeton University Press, 1958) 133-169.

[12]It could be argued that the "law" referred to here includes more than morality which applies solely to Judah's special relationship to Yahweh, but includes some of the "common morality" violated by the other nations.

[13]Carroll Stuhlmueller, "The Prophetic Price for Peace," *Biblical and Theological Reflections on The Challenge of Peace.* Eds. John Pawlikowski and Donald Senior (Wilmington, DE: Michael Glazier, 1987) 36.

[14]Walter Houston, "War and the Old Testament," *The Modern Churchman* 27, 3 (1985): 18.

[15]Duane L. Christensen, *Transformation of the War Oracle in Old Testament Prophecy* (Missoula, Montana: Scholars Press, 1975) 70.

and the nation of Israel.[16] At the same time, he draws upon a more universal and judicial tradition which judges the nations on the basis of universally recognized moral principles.

The prophet Joel projects into an apocalyptic future some of the same emphases noted above.

> For then, in those days and at that time, when I restore the fortunes of Judah and Jerusalem, I will gather all the nations and bring them down to the valley of Jehoshaphat, and I will enter into judgment with them there, on account of my people and my heritage Israel, because they have scattered them among the nations. They have divided my land, and cast lots for my people, and traded boys for prostitutes, and sold girls for wine, and drunk it down. Proclaim this among the nations; Prepare war, stir up the warriors. Let all the soldiers draw near, let them come up. Beat your plowshares into swords, and your pruning hooks into spears; let the weakling say, "I am a warrior." Come quickly, all you nations all around, gather yourselves there. Bring down your warriors, O LORD. Let the nations rouse themselves, and come up to the valley of Jehoshaphat; for there I will sit to judge all the neighboring nations. Put in the sickle, for the harvest is ripe. Go in, tread, for the wine press is full. The vats overflow, for their wickedness is great. (Joel 3:1-3; 9-13)

Note that the nations are to be judged not only for destroying the nation of Israel and scattering the people (that would be reason enough for many Israelites), but because of the way they treated children and engaged in drunkenness and sexual immorality. As in Amos, judgment comes in the form of war. Note also that it is not Israel who is summoned to prepare for war. Rather, the nations are summoned. Israel has no army. Yahweh will act on their behalf.[17]

Second Chronicles 20:5-12 combines elements of the pacifist and just war motifs[18].

---

[16]Ibid., 283.

[17]This coincides with both the holy war: passive and pacifist stance often observed in Israel's military past. See the discussion in chaps. 3 and 6.

[18]The D document does not include this interesting story. Is it because it does not fit the holy war ideology espoused by the D redactors? However, not all non-holy war ideology has been removed from the final document. See v. 29f.

Jehoshaphat stood in the assembly of Judah and Jerusalem, in the house of the LORD, before the new court, and said, O LORD, God of our ancestors, are you not God in heaven? Do you not rule over all the kingdoms of the nations? In your hand are power and might, so that no one is able to withstand you. Did you not, O our God, drive out the inhabitants of this land before your people Israel, and give it forever to the descendants of your friend Abraham? They have lived in it, and in it have built you a sanctuary for your name, saying, 'If disaster comes upon us, the sword, judgment, or pestilence, or famine, we will stand before this house, and before you, for our name is in this house, and cry to you in our distress, and you will hear and save.' See now, the people of Amon, Moab, and Mount Seir, whom you would not let Israel invade when they came from the land of Egypt, and whom they avoided and did not destroy—they reward us by coming to drive us out of your possession that you have given us to inherit. O our God, will you not execute judgment upon them? For we are powerless against this great multitude that is coming against us. We do not know what to do, but our eyes are on you."

Jehoshaphat presents his case in the courtroom of Yahweh.[19] He argues that the coalition of Ammon, Moab, and Edom has no just cause to attack Judah. Judah has clear title to its land; they possessed it peacefully; they mercifully did not destroy these nations when they had the power to do so.[20] It is as if Jehoshaphat argues that Israel had waged war with a view to establishing an enduring and equitable peace, a theme found in traditional just war theory. Israel had acted

---

[19]Jehoshaphat may have possessed the keenest judicial interest of any of the kings of Israel and Judah. He is pictured favorably in both Kings and Chronicles and apparently his widespread judicial reforms were a part of larger religious reforms carried out at the beginning of his reign (2 Chr. 17:7-9; 1 Kings 22:43-46). The Deuteronomic historians certainly applauded his "centralizing" activities, although this probably met with great resistance from local leaders. See the discussion by Keith W. Whitlam, *The Just King: Monarchial Judicial Authority in Ancient Israel* (Sheffield: JSOT Press, 1979) 185-206.

[20]There is a hint here of what James Nash refers to as "mourning and mercy, remorse and redress-humane dispositions that once were considered by some just war theorists as the only appropriate ones for facing the tragedies of war . James A Nash, "The Aftermath," *Theology and Public Policy* III, 1 (Summer 1991): 4.

justly in warfare but this coalition now mounts an unjust attack on Judah. Jehoshaphat then, as it were, appeals to Yahweh's "objective judgment." Like a judge who is "blind" with regard to the parties involved, the decision is to be reached on the basis of justice, not because of Yahweh's special relationship to Israel.[21]

The outcome of the battle is described in 2 Chron. 15: 13-30. Troops are deployed but do not engage in battle. Mirroring the motifs found in Exodus 15 and Judges 5 and elsewhere, Yahweh alone fights for Israel. This is holy war with Israel passive and it is a just war because it is unprovoked, defensive, and because the attack violates common norms of justice and standards of fairness.

The so-called "laws of war" found in Deuteronomy have been a subject of much interest to scholars.

> When you go out to war against your enemies, and see horses and chariots, an army larger than your own, you shall not be afraid of them; for the LORD your God is with you, who brought you up from the land of Egypt. Before you engage in battle, the priest shall come forward and speak to the troops, and shall say to them: "Hear, O Israel! Today you are drawing near to do battle against your enemies. Do not lose heart, or be afraid, or panic, or be in dread of them; for it is the LORD your God who goes with you, to fight for you against your enemies, to give you victory." Then the officials shall address the troops, saying, "Has anyone built a new house but not dedicated it? He should go back to his house, or he might die in the battle and another dedicate it. Has anyone planted a vineyard but not yet enjoyed its fruit? He should go back to his house, or he might die in the battle and another be first to enjoy its fruit. Has anyone become engaged to a woman but not yet married her? He should go back to his house, or he might die in the battle and another marry her." The officials shall continue to address

---

[21]Israel was repeatedly tempted to presume on God's favor. Their election was misunderstood; it was election to service, not to privilege. In a stunning one-liner, Amos goes so far as to say that Israel's status is no greater than that of the Ethiopians and that Yahweh also brought the Philistines and the Aramaeans to the promised land (9:7-8). Thus Amos declares that "Israel's religious institutions and symbols can be transferred into the culture and political history of other nations/peoples. All are capable of salvation; each has experienced a migration which can be seen as a sacred 'exodus' leading to a promised land and to peace." Stuhlmueller, 37.

the troops, saying, "Is anyone afraid or disheartened? He should go back to his house, or he might cause the heart of his comrades to melt like his own." When the officials have finished addressing the troops, then the commanders shall take charge of them. When you draw near to a town to fight against it, offer it terms of peace. If it accepts your terms of peace and surrenders to you, then all the people in it shall serve you at forced labor. If it does not submit to you peacefully, but makes war against you, then you shall besiege it; and when the LORD your God gives it into our hand, you shall put all its males to the sword. You may, however, take as your booty the women, the children, livestock, and everything else in the town, all its spoil. You may enjoy the spoil of your enemies, which the LORD your God has given you. Thus you shall treat all the towns that are very far from you, which are not towns of the nations here. But as for the towns of these peoples that the LORD your God is giving you as an inheritance, you must not let anything that breathes remain alive. You shall annihilate them—the Hittites and the Amorites, the Canaanites and the Perizzites, the Hivites and the Jebusites--just as the LORD your God has commanded, so that they may not teach you to do all the abhorrent things that they do for their gods, and you thus sin against the LORD your God. If you besiege a town for a long time, making war against it in order to take it, you must not destroy its trees by wielding an ax against them. Although you may take food from them, you must not cut them down. Are trees in the field human beings that they should come under siege from you? You may destroy only the trees that you know do not produce food; you may cut them down or use in building siegeworks against the town that makes war with you, until it falls. (Deut. 20:1-20)

When you go out to war against your enemies, and the LORD your God hands them over to you and you take them captive, suppose you see among the captives a beautiful woman whom you desire and want to marry, and so you bring her home to your house: she shall shave her head, pare her nails, discard her captive's garb, and shall remain in your house a full month mourning for her father and mother; after that you may go in to her and be her husband, and she shall be your wife. But if you are not satisfied with her, you shall let her go free and not sell her for money. You must not treat her as a slave, since you have dishonored her. (Deut. 21:10-14)

When you are encamped against your enemies you shall guard against any impropriety. If one of you becomes unclean because of a nocturnal emission, then he shall go outside the camp; he must not come within the camp. When evening comes, he shall wash himself with water, and when the sun has set, he may come back into the camp. You shall have a designated area outside the camp to which you shall go. With your utensils you shall have a trowel; when you relieve yourself outside, you shall dig a hole with it and then cover up your excrement. Because the LORD your God travels along with your camp, to save you and to hand over your enemies to you, therefore your camp must be holy, so that he may not see anything indecent among you and turn away from you. Slaves who have escaped to you from their owners shall not be given back to them. (Deut. 23:9-15)

When a man is newly married, he shall not go out with the army or be charged with any related duty. He shall be free at home one year, to be happy with the wife whom he has married. (Deut. 24:5)

Although these are located in four different loci, Rofe believes that they were initially conceived of as one group.[22] Deuteronomy 20:10-14 limits killing to the fighting population and calls for negotiation prior to attack. This is a far cry from the *herem*, but reflects rather the traditional just war criteria, which, while recognizing the necessity of conflict, tries to impose severe restraints on warmaking. The same is true in 21:10-14. "This humane ruling reflects a universal concern with limiting soldier's unbridled brutality and demonstrates consideration for the feelings of captives."[23] Michael Walzer says that this is the first attempt to be found in historical records which regulates the wartime treatment of women.[24] Chapter 20:19-20 carries this concern to vegetation. This

---

[22]Rofe, 26ff.

[23]Ibid., 30. T. R. Hobbs believes that these passages reflect not humanitarian concerns but only concerns for the efficiency of the army. T. R. Hobbs, *A Time for War: A Study of Warfare in the Old Testament* (Wilmington, DE: Michael Glazier, 1989) 227. The tone of these passages suggest that both of these concerns are present. A mere concern for efficiency would not account, however, for the types of exemptions listed in 20:5-8 nor for the treatment of women in 21:10-14.

[24]Michael Walzer, *Just and Unjust Wars* (New York: Basic Books, 1977) 134. In a footnote Walzer cites Simone Weil who objects to this kind of "rights talk," which involves claims and counter-claims. Instead, she thinks that a more

compassion is extended to newlyweds in 24:5. Furthermore, the rabbinic scholar Abrabanel (1437-1508), believes that the word translated "fear" in verse 3, usually interpreted as a warning not to fear the enemy in battle, is better translated "to hurry," meaning that the command is not to hurry to go to war because haste in war matters is very dangerous.[25]

To be sure, not all of the D materials reflect this understanding of warfare. The different strata in D reflect different traditions or ideologies regarding war. Annihilation materials appear along side accommodation materials. The final redactor could have easily removed materials incompatible to his viewpoint, but chose to include varying perspectives. Apparently, he believed that they deserved inclusion because they demonstrated defensible beliefs held by some in the community of faith.

These different traditions appealed to different motives and behavior. For some, something was right because Yahweh commanded it. This constitutes a morality of the will. For others, Yahweh commanded it because it was right. An action was right because it was in accordance with principles of reason and justice, not merely because God commanded it. This constitutes a morality of the mind. For the former, obedience was based on the promise of blessings and the fear of curses (Deut. 28). For the latter, obedience was based on a humanitarian or a more natural law rationale. Thus, ancient Israel seemed to experience its own version of the universal versus the particular. Was Yahweh's will for his chosen people different from his will for the nations? There was no uniform answer to this question. Conflicting answers and approaches found a home in Israel's traditions and the D historians faithfully recorded them.[26]

---

ultimate reference is needed, such as the image of God in humans. Weil may be right, viz., that this theological base is what shapes the understanding of the Deuteronomic historian. But Walzer takes issue with her, insisting that arguments about human rights have played a significant part in the struggle against oppression, including the sexual oppression of women. Human rights apparently played a role, to some degree, in Israel's thinking.

[25]Cited in Efraim Inbar, "War in Jewish Tradition," *The Jerusalem Journal of International Relations* 9, 2 (June 1987): 96.

[26]For an intriguing article on biblical diversity related to the present see Carl Graesser, Jr., "Biblical Roots of Our Diversity," *Currents in Theology and Mission* 15, 1 (February 1988): 27-33. He sees J as the first Lutheran, P as the first Roman Catholic, and D as the first Reformed Theologian.

These passages, to some degree, substantiate Good's conclusion that "Yahweh's role as warrior can be subordinated to his role as judge, and his authority as judge made subject to the general duty of law to function in accordance with standards of justice. In matters of war, Yahweh seems not to have been conceived as a might-makes-right sovereign."[27]

This is not the case throughout the entire Hebrew Bible, but it confirms our belief that this strand or tradition existed alongside other understandings of warfare in ancient Israel.[28] Israel's experience of being under almost constant threat from its neighbors would understandably push them toward a more militant and emotional view of warfare. But there were times when they moved beyond a visceral, gut-level approach to a more reasoned and objective understanding. Unfortunately for both ancient and modern Israel, this has not been a dominate attitude.

Although it is not in the scope of this study, it is significant to note that later Jewish political tradition reflected a strong commitment to several just war themes. In a helpful study by Ephraim Inbar, Maimonides and several lesser known rabbinic scholars are cited as demanding a more rational approach to issues in war than the mere citing of holy war passages.[29] The established Talmudic tradition insisted that decisions concerning human activity, including war, were to be governed by a rational process that rejects divine intervention, whether in the form of a heavenly voice or in the ephod of 1 Samuel 23:10-12; 30:8. Inbar concludes that Jewish tradition, as we have noted in the Bible itself, contains a "conceptual richness" on the subject of war, but that in general it favors a political system with "considerable diffusion of power." This, of course, is in harmony with just war thinking.

---

[27]Good, 399.

[28]To be sure, there are not many instances where the Israelites weigh matters of equity, motive, or probability because often they simply sought a Yes or No from Yahweh. Furthermore, "the concern of Just War exponents with the use of 'right means' moves in a different dimension from the preoccupation of the Torah with ritual purity and with wholeheartedness." F. Derek Kidner, "Old Testament Perspectives on War," *Evangelical Quarterly* 57, 2 (April 1985): 108.

[29]Inbar. The following points are taken from his article, pp. 94, 96, 97.

# SUMMARY & CONCLUSION

In the preceding chapters we have sought to trace the different understandings or traditions about warfare which existed virtually throughout the entire biblical period. Thus, our initial conclusion is that during the entire history of the Israelites there were multiple sets of beliefs about morality of warfare. These were, to some extent, competing sets of beliefs, somewhat like "an ordered bundle of biblical theologies which stand in tension with one another."[1] Our texts indicate that there must have been vigorous debates throughout biblical history on how war should be viewed under the leadership of Yahweh. Waldemar Janzen talks about, but does not develop, the idea of an "ethical refinement" regarding war as the Old Testament story advances. But he adds, "It is probably unwarranted, however, to seek a steadily unfolding peace ideal in the Old Testament, at least as far as its own time is concerned. Nevertheless, there was a check upon unbridled human warfare and its idealization."[2]

This analysis confirms some of Janzen's views, but not all. Although warriors like David are at times glorified, in general the exploits of the human warriors are downplayed, so that the credit is given to Yahweh. Thus, war is not idealized. Then, too, there are evidences of restraint in warfare.[3] We also agree that there is little evidence of "a steadily unfolding peace ideal."[4] But a "refinement" suggests a kind of

---

[1]Hans-Ruedi Weber, *Power: Focus for a Biblical Theology* (Geneva: WCC Publications, 1989) 22.

[2]Waldemar Janzen, "War in the Old Testament," *The Mennonite Quarterly Review* 46 (1972): 160

[3]See the chapter on Just War.

[4]However, Raymund Schwager speaks of a gradual emergence of a new community of peace and love in his *Brauchen wir einen Sundenbock* (Munich: Kosel, 1978). He notes that are no less than 600 O.T. passages where violence is condemned but there are at least 1000 instances in which Yahweh's own violence is mentioned, some of which Schwager is forced to qualify as irrational (pp. 58-64). See a comparison of Schwager and Rene Girard in Robert North, "Violence and the Bible: The Girard Connection," *Catholic Biblical Quarterly* 47

development which may also be lacking, because, as we saw in Genesis, some of the better examples of peacemaking initiatives occur early in Israel's history so that later events exhibit an abandonment of these ideals.[5] The "pacifist tradition" had it roots early in Israel and persisted throughout its history. At times it was more influential or prominent than in other times. Second Isaiah displays its highest expression whereas other exilic and post-exilic prophets share none of this outlook. We have also examined passages reflecting just war motifs from the time of the amphictyony to the times of the divided monarchy. Similarly, the concept of holy war is found in the beginnings of Israel's nationhood, is believed by the Deuteronomic historians in the sixth century to be a valid expression of Yahweh's will, and persists throughout the Biblical period. So instead of looking for a clear development or even a refinement, would it not be better to say that there are different strands or traditions which run more or less concurrent in Israel's reflections regarding war? The varied experiences of the people, of course, would have a profound impact on how they viewed political enemies.[6] These experiences took on the form of stories and anecdotes which circulated orally among the people. These diverse stories produced diverse attitudes about how to deal with hostilities. In other words, the sacred texts of the ancient Israelites and of the early Christians are ambiguous about war because they faithfully reflect the deep ambiguity felt by those struggling to relate their faith in the Lord of history to the brutal realities of inevitable and pervasive conflict.

## Yahweh-as-Warrior and Holy War

It is possible to view these traditions as mutually exclusive and also possible to view at least some of them as in some sense complementary. Maybe a better way to visualize the relationship between them is to employ the analogy of a tree. The trunk represents trust in Yahweh with several branches growing out of it. Holy war, in its several

---

(1985): 14-15.

[5]Thus Walter Wink is wrong when he asserts that "Jesus was the first to see violence as a problem"(Lecture, Seventh & James Baptist Church, Waco, Texas, Oct. 10, 1992). It is clear from our study that many throughout the entire Biblical period viewed violence as a serious problem which must be addressed.

[6]This has always been true. Note, for example, the diverse religious opinions about native Americans during the settlement of the United States. One who had a good experience with them would obviously see things differently than would one whose family had been killed in an Indian raid.

variations, comprises one of the largest branches. Just war principles provide a small but significant branch. Pacifism, in its various forms, is a larger branch than many readers of the Bible might think. Thus we may concur with J.M. Ford's conclusion that "on the whole, war in the history of Israel is defensive, not aggressive. I believe that this forms a sharp contrast with the nations surrounding Israel. Therefore, the seeds of the peace-ideology lie in the Hebrew tradition.[7] But, it is important to realize that all of these grew out of an effort of the Israelites to relate their faith in Yahweh the Lord/King/Warrior to historical realities. These were traditions that, to be sure, were influenced by their surrounding cultures, but which, to a large extent, grew out of a relationship with Yahweh, out of deeply felt religious convictions. But, to carry the tree analogy further, it is an open question as to whether or not we need to saw off any of these branches. We will return to this question later.

Another conclusion which we may draw is that the Bible is a realistic book when it comes to the issue of war. In one sense we can agree with Craigie when he asserts that war posed no problem for the Israelites. "War was for them a natural—if unpleasant—part of the world in which they lived."[8] Our analysis has shown, however, that it *did* pose a problem for some in ancient Israel. The pacifist and just war motifs found in the Bible indicate that there were those who sought to find either other rationales for warfare or other ways of dealing with aggression and conflict. But, it is probably safe to say that most Israelites at all times during the Biblical period would reflect Craigie's view that "to oversimplify a complex set of possibilities, states come into existence, survive, and eventually decline and die, in direct relation to the existence and use of force in such activities as warfare.[9]

This "realism" of the Bible is seen in the fact that it recognizes that "people are born into a world in which power is unevenly distributed,"[10] and that conflict of some sort is inevitable if one hopes to

---

[7]Josephine M. Ford, "Cursing and Blessing as Vehicles of Violence and Peace in Scripture," *Peace in the Nuclear Age*, Charles J. Reid, Jr. (Ed) (Washington, D.C.: Catholic University of America Press, 1986) 6.

[8]Peter Craigie, "Yahweh is a Man of Wars," *Scottish Journal of Theology* 22 (1969): 185. Recall, with W.F. Albright, that the important city of Bethel was destroyed four times between 1200-1000 BCE. *From The Stone Age to Christianity* (Baltimore: Johns Hopkins, 1940) 219.

[9]Peter Craigie, "War, Idea of," *International Standard Bible Encyclopedia*, vol. IV, ed. by G.W. Bromiley (Grand Rapids: Eerdmans, 1988) 1019.

[10]John T. Pawlikowski, "Power and the Pursuit of Peace: Some Reflections,"

change that distribution. Or to state it another way, "all hopes for the future must take into account what will be done by (people) who do *not* want peace and justice."[11] This realism explains why, as we have noted in previous chapters, the theme that Yahweh is a Warrior is *central* to many of the tenets of the Old Testament, confirming sociologist James Hunter's observation that "Few developments can change a nation-its mood, its identity, its people-like war. *War always brings to light the most basic questions of national purpose*: What is it about our nation—our history and place in the world—that should obligate it to fight?"[12]

This certainly proved to be the case for tiny Israel, sandwiched as it was between several large, hostile nations who desired her strategic location. Warfare was thus never far from the forefront of Israel's psyche and defined her identity in a basic way. Consequently, to try to jettison this concept would mean the loss of numerous affirmations in the Hebrew Scriptures.[13]

On what basis can we make a moral judgment about Yahweh wars? Two criteria often used in modern times can at least point us in the right direction. They concern motives and consequences. We will take up these separately.[14]

---

in *Biblical and Theological Reflections on the "Challenge of Peace,"* eds. John Pawlikowski and Donald Senior (Wilmington, DE: Michael Glazier, 1983) 80.

[11]Millar Burrows, *An Outline of Biblical Theology* (Philadelphia: Westminster, 1946) 318 (emphasis added). Craigie expresses this same sentiment by saying that when it comes to thinking about war "we need the cynicism of Ecclesiastes and the soaring vision of the prophets." *The Problem of War in the Old Testament* (Grand Rapids: Eerdmans, 1978) 111.

[12]James D. Hunter, *Culture Wars: The Struggle to Define America* (New York: Basic Books, 1991) 288 (emphasis added). Hunter notes that the issue of war plays a prominent role in America's debate about its role in the post Cold War world. The nation, he says, is currently divided between those, confident of America's essential goodness, who believe that America should intervene for the principles of good and fair play, and those whose vision holds that a strong military represents a misuse of America's power and resources. At brief periods during Israel's United and Divided Monarchy, she may have had the luxury of this type of "debate," but, as we have already noted, her size and location dictated a defensive posture.

[13]See Richard Nysse, "Yahweh is a Warrior," *Word and World* 7 (1987): 193. See especially our discussion in Chapter 1. Craigie agrees: "The association of God with warfare in ancient Israel is integral to the fundamental theology of the Hebrews, namely, that God participated in and through the historical experience." *ISBE*, 1019.

[14]By pursuing this avenue we demonstrate our acceptance of the type of

Ascertaining the motives of people in biblical times is a very tricky business. Either the motives may not be stated or even alluded to, or motives may be added later by subsequent editors as a way of trying to clarify or to interpret phenomenon which caused them problems. Having recognized this, however, we will make some tentative judgments about what motivated the Israelites to engage in battles armed with the belief that Yahweh was fighting on their behalf.

For some the basic motivation was that they *believed* that they had been commanded by God to fight. Usually this was in response to some authoritative figure who spoke on God's behalf. This faith resulted in blind obedience. "Their's not to reason why; their's but to do and die." If we were able to bring back from the dead an ancient Israelite, he or she would probably respond to a modern person's demand to know why they fought these wars with a blank stare. Except in rare cases, people followed their leaders. The corporate dimension of Israelite society placed greater demands on them at this point than is felt by modern individualists. One's identity and reason for living were intimately tied up with the life of the community.[15] The community was threatened often and people were told that it was Yahweh's will for them to fight. To employ Lawrence Kohlberg's categories here, which he claims are universal, the motivation to do what was "right" was to avoid punishment (stage one) or to obey because this was what was expected by those close and by the society as a whole (stages 3 and 4). We have seen stage one at work in the carrying out of punishment on those who failed to obey the demands of the *herem* (Achan in Josh. 7, Saul in 1 Sam. 15, as well as the general promises of obedience and the threats of punishment in Deut. 28).[16] If we accept the conclusions of Kohlberg's studies, which indicated that most people reason at stages 3 or 4, the "conventional level of moral reasoning," then we may assert that most Israelites did what they did because their families, clans,

---

reasoning done by just war theorists.

[15]The classic work on this is H. Wheeler Robinson's *Corporate Personality in Ancient Israel* (Philadelphia: Fortress Press, 1964).

[16]Stage Two, individualism and reciprocity, "you scratch my back and I'll scratch yours," is less likely in Israel's experience because of the nations' corporate emphasis. One, however, might point to the sages observations in Proverbs that persons will prosper if they follow certain paths (Proverbs 10:24, 27, 30; 11:8; 13:21; 16:2; 19:23; etc.). It is probably not reading back into their minds to assert that some undoubtedly were concerned primarily or completely with their own welfare and that they followed the command to fight to secure what they wanted.

tribes, or nation expected them to do it.[17] Furthermore, life was apparently perceived to be more interdependent than is the case for most western individualists today.[18]

George Carey attempts to address the corporate motivation of Israel when he asserts that holy wars were not ends in themselves but were to bring about the fulfillment of God's promise.[19] He draws on Walter Brueggemann's belief that *land* is a central if not the central theme of biblical faith. If the possession of the land makes a nation of the people of God, then Israel's wars were designed to pave the way for the fulfillment of her destiny. Thus, Israel's motives were not those of greed or desire to exploit, but sprang from the conviction that the land was hers by right. "She was not taking land that belonged to another but merely entering into her inheritance."[20] This, by itself, does not, of course, provide a satisfactory answer to the moral problem of holy war, but it does address a necessary element.[21] Motives alone cannot justify an action, but they provide a part of the picture.

Motives for doing anything, whether in individuals or in nations, are rarely, if ever, singular. Motives for engaging in warfare are particularly subject to a complex mixture. K.N. Schoville lists several possible motive: "For ... nations, the drives toward war are predominantly over *territory*, for *adventure*, to *dominate* another people, and to *maintain a ruling class in power* .... Religious factors permeate the idea of social solidarity and group loyalty. These drives toward conflict on the part of one group induce a defensive action by the threatened group."[22]

Millar Burrows approaches the issue of motivation from this angle: "The real point at issue is not force against persuasion, but resentment

---

[17]Lawrence Kohlberg's work is systematically spelled out in his three volume work, but for our purposes vol. 1 is sufficient. *The Philosophy of Moral Development* (New York: Harper & Row, 1981).

[18]Robert Bellah, et al. *Habits of the Heart* (New York: Harper and Row, 1985) is written to counter the hyper-individualism of American life and to encourage a more corporate understanding of existence.

[19]George L. Carey, "Biblical-Theological Perspectives on War and Peace, *The Evangelical Quarterly* 57, 2 (April 1985): 165.

[20]Ibid.

[21]Some might respond with the statement: "Tell that to the Canaanites who were displaced or subjugated and, furthermore, tell that to the modern Palestinians who are being deprived of their homeland!".

[22]K.N. Schoville, "War; Warfare," *ISBE*, 1013 (emphases added).

and vindictiveness against love and forgiveness."[23] Basil the Great in the fourth century seems to allude to this attitude when he praises a soldier "who proves that even in military life one may preserve the perfection of love for God, and that Christians should be marked, not by the fashion of his clothing, but by the disposition of his soul."[24]

From the standpoint of motivation, then, both Basil and Burrows imply that if a war is waged out of the genuine concern of the good of the whole and not out of an attitude which dehumanizes, then that war is justifiable. This view is consistent with Paul Ramsey's conclusion, in discussing noncombatant immunity/collateral damage/double effect, that intentionality is the key moral concept.[25] But this fails to address the brutal fact that, whatever the motivation/intention, innocent victims die. In matters of death, motivations, important as they are, cannot be the sole criterion. An ethic that gives undue prominence to intentionality is a bankrupt ethic.[26] This forces us into the second criterion, that of consequences.

One cannot make a moral judgment on an action without examining the consequences, both short-term and long-term. W.F. Albright stated the matter in surprisingly strong terms: "It was fortunate for the future of monotheism that the Israelites of the Conquest were a wild folk,

---

[23]Burrows, 320. L.H. Marshall shares Burrows view: "It is possible for a man to fight evil with the vision of truth and justice before his eyes, with malice towards none and with charity for all. The passion for revenge is the thing that Jesus seeks to destroy, root and branch. The futility of revenge has been made clear thousands of times in the history of men and of nations. All who, in social life, have ever met insult with insult, or wrong with wrong, know the senselessness of such a procedure - it just adds fuel to the fire that needs to be quenched .... The tragedies of European history are due, to no small extent, to the tendency of nations to find no rest for their spirits until they are even with their adversaries, and have avenged defeat, whether that defeat was deserved or not. But Jesus condemns the spirit of revenge not just because of its senselessness and futility but because it is a wicked fiendish thing, a denial of brotherhood, a withholding of love, a sin against man and against God." *The Challenge of New Testament Ethics* (London: MacMillan & Co, 1960) 119.

[24]Letter 106, cited in George W. Forell, *History of Christian Ethics*, vol. (Minneapolis: Augsburg Publishing House, 1979) 124.

[25]Paul Ramsey, *War and the Christian Conscience* (Durham, NC: Duke University Press, 1961) 34-59. All of this, of course, raises the larger question of whether killing can ever be an act of love.

[26]Refer to Robert Jewett's work on the tendency to reduce morality to motives and how this has played itself out in American foreign policy in *The Captain America Complex* (Philadelphia: Westminster, 1973).

endowed with primitive energy and ruthless will to exist, since the resulting decimation of the Canaanites prevented the complete fusion of the two kindred folk which would almost inevitably have depressed Yahwistic standards to a point where recovery was impossible. Thus the Canaanites, with their orgiastic nature-worship, their cult of fertility in the form of serpent symbols and sensuous nudity, and their gross mythology, were replaced by Israel, with its nomadic simplicity and purity of life, its lofty monotheism, and its severe code of ethics."[27]

Albright expresses a common view that Canaanite culture and religion were so depraved and so incompatible with Yahwism that both Israel's short-term good and the good of humankind's future necessitated the complete destruction of the Canaanites. Thus, from the benefit of subsequent history, we can make the judgment that Israel's legacy on the world, however negative some of it might be viewed, is far superior than what the Canaanites could have bequeathed.

Whereas Albright emphasized the positive consequences of Israel's conquest of Canaan, others could equally amass evidence of the destructive consequences of these wars. Many Christians, from the very beginning of the Christian era, found the brutality of the wars of conquest so objectionable that they rejected the entire Old Testament, as Marcion did, and in so doing sowed the seeds of militant anti-Semitism.[28] At least some of the blame for this sad chapter in Christian history can be laid at the door of the holy wars. Ironically, Christians have also appealed to these wars as a justification for the brutal carrying out of their own wars. The medieval Crusades and the attempted genocide of native Americans are only two of many examples which could be cited.[29] As Gottwald notes—and in so doing illustrates the inherently close relationship between motives and consequences—that these wars in Scripture "give license to two revolting developments in modern war: the murder of civilians and the cold, calculated killing of people according to dogma .... The "Holy War" idealism has always been a front for naked self-interest .... By the way it (the church) has used holy war texts it has often conveyed, consciously or unconsciously, the nobility and religious grandeur of war."[30]

---

[27] Albright, 214.

[28] Nysse, 192.

[29] Craigie devotes an entire chapter (pp. 22-32) in his book *The Problem of War*, noting that Islam, Judaism, and Christianity are all guilty of misusing the holy war theme of the Old Testament.

[30] Norman Gottwald, "'Holy War' in Deuteronomy: Analysis and Critique," *Review and Expositor* 61 (1964): 309, 310. It is sad, but true, that "the higher the

One effort to soften the negative consequences of the emphasis in the Bible on Israel's warmaking is to try to place Israel's wars in the total context of history and of comparative studies. Albright cites numerous historical examples, including the reciprocal massacres of Protestants and Catholics in the seventeenth century and the bombing of Rotterdam in 1940.[31] McKenzie agrees that Israel's holy wars are "doubtfully more primitive than the modern concept of war."[32] This is no doubt true, but it begs the question. While moderns seek religious justifications for war, the Israelite wars claim in Holy Writ to be sanctioned by Yahweh. Thus, the comparative analysis, while providing some helpful perspective, and preventing the modern reader from becoming too judgmental, does not provide us a satisfactory answer.

Thus, the consequences are decidedly mixed. What is the "net effect"? How one would calculate the net effect would depend on how much weight is given to the many variables in the equation. Despite the claims of some utilitarians, there is no "objective" way to do this. One's overall worldview and orientation will influence in large measure how one views these consequences. A pacifist orientation, for example, could ask if Yahweh's purpose for Israel (i.e., good consequences) might have been accomplished without resorting to warfare. One pacifist, Millard Lind, would rather state the issue differently by insisting that Israel should have trusted Yahweh to fight for them. This means, of course, that Yahweh alone has the moral right to take life. This understanding leads to the conclusion that the same activity which was morally right for Yahweh was morally wrong for the

---

motives of those who fight wars, the more inhumane the war becomes." Cited in John L. McKenzie, *The Old Testament Without Illusions* (Chicago: Thomas More Press, 1979) 215. McKenzie is puzzled by the fact that Christians point to holy wars as normative in Scripture while ignoring other elements: "I do not know why Christians, who have so often appealed to the holy war as a principle of conduct in modern situations, never appeal to the Israelite prophets as establishing principles of political decisions. Napoleon was wiser, if cynical, when he said that God is on the side of the big battalions. Abraham Lincoln was wiser and not cynical when he told the minister who prayed that God would be on 'our side' to pray that 'we might be on God's' side. To say that a people or a nation is of a moral quality such that it deserves not God's assistance but his punishment would make us ask what people or nation could be excluded from this judgment" (p. 216).

[31] Albright, 213.

[32] John L. McKenzie, *Dictionary of the Bible* (Milwaukee: Bruce Pub. Co., 1965) 921.

Israelites. From the standpoint of moral consistency, this leaves much to be desired. As noted earlier,[33] another pacifist, J. H. Yoder, sees indications that the conquest of Canaan could have been accomplished quite apart from warfare. From this perspective, then, it would seem that both the short-term and long-term consequences of Israel's warfare were negative. In the short-term, Israel's violence begat violence against them, which eventually resulted in national destruction. In the long-term, the violence of holy war, because it is in Holy Writ, has been used and abused to justify incalculable destruction. Possibly, then, if Israel had followed its more noble impulses, as described in chap. 6, she would have left a healthier legacy. Furthermore, with regard to our New Testament analysis, if the church had followed Luke's understanding of Jesus with reference to violence rather than Matthew's and Mark's, it would also have left a more honorable legacy. I must conclude, then, that the net effect of the Biblical holy war tradition is negative, especially in the light of the way it has been used and abused by subsequent readers.[34]

What, then, are our options in assessing the Yahweh-as-Warrior analogy which we have found throughout the entire Bible?[35] There appear to be two options.

(1) One option is to reject the analogy. This may be done in two ways. One may admit that the analogy and understanding of God as participating in and/or commanding wars served some possible useful function in ancient times but no longer can and does. Roland Bainton briefly traces this view through Christian history and cites those who believed that these wars "were allowed by reason of special revelation from God which had not been subsequently repeated."[36] Bainton is

---

[33]See Chapter 2.

[34]I refer to this as " the second generation syndrome." Subsequent generations fail to discern the intent of the original concept or fail to place it in the total context out of which the concept arose. The result can be a disastrous misinterpretation or misapplication of basic principles.

[35]Some may object to the use of the concept of analogy here because Yahweh is not merely *like* a Warrior, but he *is* a Warrior. If a symbol participates in the reality to which it points (Tillich) then we can say that the use of the Warrior analogy says something about the nature of Yahweh. This is to say that those O.T. writers who employ this concept believed that Yahweh *was* indeed a Warrior.

[36]Roland Bainton, *Christian Attitudes Toward War and Peace* (Nashville: Abingdon Press, 1960) 154f. With some variations this seems to be the view of C.J. Cadoux in his 1919 classic *The Early Christian Attitude To War* (New York: Seabury, 1982). He acknowledges that the early Christians accepted the view

alluding to the often employed concept of "progressive revelation."
Most who utilize this concept see no clear developmental line in the Old
Testament from holy war to pacifism, but try to make a case that
"rejection of holy war concepts was in fact the mature view of Israel's
own representatives (e.g., Isa. 2:1-4; 19:18-25)."[37] They insist that the
objectionable passages throughout the Hebrew Scriptures must be
placed in their cultural contexts. They remain people of their age who
shared its conceptions; consequently as divine emissaries they could
often demand certain measures which to them were entirely natural,
but which are altogether foreign to us. This God permitted.[38]

On the other hand, McKenzie seems to reject the analogy as ever
functioning in a positive way to reveal the true nature of Yahweh and
concludes that "where the Bible relates the thought patterns of early
Israel, it does not seem to rise above the thought of its time; and its
conception of Yahweh as a warrior was an imperfect apprehension of
His reality and activity."[39]

McKenzie's view calls into question the nature of revelation by
rejecting this part of Scripture without providing a rationale for
determining when an analogy should be retained or rejected.[40]

In the light of many of the concepts which we have examined in this
study, it is understandable why some would take this position. One

---

that the wars waged by the ancient Hebrews had Divine sanction, but were
unable to harmonize the divergent views of the Old and New Testaments in
regard to the use of violence. He posits that the early church's instincts not to
copy the military precedents of Scripture "were perfectly sound and could have
been logically justified if the requisite philosophical apparatus had been
available"(178). This "apparatus" apparently includes modern philosophical
thought as well as historical-critical hermeneutical methods.

[37]Gottwald, 308.

[38]Louis F. Hartman, "Ban," *Encyclopedic Dictionary of the Bible*. A
translation and adaption of A. Vander Born's *Bijbels Woordenboek* (New York:
McGraw-Hill Book Co., 1963) 196.

[39]McKenzie, 921. This seems to be the view of Flanders, Crapps, and Smith,
*People of the Covenant*, 2nd ed. (New York: John Wiley & Sons, 1973) 192: "The
brutality of the conquest, then, was more the result of *Israel's limited grasp of the
nature of Yahweh* than of Yahweh's purpose. Although the savagery of Israel
cannot be excused, it can be understood as an act of faith and obedience.
Hopefully *later generations* would behold greater light, but *the shutters of
understanding are always conditioned by the environment*. God remains the same;
man changes as God's revelation breaks forth upon him" (emphases added).

[40]McKenzie would probably appeal to a natural law or common sense basis
to reject elements in Scripture which are offensive to him and to many others.

serious difficulty, however, with this view is that the rejection of the warrior analogy, which, as we have seen, is a central concept in the Hebrew Scriptures, would necessitate the elimination of huge portions of the biblical texts (along with a strong impulse to replace them with new ones). This approach would produce canonical and hermeneutical problems of the first order. This option is neither desirable nor necessary.

(2) A more adequate and promising option is to try to retain the analogy of Yahweh-as-Warrior but seek to penetrate behind the terminology to discover what fundamental truths were being affirmed. Dianne Bergant seems to come to this conclusion by way of examining the broader context of God-language. "To ask: 'Is Yahweh a warrior?' is not unlike asking: 'Is God a father? Or a mother? Is God personal? Is God just?'"[41] These and other analogies need to be examined to see if they affirm today what they were trying to affirm when originally written. Or, to state it differently, what was the faith which inspired these expressions? Or again, what does the analogy of Yahweh-as-Warrior point to which is of abiding significance? Yet again, as Hanson states the issue: "War in the Bible, not unlike war in our world, is a very complex issue and is not amenable to analysis in terms of war and peace alone. One must seek to grasp the broader structures of value and purpose within which any given war functions; that is to say, one must examine the ideologies of war coming to expression."[42]

Several possible ideologies have been suggested.

(a) According to some, one of the more obvious truths suggested by this analogy is God's power and might. As Bergant elsewhere states it, "Warrior-god traditions *are* revelatory, but they reveal the splendor of God, not of war. They tell of a God of unprecedented majesty and unsurpassed solicitude."[43] Richard Sklba notes that in another age different symbols could have been used to express this but the ever-present military facets of Israel's life in Canaan provided a readily available and extremely apt metaphor to the writers to express God's

---

[41]Dianne Bergant, "Yahweh: A Warrior God?" *The Bible Today* (May 1983): 160. In the end Bergant affirms the theology the analogy was trying to express but rejects the image of Yahweh as warrior as "no longer apt expressions of such theology." (p. 161).

[42]Paul Hanson, "War, Peace, and Justice in Early Israel," *Bible Review* (Fall 1987): 45.

[43]Bergant, "Peace in a Universe of Order," in *Biblical and Theological Reflections on the "Challenge of Peace,"* eds. John Pawlikowski and Donald Senior (Wilmington, DE: Michael Glazier, 1983) 24.

power. But, it must be noted, "the substance of their affirmation transcended the imagery."[44]

The implications of God's power and freedom to act in war comprise one reason why the Yahweh-as-Warrior theme is offensive to many. As Nysse observes: "Perhaps we ... wish to avoid the radically unconditional character of the Yahweh-is-a-Warrior theme—the unconditional dimension means that we are totally dependent and that total allegiance to God is necessary. That does not mesh well with modern refrains emphasizing the independence and freedom of the individual self.[45] Thus, some rejections of this concept flow from motives born of pride and self-sufficiency.

(b) G. Ernest Wright and others subsume the imagery of Yahweh-as-Warrior under the imagery of Yahweh-as-Lord, whose "chief concern is universal order."[46] Yahweh is the Divine Sovereign and the purpose of the suzerainty(rulership) language "is to depict why creative, positive, righteous goals have an ultimate support in our world, why life is given for service for which one is accountable, and why, despite the suffering and injustice in the world, life in the service of the Ultimate understood as Suzerain [Sovereign] is possible and triumphant."[47]

---

[44]Richard Sklba, "A Covenant of Peace," *The Bible Today* (May 1983): 152.

[45]Nysse, 201.

[46]G. Ernest Wright, *The Old Testament and Theology* (New York: Harper & Row, 1969) 129. A more recent statement of this view, although Yahweh's Lordship is tied more to His creative work, is by Ben Ollenburger, "The Concept of 'Warrior God' in Peace Theology," in *Essays on Peace Theology and Witness*, ed. Willard M. Swartley (Elkhart, IN: Institute of Mennonite Studies, 1988) 114: "One cannot properly speak of the Old Testament concept of God the Warrior apart from the larger symbolic construction of which it is a part. For that reason, it is also important to relate God the Warrior to God the Creator. It is in the dual roles of warrior and creator that the royal God is portrayed as acting in the Old Testament."

[47]Wright, 110. Waldemar Janzen challenges Wright's telescoping the Divine Warrior and Cosmic Government. He sees the classical Divine Warrior passages as picturing Yahweh as the Warrior who conquers and *then* establishes his dominion. For him a better metaphor for present reality is that of bondage and exile, i.e., of the apparent domination of oppressive powers. Janzen, a pacifist, views the present world as alienated from a God who will eventually bring victory and peace. Wright seeks a high degree of integration of present historical reality into God's ultimate reality. There are two very different worldviews at work. See Janzen, "God as Warrior and Lord: A Conversation with G.E. Wright," *BASOR* 220 (1975): 73-75.

Patrick Miller agrees: "In the conception of the divine warrior, Israel explicitly maintained that God was completely and totally in charge of things and that this fact had practical implications for Israel's life."[48]

Here, the focus is not so much on God's power, but on the orderliness of the world which is under God's ultimate control. The suzerainty treaty language is relationship language, so that Yahweh's people are to receive his gifts but are also to be responsible in His world. In other words, it is a relationship "which holds grace and duty to be a part of each other and inseparable."[49] The Lordship-Warrior language acknowledges, then, that there are powerful evil forces in the world and that they can and must be resisted. "Life, then is a battleground, but the Divine Warrior will not be defeated."[50] This theme, then, brings with it a tremendous hope for the future. Evil, however often it appears to triumph, is not the last word in history. Yahweh is in ultimate control of the universe and He is the guarantor that good will win out in the end. As Sklba phrases it, this language proclaims "their conviction in his ability to bring all evil to definitive subjugation."[51]

A variation on Wright, who subsumes Yahweh's martial activity under *Lordship*, is Tryggve Mettinger's preference to subsume it under *Kingship*.[52] Kingship is thus a "root metaphor" which serves as a basic model to describe the nature of the world and which feeds a whole family of extended metaphors, including the metaphor of Yahweh-as-Warrior. Following the work of Victor Maag and others, Mettinger examines the question of whether or not the Yahwistic faith was influenced by Baal religion, since Baal is also depicted as a warrior god.

---

[48]Patrick Miller, Jr. "God the Warrior," *Interpretation* 19 (1965): 44.

[49]Wright, 119.

[50]Ibid., 130. In a related vein Denis Baly notes that "In a vast number of societies the warrior is thought of as sacred, set aside and empowered to preserve the order and harmony of the world from the disorder which threatens it from outside. 'Think also of thy duty and do not waver. There is no greater good for a warrior than to fight in a righteous war' (Bhagavad Gita, 2:31). *Dulce et decorum est pro patria mori* (It is a sweet and fitting thing to die for one's country - Horace, Odes, III, ii. 13). Even in the strongly secularized societies of the West death in battle in the defense of freedom is held to have a sacred quality." *God and History in the Old Testament: The Encounter with the Absolute Other in Ancient Israel* (New York: Harper & Row, 1976) 48.

[51]Sklba, 152.

[52]Tryggve N.D. Mettinger, *In Search of God: the Meaning and Message of the Everlasting Names*, trans. by Frederick Cryer (Philadelphia: Fortress, 1988) especially Chapter 6: "The Lord As King: The Battling Deity."

Religions, Mettinger notes, react to other religions in three patterns: *Identification* (the god of one religion becomes identified with the god of another); *Elimination* (one of the religions in question actively repudiates motifs and conceptions present in the other; and *Integration* (in the course of the encounter, one of the religions receives from the other stimuli that lead to new formulations of the original faith.[53] Mettinger believes that all three of these can be noted in the Hebrew Scriptures but that integration was the more dominant reaction throughout Israel's history. Proceeding on the hypothesis that the Israelites did indeed inherit the designation "king" for their God from the Canaanites, Mettinger believes that it was a "conscious confiscation, that is, that the confession of the Lord as King was at one and the same time a protest against Baal's claim to this title. Yahweh is King, not Baal!"[54] Although he believes that Israel did *not* adopt the Baal myth(found in the Ugaritic texts) as a unit, it is possible to point to four structural elements which may have played a role in the development of Israel's faith in Yahweh-as-Warrior: *The creation battle* (descriptions of a divine conflict in the primeval time—Ps. 74, 89, and 104); *The Zion battle* (descriptions of how God defends his temple-mountain against hostile assaults—Ps. 24; Is. 17:12-14; and the "Zion Psalms," Ps. 48 and 76); *The exodus battle* (passages in which the exodus and the miracle at the Sea of Reeds are described in terms of symbols deriving from the chaos battle—Ps. 114; 77:16-19; Ezek. 2:32-44; Is. 51:9-10); and finally *The battle of the Day of the Lord* (descriptions of the great eschatological drama in which it is seen as a rehearsal and conclusion of God's continually varying struggle with the forces of chaos—Is. 24-27; Zech. 14; Zeph. 1-3). Mettinger concludes that "This 'monarchial' understanding of God was formulated with a root metaphor consisting of God's chaos battle, his kingship, and his palace (temple). God asserts sovereignty through battle with the forces of chaos, which continually threaten his creation. This divine activity stretches from creation, across the pages of history, and ahead to the eschatological completion. Protology, history, and eschatology are unified in God and ruled by God the warring King."[55]

---

[53]Ibid., 94.

[54]Ibid., 95.

[55]Ibid., 115. But refer to the discussion in Chapter 1 regarding the debate within ancient Israel as to whether or not the transition from the amphictyony to the monarchy was a valid one. Those who think that the establishment of the monarchy reflected a rejection of Yahweh might resist Mettinger's use of this analogy for Yahweh because of the overtones of Ancient Near Eastern absolute

Thus, both Wright and Mettinger attempt to get to the heart of the Yahweh-as-Warrior metaphor by placing it in a more comprehensive context of lordship or kingship, which developed to some extent as a reaction to and integration of Canaanite religion. Whether one prefers Wright's term "Lord," which is used almost exclusively of deity, or Mettinger's term "King," which is used of both heavenly and earthly rulers, the same basic concepts are being affirmed.

(c) Both Wright's and Mettinger's analyses are compatible with Paul Hanson's suggestion, with a slightly different twist, regarding the essence of what the concept of holy war affirmed. It relates to what Hanson believes was the major fear and concern of the ancient world, namely, chaos. As noted earlier, the basic Near Eastern cosmology which Israel shared with its neighbors was that "the world was situated precariously between order and chaos."[56] Only a God who was able to fight and defeat the forces of chaos was worthy to be worshipped. The Warrior analogy affirms, then, that Yahweh was worthy of trust and worship because He overcame the forces of chaos in the realm of historical events. In a later more popular oriented article Hanson expands on this theme by referring to Yahweh's work in fighting against the forces of chaos as the establishment of the "order of *shalom*."[57] Hanson believes that Israel's basic understanding of war is found not in the period of the Israelite monarchy, where the stories were shaped so as to give the expression of a triumphant royal ideology, but in the ancient songs of Miriam and Deborah. In the events surrounding these songs, war was not perpetrated by the Israelites, but "inflicted upon them by forces of chaos seeking to reimpose the bonds of servitude."[58] Consequently, these songs actually function "to describe the process by which *shalom* is preserved in a hostile world."[59] The Israelites became convinced that what decides the

---

monarchy. But recall that the rejection of Yahweh was rejection of Yahweh *as King*. Even those Israelites who rejected the earthly monarchy understood that Yahweh was indeed a King, but *not* in the same way as a pagan earthly king or as the pagan gods who functioned as kings.

[56]Paul Hanson, "War and Peace in the Hebrew Bible," *Interpretation* 38, 4 (1984): 345.

[57]Hanson, "War, Peace, & Justice," 41.

[58]Ibid., 45. Hanson is here in basic agreement with Millard Lind's thesis that the Exodus provides the fundamental paradigm of holy war which sees Yahweh alone fighting for His people, and that the monarchy results in an abandonment of this belief. *Yahweh is a Warrior* (Scottdale, Pa.: Herald Press, 1980).

[59]Ibid.

battle "is not the divine power invested in a tyrant king, but the power of the God of justice who embraces the cause of the powerless."[60]

The decisive and determinative experience of deliverance, then, by a powerless or a clearly militarily inferior people at the Sea of Reeds and at the battle of Deborah and Barak gave rise to the theme of Yahweh-as-Warrior. In other words, it was, in Nysse's words, something that was *experienced, not argued,* and which resulted in *worship and doxology.*[61] It follows that, "The theme is not, therefore, static or abstract in the sense of being a theological position that one can presume upon .... The theme is problematic because the human community wishes to involve the theme outside of the posture of petition and doxology. The Old Testament addresses this problem not by abandoning the theme but by asserting that the community which stands outside of petition and Doxology will experience the theme as against itself."[62]

In sum, Yahweh will not allow the forces of chaos to engulf the creation. The Israelites could affirm this because they experienced God's *shalom* in various ways throughout their history.

(d) Although included in the above viewpoints, it is worth emphasizing separately that the warrior language focuses strongly on Yahweh's ability to act in *history.* This was in stark contrast to the nature religions which held sway in Israel's world. Israel believed that Yahweh was present in every detail of its history, "from the secret ponderings of the human heart (Ps. 139:1-6) to the momentous selection of the divinely graced king (1 Sam. 16:1). Yahweh was a God who caressed with tenderness (Hos. 11:3-4) and also chastised with severity (Hos. 11:5-7); a God who meekly endured rejection (Mic. 6:3-5) and furiously punished infidelity (Mic. 6:13-16). We should not be shocked

---

[60]Ibid. Elsewhere in the article (40) Hanson emphasizes that Yahweh acts in accordance with the norms of justice and compassion, so that Yahweh's victory over Pharaoh is not merely an arbitrary display of raw force for an arbitrarily chosen people, but rather a demonstration of the validity of the principle of universal justice over the principle of special privilege. This, it should be noted, is the kind of logic found in just war doctrine.

[61]Nysse, 201.

[62]Ibid. Craigie notes here that the Old Testament must be taken as a whole which includes both "defeat narratives" as well as "conquest narratives." The prophets took the Yahweh-as-Warrior theme and turned it against Israel. *The Problem of War,* 97.

to find Yahweh present and active in the midst of battle, or at least perceived as such."[63]

Furthermore, to act in history means that Yahweh works in the world *as it is*, not as if in some ideal world. At times Yahweh intervened in Israel's behalf through some miraculous act in nature. But more often, human beings were the means whereby he accomplished His purpose, because to work *in* the world requires that human means be employed. From this standpoint, then, Israel's holy wars "can be conceived as an agency which God made use of at one time for his own purposes and without in any way sanctifying the participants."[64] In a complex and sinful world could there be any other way? Since so much of history is the history of warfare, if God is involved in history, he must be involved in some degree in warfare. There is no escaping this conclusion given the Biblical understanding of the nature of God. However much Israel's understanding of war may have been influenced by the surrounding cultures, her steadfast belief that Yahweh was a God of history is a contribution of the first magnitude.

(e) It is important to stress what the analogy of Yahweh-as-Warrior does *not* affirm. The major contribution of Millard Lind's *Yahweh is a Warrior* is the demonstration that many of the biblical texts functioned in the Israelite community not to motivate or legitimate warfare, but rather to correct or repudiate it. Ollenburger summarizes Lind's work as challenging "the assumption that God the Warrior is inevitably or even primarily a symbolic call to arms."[65] More often, Lind believes, it was a call to *denounce* arms.

To use more modern terminology, the Biblical idea of God as a Warrior constituted what may be designated as a *core belief*. This concept is utilized forcefully by Nicholas Cooper-Lewter and Henry Mitchell in their analysis of American black culture in *Soul Theology*.[66] They describe core beliefs as "bedrock attitudes that govern all deliberate behavior and relationships and also all spontaneous

---

[63]Diane Bergant, "Peace in an Universe of Order," in *Biblical and Theological Reflections*, 23.

[64]Wright, 130.

[65]Ollenburger in *Essays on Peace*, 117. Baly agrees: "The Wars of Yahweh therefore describe the desperation of a people without any legal protector, and the Power which thrusts backward those who would overwhelm them. In no sense at all do these stories suggest that violent action is something which men may safely imitate for purposes of their own." (42).

[66]Nicholas Cooper-Lewter & Henry H. Mitchell, *Soul Theology: The Heart of American Black Culture* (Nashville: Abingdon, 1986).

responses to crises ... (they) are *our working opinions about whether God can be trusted.*"[67]

This is an apt description of the Israelite effort to forge an understanding of a God who could be trusted in the midst of hostile neighbors who continually threatened and attacked them. As Cooper-Lewter and Mitchell state it, "core beliefs are seen as a necessary anchor in life's storm. Without formal or sophisticated rationale, the oppressed people holding core beliefs tend to assume that God takes good care of them."[68]

The authors, in examining African religion and American black religious beliefs, illuminate contemporary biblical scholarship's emphasis on "narrative theology." Stories in "primitive" cultures, whether Biblical or otherwise, "made indelible impressions on memory and had a calculated impact on behavior ... (they were) not concerned with defense against intellectual attack. Apologetic was not an issue, nor was intellectual respectability. The doctrine-in-narrative form instead used familiar people ... as symbols with which to improve the quality of life. No other purpose was conceivable.[69]

One might be hard pressed to find a better explanation of what was happening in Biblical times. An Israelite core belief was that Yahweh protected them against their enemies. This belief was communicated, not in abstract analysis dealing with nuances and ambiguities, but in stories of Yahweh's deliverance of his people. Without this core belief there is real doubt that the nation could have survived.

Cooper-Lewter and Mitchell do, however, address some problems inherent in core beliefs. Core beliefs may give so much attention to perceived need that selfish concerns may distort God's revelation. An ideal balance enables a people to affirm their own specialness and still be other-centered and self-giving.[70] We have observed this phenomenon in the previous chapters. The Israelites were constantly tempted to view Yahweh as a tribal god who fought only in their behalf. But some of the prophets insisted that Yahweh fought for justice and righteousness, and that Yahweh's wars were ultimately redemptive and inclusive. To be sure, the astonishing universalism seen in such passages as Isa. 2:2-4 and Mic. 4:1-4 are few in comparison to the texts which speak with triumphalism or hostility toward other nations,[71] but,

---

[67]Ibid., 3 (emphasis added).
[68]Ibid., 5.
[69]Ibid., 8.
[70]Ibid., 5.
[71]See the discussion on the reign of God by Marjorie H. Suchocki, *God, Christ,*

nonetheless, they were preserved in the sacred text and served as a much needed corrective.

So, our final assessment suggests that Yahweh-as-Warrior language, properly understood in its broader context, affirmed enormously important truths for ancient Israel and can do the same in the modern world. Because of our radically different situation in the modern world, however, we may do better to look for other metaphors which will affirm these truths. Modern warfare, including nuclear and chemical weapons capable of incredible destruction, conveys an image that fails to affirm what the biblical imagery affirmed. We should not abandon the warrior image altogether, because it expresses a core belief and because it is a permanent part of Holy Writ. Instead, it is necessary to interpret what the language was trying to communicate in order to challenge the horrible abuses of this imagery by uninformed, misguided, and perverted people. As Gottwald states, "it is default of duty for anyone to teach these stories of holy war without suitable correctives and warnings."[72] Or, as Ollenburger states, "so long as there are churches in which the Bible is read there will remain a theological responsibility to address the questions of how its reading bears on the faithfulness of believers, and on the faithfulness of their talk of God - including God the Warrior."[73]

---

*Church: A Practical Guide to Process Theology* (New York: Crossroad, 1989) 185f.

[72]Gottwald, 310. This is possibly one reason that for centuries Roman Catholics did not encourage untrained lay people to study the Bible. Without some guidance from the church as a whole, and even when there is guidance, some horrible misuses of the Bible can and do occur. But as Baly notes: "But the danger inherent in these concepts, and the tragic misuse of them made in later years does not affect the questions of whether in their primary form they might perhaps be valid. This is a matter for serious thought." (50)

[73]Ollenburger in Swartley, 127. In his essay Ollenburger examines the hermeneutics of Menno Simons for help in this matter. He concludes: "Theology, for Menno, is an exercise in hermeneutics--not in bridging a gap between Scripture and what we know on other grounds to be true, not in casting about for concepts by which to construct an image of God that enshrines the values we cherish, and not in giving specific expression to a common religious experience, but in having sufficient mastery of the biblical concept of giving intelligible expression to that faith whose actions verify the religious claims we make. It is because the real agent in these narratives is God the Creator and Warrior King that, for Menno, both suffering and peacemaking can and must be cruciform." (124f)

But, returning again to Cooper-Lewter & Mitchell's approach, *if core beliefs are reshaped only at great cost,*[74] then the responsibility of the church is to "take the heat" and work for peace while affirming the intent of the Yahweh-as-Warrior language.

## Some Hermeneutical Principles

An analysis of the Yahweh-as-Warrior language leads us to consider John H. Yoder's observation that Christian interpretations of these warrior concepts in the Old Testament are generally warped when the effort is made to derive direct moral guidance from these ancient stories.

This is nowhere more clear than in the reverse legalism with which majority Christianity has argued that killing must not be wrong for Christians since it was once proper for Hebrews, and God must not change.[75]

Yoder goes on to assert that this reverse legalism could be countered in at least three ways:

(a) by noting in how many other ethical realms ancient Hebrew morality is not applied by Christians;

(b) by showing the profound structural differences between the wars of Yahweh and those of our own time;

(c) by doubting that God's faithfulness over time should best be described as imparting timelessness to certain specific cultural forms that obedience once took.[76]

Yoder's insights highlight the important issue of hermeneutics, how we interpret the biblical texts. The work of a contemporary theologian, David Tracy, is most helpful in the task of establishing a relevant and responsible hermeneutic and his insights assist us in the difficult task of assessing the issue of war in the Hebrew and Christian Scriptures.[77] Drawing on the work of Hans-Georg Gadamer and others, Tracy sees three strands which must meet in a theological interpretation of the Scriptures. First, interpretation itself is a process best understood on the model of the conversation whereby the *preunderstanding* of the

---

[74]Cooper-Lewter/Mitchell, 4, citing Sara Little (emphasis added).

[75]In Yoder's introduction to Millard Lind's *Yahweh is a Warrior*, 18.

[76]Ibid.

[77]The following discussion draws on Tracy's contribution to the revised and enlarged edition of Robert Grant's *A Short History of the Interpretation of the Bible* (Philadelphia: Fortress, 1984) 153-87, especially the summary in 181-87. References to these pages will be included in the text. Emphases will be added to highlight the key elements.

interpreter and the claim to attention of the *text* meet in that peculiar interaction called a conversation, where the *subject matter itself* takes over (181). Second, theology is an interpretation that can be further classified by specifying the model of theological conversation as a "correlation." Every theologian attempts to interpret the scriptures by *correlating an interpretation of the contemporary situation with an interpretation of the scriptural texts* (181). The third strand recognizes that the theologian interprets Scripture within the church. These texts witness to an event; they do not replace the event itself, nor are they simply replaceable by later concerns of later communities (182).

Tracy's discussion contains two necessary and important elements of this method of correlation, namely the hermeneutics of *retrieval* and the hermeneutics of *suspicion*. The interpreter must seek to retrieve, by every conceivable method, the revelatory event of Jesus Christ and the scriptural texts which witness to it while at the same time "suspecting all" in the light of the revelatory event of Jesus Christ (184). These two elements are particularly useful in the examination of the issue of war in the Old Testament. We have attempted earlier in this chapter to *retrieve* the fundamental insights provided by the analogy of Yahweh-as-Warrior. At the same time we have been *suspicious* of those places in the texts where the authors understand Yahweh as commanding the annihilation of entire groups of people. C. S. Lewis applied the principle of suspicion when, commenting on the Psalms which cursed enemies, he concluded that, "We must not either try to explain them away, or yield for one moment to the idea that, because it comes in the Bible, all this vindictive hatred must somehow be good and pious."[78]

Obviously there are great risks involved in this task. An interpreter must avoid the extremes of substituting the texts for the event itself, which the "fundamentalists" do, or simply replacing the authoritative texts with modern concerns, which the "liberals" tend to do. One avoids these extremes by applying *the criteria of appropriateness* (176). This appropriateness does not mean that a later Christian witness must be found in identical form in the scriptures nor does it suggest that there can be no criticism of scriptural expressions in the light of later developments.[79] But all Christian theologies are obliged to show why

---

[78]C.S. Lewis, *Reflections on the Psalms* (London: Fontana Books, 1961) 25.

[79]Tracy asserts that Christianity cannot be considered strictly a religion of the book. Like Judaism but unlike Islam, he asserts, Christianity considers the scriptures not the revelation itself but the original witness to the revelation. It is the revelatory event and not the witnessing texts that must play the central role in Christian self-understanding (176). The central Christian affirmation has been

they are not in radical disharmony with the central Christian witness expressed in the scriptures.

Applied to our subject, the view (preunderstanding) I prefer is that the God of Abraham, Isaac, Jacob, Moses, David, and Jesus Christ is preeminently the God of *shalom* and not of war. I have sought to interpret the passages relating to war and the analogy of Yahweh-as-Warrior in the light of this basic affirmation. In this dialogue with the text I have concluded that some of the texts dealing with war do indeed point to a stance of active faith in Yahweh which renounces the use of force, or which depends upon Yahweh for deliverance, or which places severe restraints on war making. These passages then provide the norms whereby we judge the other passages.[80] In Tracy's words I have attempted to let the event of Jesus Christ judge the texts and the traditions witnessing to it and not vice versa (185). Although we find no single understanding of war in the Bible, we can assert with Hans-Ruedi Weber, that Jesus becomes the prism which lets them "converge" in a remarkable way. But this convergence results in a transformation because "Jesus transforms the love of power into the power of love."[81] Or, to return to Yoder's terminology, we have concluded that one strand of ancient Israel's understanding of war, namely holy war, is among those realms of ancient Hebrew morality which has been superseded by a better way.[82] Indeed, as we have seen, the Old and New Testaments themselves contain texts which already point to a better way.

It must be maintained, however, that obedience to Yahweh as ancient Israel understood him at times did involve preparations for and engagement in defensive warfare.[83] At times this meant involvement

---

and remains, I believe *in* Jesus Christ *with* the apostles (175).

[80] I can now be accused of possessing "a canon within the canon" but I see no alternative to this when dealing with disputed moral issues in the scriptures. The diversity within the Bible itself leads us to this path.

[81] Weber, 167.

[82] As we do in such matters as slavery, polygamy, view of women, etc.

[83] It is not in the purview of our study to assess every conflict in the Old Testament. Suffice it to say that our criteria lead me to say that, in general, the contest with Pharaoh ("an unplanned war of liberation," Craigie, *The Problem of War*, 68) and the wars during the amphictyony are capable of justification while the expansionist wars of the monarchy are not. The conquest narratives in Joshua present a more difficult problem but the problem is mitigated somewhat by the growing scholarly consensus that the "conquest" was more complex and was not only the result of several, undisputed, key military victories in the hill country, but also the result of gradual infiltration, peaceful settlement, and

in an evil activity, howbeit a lesser evil than the alternatives available to the Hebrews. War was and is evil because it results in the death and injury of God's creatures and damages the earth which is to be protected. But in the case of ancient Israel, the choice was often to do battle or to suffer annihilation.[84] Indeed, as we have seen, a tradition in Israel called on her not to engage in battle, but to trust Yahweh for deliverance. But this does not lessen the moral difficulties. Whether Yahweh killed them, or the enemies killed each other, or whether Israel participated in the battle, the results were the same—fathers and mothers, sons and daughters, were killed. This is an evil. But at least in some instances, it was a lesser of two evils. Wars were "emergency measures evoked by human sin."[85] This is a different moral logic than trying to maintain that since Yahweh was involved in the activity that this meant that it was therefore in essence good. God is good, but if he is to be involved in the real lives of his creatures, he allows evil means to accomplish ultimate good. William Temple stated it thusly a generation ago, "War is horrible, evil, and an appalling thing, and we must do all we can to end it. But a Nazi concentration camp is a horrible thing, and the suppression of a national community is an appalling thing. Our question is here as always: How can I prevent the greatest imminent evil or promote the greatest practical good?"[86]

Bergant concurs: "If Israel believed in the all-encompassing presence of God, then they had to deal with this presence in the midst of dilemmas where the only options were between various evils and not between evils and goods. They believed that God was there, inspiring them to seek what was best in situations where, from our perspective, nothing looked good."[87]

No doubt this type of argument leads to the slippery slope of "the end justifies the means" that tends to resist safeguards.[88] But, wherever

---

peasant revolt.

[84]In the third century Origen came to this conclusion: "To take from them [the ancient Jews] the right of making war upon their enemies, of fighting for their country ... would be to subject them to sudden and utter destruction whenever the enemy fell upon them." Cited in Forell, 87.

[85]Janzen, 165.

[86]William Temple, *Thoughts in Wartime* (London: MacMillan & Co., 1940) 35. Temple states elsewhere in the book that "if loss of life is not the greatest injury to suffer, it cannot be the greatest injury to inflict."(33)

[87]Bergant, "Peace in a Universe of Order," 23.

[88]Seemingly the only safeguard available is the rigorous application of the just war criteria and the application of Tracy's general criteria of appro-

it leads us, it does not lead to the claim that God commands Christians to fight. Some Christians may feel that they must respond to aggression by engaging in war, and they can do so because just war criteria have a sound biblical and historical basis. But they cannot claim that God commands them to do so or that in so doing they are engaging in God's good work. Participation in war by a Christian must always be, as Edward Long reminds us, "agonized participation."[89] To repeat, war was an evil then and is an evil now. Tragically, sometimes it is the lesser of two evils. Or, to use Tracy's language—the criteria of appropriateness—means that both pacifism and just war are legitimate Christian[90] stances toward war, but holy war is not. We must reject holy war because it has no awareness of its own sin or of the worth of the enemy and because its absolute ends eclipse other real human goods.[91] Furthermore, as Joseph Allen reminds us, no matter how deep

---

priateness. J. H. Yoder addresses this issue in *The Politics of Jesus* (Grand Rapids: Eerdmans, 1972) 246: "In the past, Christian and especially pacifists have debated the theoretical issue of whether evil may be done for the sake of good. But really the deeper question is the axiom that underlies the question, namely that it is a high good to make history move in the right direction. For only if that assumption is made does the further 'opportunistic' justification of evil follow." Yoder makes a strong pacifist case for refusing to try to make history move in the right direction, but at this point I am unable to conclude that it is *the* normative biblical and Christian alternative. Stephen Mott concludes that nonviolence might prove to be the only legitimate Christian position "when the full implication of biblical values have been understood. But this must be established through other means than exegesis and exposition of particular passages. If the case for nonviolence must be built on the general structure of biblical values, this will require reflection upon the historical and philosophical implications of biblical principles as applied to situations concerning which the Gospels are silent. Only by such reflection can one arrive at valid conclusions about the use of arms; it is not enough merely to point to the teaching and life of Jesus or to call for obedience to canonical Scripture." *Biblical Ethics and Social Change* (New York: Oxford University Press, 1982) 183. In other words, one can make a good case for pacifism, but it cannot be established solely on biblical grounds.

[89]Edward L. Long, Jr., *War and Conscience in America* (Philadelphia: Westminster, 1968) 41-47.

[90]On the basis of our study I would also add that the criteria of appropriateness within the Hebrew Scriptures themselves leads to the belief that both pacifism and just war are appropriate *Jewish* stances toward, but holy war is not.

[91]Joseph L. Allen, *Love and Conflict: A Covenantal Model of Christian Ethics* (Nashville: Abingdon, 1984) 188.

and persistent the disagreement is between pacifism and just war, it is "always 'within the family' theologically to a degree to which that cannot be said about either in relation to crusade ethics."[92] In addition, it must be emphasized over and over that no matter how much just war criteria have been manipulated and subordinated to nationalistic goals, that they were and are "violence reduction criteria."[93]

It is instructive to note here that different ethical approaches tend to lend themselves to different viewpoints regarding war. The obedience model as seen in the Deuteronomistic history is especially compatible with holy war, but it is ironic that this model is also employed by some pacifists who ground nonviolence in obedience to explicit sayings of Jesus.[94] It is no secret that natural law ethics provides the strongest basis for just war teachings, although we saw in Chap. 7 that natural law ethics existed in germinal form in the biblical texts. An ethic built on the imitation of God can, like the ethic of obedience, be used to support both holy war (i.e., imitate God the Warrior) and pacifism (i.e., imitate God the peacemaker).[95] One's ethical starting point goes a long way in determining where one comes out on this issue.

Furthermore, peoples' general worldview predisposes their stance on the issue of war. To employ H. Richard Niebuhr's categories in his

---

[92]Ibid., 191. Allen also rightly notes (190) that the effort by some to hold to a position of "selective pacifism" is not valid because the term allows for the possibility of justifying war under certain conditions, which is exactly what just war theory attempts to do.

[93]Walter Wink, *Engaging the Powers* (Minneapolis: Fortress, 1992) 220-27.

[94]Frederick Schuele worries that this kind of ethic pushes one in the direction of a purely heteronomic ethic in which one acts virtuously simply because one is commanded to do so. "That is, the motive for an ethical act comes entirely from outside, in this case, from God. When pushed to extremes, this view ends in what can be called a theonomic moral positivism, a position not only at odds with popular modern view of human autonomy and human dignity, but also quite inconsistent with a mature understanding of what it means to be created in God's image and likeness (Gen. 1:26) and to have God's own Spirit dwelling within us." "Living Up to Matthew's Sermon on the Mount: An Approach" in *Christian Biblical Ethics*, ed. by Robert J. Daly (New York: Paulist Press, 1984) 212.

[95]John Barton thinks that the imitation of God ethic deserves much more attention than it has received in examining Old Testament ethics. "Understanding Old Testament Ethics," *JSOT* 9 (1978) 60f. One might also add that H. Richard Niebuhr's ethics of response deserves more attention. See *The Responsible Self* (New York: Harper & Row, 1963).

classic *Christ and Culture,*[96] it is easy to see how pacifists most often display a "Christ Against Culture" mentality because of the enormous preoccupation with violence that all cultures have had and continue to have. Conversely, it is also obvious that the holy war mentality reflects the "Christ Of Culture" model. It is also clear that the just war criteria provide a classic example of "Christ Above Culture" reasoning. It is much more difficult to identify Niebuhr's other two models, "Christ and Culture in Paradox" and "Christ the Transformer of Culture" with any one understanding of war, but it is safe to say that a holy war mentality would fit in neither one and that both pacifism and just war could properly lay claim to both. This confirms Joseph Allen's observation that pacifism and just war belong to the "same family," whereas holy war expresses a substantially different outlook on the nature of warfare. The point here is to stress that an individuals' fundamental outlook on life (i.e., ones' character, the sum total of ones' core belief) is probably the single most important factor in determining how one will approach the issue of war. Consequently, if one of the major functions of the church is to mold and nurture character, it is evident that this task is both urgent and enormous in a world enamored by and addicted to violence and warfare.

---

[96]H. Richard Niebuhr, *Christ and Culture* (New York: Harper & Row, 1951).

# Appendix

## Methods of Warfare

*Weapons of War*

Israelite wars were carried on during the bronze age[1] and iron age[2] and a wide range of both offensive and defensive weapons is referred to in the biblical texts.

*Offensive Weapons*

Offensive weapons may be divided into short, medium, and long-range weapons. Swords, daggers, and spears were employed in short-range, hand-to-hand combat. The word *hereb* is used for both dagger and sword and since it was the main offensive weapon, it became the symbol of war (Isa. 51:19; Jer. 14:15; 24:10; Ezek. 15:33, etc.).[3] A dagger would probably be a short sword of twenty inches or less in length. Ehud's *hereb*, which he concealed by tying it to his leg (Judg. 3:16, 21-22), was such a weapon. T.R. Hobbs concludes that Israelites preferred slashing swords (for cutting muscles and blood vessels) over thrusting swords (for penetrating vital organs).[4] The mace ("hammer" or "club"),

---

[1]Bronze is made by adding tin alloy to copper, usually about 5-15%. The greater the percentage of tin made the metal harder but also more brittle, thus a proper balance between flexibility and hardness had to be found. Bronze, as J.W. Wevers notes, was particularly useful for the longer piercing weapons. "Weapons and Instruments of War," *Interpreters Dictionary of the Bible*, IV ed. by G.W. Bromiley (Grand Rapids: Eerdmans, 1988) 822.

[2]Ibid. Wevers notes that ancient smelting techniques could only produce wrought iron, which was not hard enough for weapons. This was overcome by heating the object in contact with carbon which, in effect, transformed the surface into steel. The chief advantage of iron over bronze was its hardness and strength.

[3]Roland de Vaux, *Ancient Israel: It's Life and Institutions*, trans. by John McHugh (New York: McGraw-Hill, 1961) 241. This appendix draws heavily on this definitive work by de Vaux.

[4]T.R. Hobbs, *A Time for War: A Study of Warfare in the Old Testament* (Wilmington, DE: Michael Glazier, 1989) 113.

especially those with spikes in them, could penetrate a helmet and crush a skull. Even crude weapons, like the fresh jawbone of an animal, could be effective in the hands of a powerful man like Samson (Judg. 15:15).

Medium-range weapons included spears that were light enough to be thrown and the bronze *kidon*, usually translated "javelin." However, this is found only in the hands of the Israelites in Joshua 8, but a similar weapon, the *hanith*, a "lance," is mentioned (1 Sam. 18:11; 20:33; 2 Chron. 23:9).[5] The *shelah*, was also a projectile of some sort (2 Sam. 18:14).

The most significant long-range weapon was the primitive bow and arrow, which dates back at least to the middle of the second millennium BCE. Although Saul's son Jonathan used a bow and arrow (1 Sam. 20:20), they are rarely mentioned until the time when chariots came into general use among the Israelites. Arrow heads were first made with bronze but later gave way to iron, which were designed to pierce armor. The *qela*, "sling," an ancient weapon used by David originally to protect his flocks was employed effectively to knock out Goliath (1 Sam. 17:40-51). The warriors from the tribe of Benjamin developed a reputation for their incredible accuracy with the sling (Judg. 20:16).[6]

*Defensive Weapons*

The most common defensive weapon was the leather shield of varying sizes and shapes (1 Kings 10:16-17; 1 Chron. 12:9; 2 Chron. 14:7). Helmets were made of both leather and bronze.[7] The body was often protected with various kinds of breast-plates, usually small plates of bronze, and later iron, which were sewn on to cloth or leather.

Although most of the fighting in the Old Testament period was on foot, chariotry took on more importance from the time of Solomon until the end of the divided monarchy. Judges 1:19 refers to the "iron chariots" of the Philistines, but the iron here probably refers only to the wheels and fittings or possibly to an iron plate which reinforced the

---

[5]de Vaux, 242.

[6]See Hobbs, 119-27 for a good discussion of both the bow and arrow and sling.

[7]Hobbs is not convinced that the Israelites wore helmets, except maybe important personnel. See his interesting discussion of helmets and other armor on pp. 128-33.

wooden body of the chariot.[8] The term might also be synonymous for the modern idea of "the latest in military hardware." In many sections of Palestine, particularly the central mountain range, chariots were useless. But for the Philistines who lived on a plain, and for the monarchs who had to defend their borders, chariots represented military sophistication and power. Since most of Solomon's large chariot force was concentrated in the north, the split of the kingdom meant that Israel, not Judah, inherited the major part of the chariotry.

## Battle Strategies

The Israelites did not seem to fare very well in pitched battles (1 Sam. 4:1-11; 31:1-7; 2 Kings 23:29). But the Israelites were able to overcome superior forces and fortified cities by a combination of more indirect methods. In an excellent article Abraham Malamat lists several of these:[9] (1) The Israelites exploited the disunity among the city states (e.g., Josh. 9); (2) They employed many forms of guile to surprise the enemy (e.g., feints, decoys, ambushes, and diversionary maneuvers); (3) Covert infiltration (Jericho); (4) Enticement (Ai); (5) Night movements (Ai, Gibeon) and night attacks (1 Sam. 14:39); and (6) The battle cry (Judg. 7:21; 1 Sam. 3:5), which could either frighten or dishearten the enemy.

*Israel's Armies*

During the early stages of Israel's existence fighting had to be a part of the life of every capable male. A few exemptions might be granted (see the laws of war in Deut. 20-24), but the survival of the people depended upon the participation and cooperation of all (note that even a "housewife" contributed to victory in Judg. 4:21). The use of voluntary forces, task-oriented militias supplemented at times with a sort of "national guard,"[10] enabled the Israelites to survive in the period of the amphictyony. But, as noted in Chapter One, a major shift occurred when Israel changed to a monarchy. Saul is apparently the first leader to recruit mercenaries, apparently primarily from his own tribe (1 Sam. 14:52; 22:7). David expanded this practice, forming his own personal

---

[8]James Moyer, "Weapons and Warfare in the book of Judges," *Discovering the Bible*, ed. by Tim Dowley (Grand Rapids: Eerdmans, 1986) 44.

[9]Abraham Malamat, "How Inferior Israelites Conquered Fortified Canaanite Cities," *Biblical Archaeology Review* (March/April 1982): 24-35.

[10]Hobbs, 71.

bodyguard (1 Sam. 22:14;   2 Sam. 23:23) and developing a professional army second to none. It is no surprise that huge expenditures were necessary to maintain a well-equipped, professional army. De Vaux thinks that this draining of resources was such that Judah was no longer able to maintain a professional army after the events surrounding the Assyrian attack in 701 BCE.[11] Consequently, conscription became necessary on a wide scale, although it had probably existed as far back as David.[12] These "men of war" fought when called, but returned to their homes and fields after the war (Jer. 40:10).

A few indications are given in the biblical texts as to how the army was organized. De Vaux lists groups of 10, 50, 100, and 1000, although Hobbs thinks that groups of ten were rare and that fifty was the most common designation.[13] It is noteworthy that kings, whether Israelites or those of the enemy, although they may have had commander-in-chiefs, usually fought in war.[14] In fact, 2 Sam. 11:1 reflects a widespread custom by stating that "In the spring of the year, the time when kings go out to battle ..."

*Defense of the City*

Major cities were forced to resort to enormous efforts to defend themselves against recurring assaults by powerful armies. Of course, many Canaanite towns were already walled when Israel invaded under Joshua and the Israelites merely repaired and strengthened these existing structures. In addition, the Israelites built a number of casemated walls which de Vaux describes as a wall along which stand blind rooms, which used to be filled with earth or rubble, or which served as stores. The purpose of these rooms is to widen the rampart, and thereby to strengthen it, while economizing in building by furnishing the store-rooms necessary for any garrison town.[15]

---

[11] de Vaux, 225.

[12] Most likely David's census (2 Sam. 24:1-9) was, at least partially, for the purpose of conscription. See de Vaux, 228.

[13] Hobbs discusses this in some detail on pp. 84-86.

[14] Ahab, Josiah, Sargon II, Esarhaddon, Cyrus, and Cambyses are a few of those who fell in battle. See Israel Eph'al, "On Warfare and Military Control in the Ancient Near Eastern Empires: A Research Outline," *History, Historiography, and Interpretation: Studies in Biblical and Cunieform Literature*, ed. by Hayim Tadmor and Moshe Weinfeld (Jerusalem: the Magness Press, Hebrew University, 1986) 100.

[15] de Vaux, 232.

Furthermore, a glacis added more protection to the wall, i.e., a slanted earthen support for the wall which also served to prevent the enemy from placing ladders at the bottom of the wall. When possible and useful, a fosse, a dry moat, could be added to slow down advancing attackers and make them easier targets for arrows. In addition, some cities erected screen walls, i.e., low walls outside the city so that defenders could keep attackers away from the main wall.

The most vulnerable part of the wall was, of course, the gate. Pillars could be erected in the entry area to establish barriers in case the gate was overcome. Usually the gate was flanked by towers upon which defenders could rain down anything that might prevent or slow the destruction of the gate or to aim at those who broke through the gate. Some cities, such as Megiddo, had gates with indirect access, forcing entrants to go through a small courtyard before entering into the main gate, or other such variations of a zigzag type entry.

Some cities had a citadel built on the highest point as a place of last resistance, while capital cities (Samaria, Jerusalem) often erected walls around the royal palace and its outbuildings.

All of these defenses, and more, were designed to discourage large armies from a frontal attack or from laying siege to a city for months at a time. The Israelites themselves rarely, if ever, engaged in siege warfare, but they were often the recipient of sieges by Assyrian and Babylonian forces. The purpose of a siege was to intimidate a city into surrender or starve them out by blocking all traffic into and out of the city. After a lengthy siege, with the inhabitants physically and psychologically weakened but unwilling to surrender, an attack was mounted. De Vaux describes it well:

> The Assyrians were past masters of siege by encirclement, and their monuments give a vivid picture of their methods of attack. The besieged city was encircled by a mound, ramps were constructed and machines brought up. These machines were mobile redoubts sheltering archers and men who maneuvered a ram, i.e., a long wooden beam with a metal-covered head for battering the wall. Those inside the city would throw flaming torches and stone down on the machines, or try to immobilize the rams by means of grappling hooks ... Once the rams had opened a breach in the walls, the assailants could enter there; alternatively, they would scale the walls with ladders.[16]

---

[16]Ibid., 237f.

The city under siege had one hope—that the attackers would tire from the wait or be forced to move on for external reasons.[17] Thus, a city did everything within its power to make provisions to lengthen the holdout. Food storage was a persistent problem but guaranteeing an unbroken water supply was even more critical. Hezekiah's famous 1700-foot water tunnel, which brought water from the Gihon Springs into the Pool of Siloam, meant that Jerusalem would never be without water. Deep-water wells have been found at Gezer, Gibeon, and elsewhere. In addition, cisterns were hewn in many cities to catch rainwater runoff.

In sum, because of Israel's strategic location, and the designs of some surrounding neighbors, it was forced to spend an inordinate amount of time and resources to defend itself throughout the biblical period. In many ways Israel's history was and is a history of military engagements.

---

[17]One explanation given for Sennacherib's withdrawal from Jerusalem is that trouble had broken out on another front (2 Kings 19:7). The bulk of the text in 2 Kings 18-19, however, attributes the withdrawal to a plague that decimated the Assyrian camp.